American Empire and the Arsenal of Entertainment

American Empire and the Arsenal of Entertainment

Soft Power and Cultural Weaponization

By Eric M. Fattor

First published in 2014 by
PALGRAVE MACMILLAN®
in the United States—a division of St. Martin's Press LLC,
175 Fifth Avenue, New York, NY 10010.

Where this book is distributed in the UK, Europe and the rest of the world,
this is by Palgrave Macmillan, a division of Macmillan Publishers Limited,
registered in England, company number 785998, of Houndmills,
Basingstoke, Hampshire RG21 6XS.

Palgrave Macmillan is the global academic imprint of the above companies
and has companies and representatives throughout the world.

Palgrave® and Macmillan® are registered trademarks in the United States,
the United Kingdom, Europe and other countries.

ISBN: 978–1–137–38725–7
ISBN: 978–1–137–38726–4

Library of Congress Cataloging-in-Publication Data is available from the
Library of Congress.

A catalogue record of the book is available from the British Library.

Design by Newgen Knowledge Works (P) Ltd., Chennai, India.

First edition: March 2014

10 9 8 7 6 5 4 3 2 1

For the Fattor Family:

Terry, Susie, Kristie, Nick, and Troy

Contents

Acknowledgments

This book is the material manifestation of over a decade of struggle. The academic career path has always been a very difficult one, but for myself (and many of my colleagues), this difficult path has been made almost impossible to navigate by an abundance of institutional and financial obstacles that epitomize the torpor of the twenty-first century. As I now finally reach an important professional plateau (though by no means the summit) with the completion of this book, I can look back at what has been overcome and recognize that my ability to get this far would have been impossible without the sustained help and support from a wide selection of friends and family.

Three excellent professors oversaw my professional development and helped me complete my degree in an institutional environment that was occasionally hostile to its doctoral students. David Goldfischer always had an insightful comment and an encouraging message about my work. Jack Donnelly's coaching on scholarly writing was nothing short of invaluable, as was his efforts at ensuring that I always had some kind of teaching job in a region of the country where such jobs are not readily available. And of course, I never would have had a chance at an academic career without my mentor Micheline Ishay. She helped transform me from a shy and humble student who never spoke up in class into an angry interrogator of the absurdities of the world—then calmed me down on those occasions when that anger got the best of me. My gratitude for her help is real and profound.

Once the frustrations of completing a degree have been met, the despairs of the academic job market quickly take their place. I was fortunate to be spared most of these thanks to Robert Duffy at Colorado State University who looked past a bad interview and hired me anyway, thus allowing me to gain some valuable teaching experience as a lecturer. Once employed, Bob also saw to it that I had enough work to eke out decent living. In 2012, I had the great opportunity to join the faculty of Hendrix College for a year, giving me for the first time the sense that the decision to pursue an academic career may not have been a mistake after all. My deepest thanks go to Jay Barth, Daniel Whelan, Kiril Kolev, and the other faculty members of Hendrix College for giving the time, space, and resources to mature into a seasoned scholar. Indeed, it was the collegial environment at Hendrix that allowed me to finish the manuscript and get it ready for scrutiny of the publishing world.

I also got important help from several people at crucial moments in the writing of the book. The comments of my colleagues who critiqued my work at Jack Donnelly's writing group had an important hand in shaping what is written here (you know who you are, so you'll forgive me if I do not name everyone). I dreaded taking the manuscript to the market, but Brian O'Connor at Palgrave showed enthusiasm for the project from the very beginning. And as the publication deadline approached, Mary Ann Jerrick in Wichita and Shawn and Glenda Kelly in Sioux Falls gave me free places to stay as I concentrated on the final corrections.

This structure of support, however, was built on a solid foundation of love and attention from my family. Because of this, I want to dedicate this book to them. My sister, Kristie, and brothers, Nick and Troy, each in their own way made it possible for me to succeed. As for my parents, Terry and Susie Fattor, anything good I produce in this world is directly attributable to their care and guidance. My gratitude to them is beyond measure.

Abbreviations

ABC	American Broadcasting Company
BBC	British Broadcasting Corporation
CBS	Columbia Broadcasting System
CIA	Central Intelligence Agency
CNN	Cable News Network
CPD	Committee on the Present Danger
CPI	Committee on Public Information
EMB	Empire Marketing Board
EPCOT	Experimental and Prototype Community of Tomorrow
ESPN	Entertainment and Sports Programming Network
FBI	Federal Bureau of Investigation
GAC	General Advisory Council
HUAC	House Un-American Activities Committee
MOI	Ministry of Information
MTV	Music Television
NBC	National Broadcasting Corporation
NIEO	New International Economic Order
NWICO	New World Information and Communications Order
OIAA	Office of Inter-American Affairs
OPEC	Organization of Petroleum Exporting Countries
OSI	Office of Strategic Influence
OSS	Office of Strategic Services
OWI	Office of War Information
RCA	Radio Corporation of America
RTL	Radio Luxembourg
UNESCO	United Nations Economic, Social and Cultural Organization
VOA	Voice of America

Introduction

The American Empire and the Weaponization of Entertainment

The world has witnessed with great interest, in the last few years, the growing power of digital media capabilities and the political consequences of their use. Aside from the well-known events of the Arab Spring—especially the so-called Facebook Revolution in Egypt—digital media and social networking have been essential tools in all sorts of political activity.[1] Barak Obama's shrewd use of social media capabilities played a pivotal role in his electoral victories in 2008 and 2012.[2] Outside of mainstream American politics, antiausterity campaigners in Great Britain have used Twitter to announce and coordinate direct action against banks and business they accuse of not paying sufficient tax. Students in Chile, Montreal, and California take digital cameras everywhere they go and post all their interactions with each other and with authorities on YouTube for public viewing. Even slum dwellers are finding ways of using Facebook and other social networking platforms to challenge attempts by local governments to relocate them to more distant peripheries of the city.[3] Given these events, it is easy to conclude that the digital capabilities of the twenty-first century are radically changing the world before humanity's eyes.

Yet, amid these flights of revolutionary fancy stands an inconvenient fact—the larger architecture of international politics and the position of the United States at the top of this structure has remained largely in place and unmolested. Indeed, since the end of the Cold War, the combination of American military might, international institutions, and neoliberal values—a combination that in other places has been labeled the "American Empire"—has not faced any major challenge to its global dominance despite the apparent preference to see social media as a force for change or subversion.[4] More importantly, the influence of media power, including the capabilities associated with twenty-first-century digital platforms, actually helps to solidify American dominance and makes genuine change more difficult to take root. Occasional outbursts of populist protest or radical demonstration may transpire from time to time, but on balance, the world's population seems content to let the American Empire continue to "rule the world."

This is an unusual situation for a polity that sits atop a global imperial structure. Asserting power at the global level almost always arouses opposition and conflict with competing communities who refuse to surrender their autonomy or their own bids for expansion. Moreover, at the heart of most imperial powers is the deployment of coercive force—usually in the form of military capability—to accomplish the goals of expansion and enforce some arrangement of hierarchical rule. While appeals to nonmaterial factors like superstition, ideology, or some primitive form of international law are often used to legitimize the use of violence, in the end, the justification that mattered most—to paraphrase a line from the famous Melian Dialogue in Thucydides's *History of the Peloponnesian War*—was that the strong did what they willed and the weak suffered what they must.[5] In the twenty-first century, however, such severe imperial discipline is largely absent from the international scene. Yes, there are handfuls of small but potent global terrorist organizations and insurgent groups scattered around the world, and states like North Korea and Iran seem destined to defy forever American imperatives. However, these are isolated exceptions. When it comes to the fundamental assumptions about the nature of world politics and the global economy, there is no coherent or organized resistance to American power.

This is not to say the United States lacks the ability or will to exercise coercive force. The US military is easily the most powerful in human history and within the last 60 years, there have been substantial American interventions in Korea, Vietnam, Iraq (twice), and Afghanistan, as well as the clandestine overthrow of the governments of several otherwise sovereign states (some of which were democratically elected). This demonstrates the United States has never shied away from imposing its will (or at least attempting to do so) upon recalcitrant nations.[6] Yet, as American political and military leaders gaze out over a world that is largely subject to their command, there is little in the way of mass organized resistance that poses an existential threat to American power. Indeed, one of strongest tensions present in the current "war on terror" is the notion that loosely organized and lightly armed bands of terrorists that often find shelter in caves (or as revealed with the killing of Osama bin Laden, in nondescript suburban houses) require the trillions of dollars the American security apparatus has spent over the past decade to fight.[7]

What, then, explains this collective passivity and mass disinterest in challenging the prevailing structure of world order, especially when it increasingly seems to deliver most of its benefits to a privileged few while billions of others face a lifetime of struggle?[8] This book argues that the United States has not had to rely as readily on coercive force thanks to a phenomenon that arose within the context of industrialization and is now a totalizing force in the world today—mass media entertainment conveyed through a global information network. Utilizing ever newer and more powerful communications platforms—from motion pictures and radio to television and theme parks to personal computers and Internet technologies—the United States, taking cues from Great Britain in the nineteenth and early twentieth century, has skillfully created a communications infrastructure that in the twenty-first century can now cast a net of seductive imagery and intriguing information over the entire planet. While such media capabilities have traditionally been seen as a platform for the transmission of overt propaganda reminiscent of Nazi Germany, the real key to the potency of this global media apparatus has been its ability to disseminate entertainment and spectacle. Whatever the crises and cataclysms of the current epoch, their severities have yet to reach a point where they steal the gaze of the masses from their pages, their stages, and their screens. This combination of spectacle and technology, this book argues, constitutes an arsenal of entertainment, and is the real key to the success of the American Empire.

At the heart of this argument is a historical claim—that the global political environment of the twenty-first century is configured in such a way as to make possible the exercise of imperial power without complete reliance on violence and coercion. Utilizing an analytical framework put forth by Antonio Gramsci and adapted by Robert Cox for inquiries into the realm of international politics, this book historically tracks the increasing importance of communications technologies and methods of generating entertaining content within the changing complex of international relations.[9] The present assemblage of global power—the American Empire—came about through the ability of the United States to not only accumulate more power than any other rival over the past century, but also to have the rest of the world recognize the legitimacy of American dominance and voluntarily acquiesce to the imperatives of American command. More importantly, this victory was not exclusively the result of military conquest and violently suppressing resistance but also due to the discovery by the ruling interests of the United States of the political impact of information technologies, their capacity to disseminate mass entertainment, and the ability of this mass spectacle—often laden with the seductive rhetoric of liberal humanitarianism, popular culture, and consumerism—to neutralize any dissent to the projection of American power. This discovery did not take place overnight, but through the various stages of development the United States (and the precedents established by the British Empire) experienced as it transitioned from a small and isolated ex-colony to the world's most powerful state. Without the invention of information technologies like radio, television, and the Internet and the techniques of managing the content emitted through these platforms, the uncontested dominance of the United States may not be something so easily taken for granted.

Information technologies can disseminate multiple types of content—news, educational programming, formal propaganda, or showcases of culture and lifestyle, so what makes entertainment so crucial beyond these other types of information in legitimizing American power?[10] The interesting answer to this question lies less with any overt partisan content found in the entertainment programming of today and more from the ability of spectacle to either neutralize the power relations of daily life or naturalize them so as to obscure the possibility that the conditions one lives in are malleable and that a better world might be possible through coordinated action.[11] In other words, entertainment does not repetitively or forcefully circulate the same propagandistic messages ad nauseum until the battered audience acquiesces to the message like some kind of *Clockwork Orange* scenario, but rather amuses the consciousness and stimulates the imagination of the spectator to a point where the critical capacity of an individual atrophies to a point of paralysis. On a mass scale, whole communities are unable to recognize their own exploitation or subordinate status, and even at those rare moments when such recognition does take place, the community is unable to mount effective resistance or make substantive change.[12] In other cases, entertainment may be the catalyst for individual or collective action, but this activity often takes the form of accumulating material goods or emulating the lifestyles and behavioral habits of the protagonists of the original entertainment programming or content.[13]

Understanding the enhanced capability of entertainment in an age of mass communication, however, only accounts for a part of this argument. The other part focuses on the United States and what makes the United States so special that it has been the greatest beneficiary of the power of spectacle. Surely, the great empires of the past also utilized means of entertainment of their respective eras to legitimize their rule and neutralize the dissent of their subjected peoples. After all, was not Rome famous for its gladiator contests in the Coliseum or chariot races in the Circus Maximus? The difference for the United States is the context in which its power rose to supremacy and how that context created opportunities to exploit new ideas and relations of material production that were not possible in previous eras. More specifically, the United States was the fortunate beneficiary of the radical political and socioeconomic shifts that took place in Europe with the rise of scientific inquiry and the Industrial Revolution. Unlike the coliseums and circuses of Rome, which could only hold so many people in a specific place, the research methods that spawned the technological developments of the Industrial Revolution meant ever-new methods of processing and disseminating information and spectacle to a mass global audience became possible. In Rome, only the privileged few could witness the fantastic and violent exploits of the arena floor, but in the American-administered globalized world of today, with its ubiquitous radios, televisions, personal computing terminals, and wireless communications devices, an addictive spectacle that would be the envy of any Roman emperor is now available on demand almost anywhere in the world at almost any time of the day.

The importance of the Industrial Revolution and the rise of the liberal economic order in the nineteenth century is an essential component in understanding the growth and maturity of the present-day complex of power. Without the first great innovations in communications technology coming out of Europe amid the political turmoil of the early nineteenth century—innovations like the mass printing of pamphlets and newsprint or the creation of the international public exhibition—the United States may not have been able to rise so quickly with so little opposition. This book, therefore, begins by analyzing how certain social and political interests in the British Empire of the nineteenth century used platforms like newspapers, public exhibitions, stage shows, motion pictures, and radio to create a mass media capability to legitimize their rule and facilitate the expansion of the British Empire. In doing so, key decision makers discovered that as the scale and concentration of the media technology grew, the most effective means of capturing and holding the attention of the public (or eventually, colonial subjects) was an appeal to emotion, imagination, and fantasy as much as the objective dissemination of facts and data. For the British Empire, however, the contradictions of imperial rule in the industrial age, including racism, colonial occupation, and great power conflict, were beyond the ability of Britain's communications apparatus to overcome, and thus the empire could not survive the world wars intact.

The challenge in the building of the American Empire both before and after World War II was to achieve a similar ability to command and influence the affairs of the world without creating the same tensions and conflicts that brought the British Empire down. To accomplish this, media technology did not merely supplement coercive military and exploitative economic relationships in the emerging American Empire, but became a central component in the overall apparatus of power. Beginning in the Spanish-American War with tabloid newspapers and early motion pictures, successive new technologies including radio, television, computers, and mobile communications devices as well as new methods of organization and ownership of these platforms became the most effective weapons in the American imperial arsenal and made the defining difference in the balance of power between the United States and the Soviet Union in the Cold War. Indeed, by the end of the Cold War, the advent of the World Wide Web created the potential to transmit an endless stream of highly personalized imagery and data into the consciousness of every individual on earth.

Of course, many mainstream scholars of international politics and policy makers in Washington, DC, have also taken note of the absence of sharp dissent to American power outside the narrow confines of Al Qaeda and other radical Islamist groups (and how those factors that contribute to popular acquiescence to American power in the rest of the world might be applied to neutralizing the terrorist threat). Their explanations for this more tranquil state of affairs rely in large part on the concept of "soft power"—an idea coined by prominent international relations scholar and former State Department policy advisor Joseph Nye.[14] Soft power, according to Nye, is "the ability to get what you want through attraction rather than coercion or payments. It arises from the attractiveness of a country's culture, political ideals, and policies."[15] Unlike the coercion and violence of "hard power," soft power "tends to be associated with intangible assets such as an attractive personality, culture, political values and institutions, and policies that are seen as legitimate or having moral authority. If a leader represents values that others want to follow, it will cost less to lead."[16] Nye makes frequent references to several values and institutions that embody American political culture and that act as magnets of admiration and emulation from other countries including individualism, consumer choice, freedom of speech, democracy, and freedom.[17] Since these values and institutions often hold the imagination and aspirations of individuals beyond the borders of the United States, many foreign populations pressure their leaders to emulate the policies of the United States and attach themselves to the national interests of the United States in the hope that American success will translate into their own success.

Soft power dramatically alters the calculus of power in an age of globalization and the rise of an information society. With diverse communities around the world able to interact and share information with each other, states that once enjoyed a preferred position in the structure of world politics thanks to large militaries or economic strength may find their ability to pursue their interests diminished. "Politics," Nye argues, "becomes in part a competition for attractiveness, legitimacy, and credibility. The ability to share information—and to be believed—becomes an important source of attraction and power."[18] For the United States, then, its dominant status in the world is due in significant part to the potency of its soft power— its attractive culture, liberal values, and foreign policies that encourage cooperation and institutional governance, and if it hopes to maintain its dominant position, it must continue to uphold these principles.[19] Because of this, scholars like Nye look askance at the idea of American Empire and insist such an idea is out of touch with the complicated realities of the emerging global information society. Likening a state to the player of a three-dimensional chess game, Nye argues, "Soft power is particularly important in dealing with the issues that arise from the bottom chessboard, transnational relations. To describe such a three-dimensional world as an American empire fails to capture the real nature of the foreign policy tasks that we face."[20]

The idea of an arsenal entertainment deployed through advanced media technologies certainly conforms to Nye's notion of soft power—indeed the phenomenon described in these pages represents perhaps the most potent variation of soft power available in the world today. The correction that needs to be made, however, is the idea that soft power cannot be the foundation upon which a structure of imperial power rests. If a single state—or an assemblage of power supervised by a single state—controls the means of communication and uses this control to neutralize opposition to policies that have major consequences for the daily life of most of the world's population, then why is the concept of empire inappropriate? The rise of soft power means that in addition to soldiers, tanks, battleships, and aircraft deploying violence to impose a political order on a population, newspapers, radio, television, motion pictures, theme parks, and digital media deploy the entertainment to bring about the same goal. Ideas, values, culture, and lifestyle require carriage through media if they are to reach a global audience and on the chessboard of soft power, like the chessboards at other levels, the United States has multiple queens, rooks, bishops, and other powerful pieces while much of the rest of the world has only a few besieged pawns.

More importantly, however, it is now possible to talk about how the most important expressions of global command now take place on the chessboard of soft power. While the "great games" of the past were struggles among imperial powers to control strategically vital territory or exercise behavior-altering influence over important local leaders, the struggles of today are for ideas, emotions, aspirations, and imaginations of the world's people. This is the chessboard that matters most in the twenty-first century and the means to win this board come not from the deployment of military force to hold territory but through the means of communication available and the production of the sweet and easily digestible elixir of entertainment products instantaneously delivered across the map. Soft power is the new hard power.

In clarifying this idea, the luminary that is most helpful is a man from one of the most important periods in the development of American media prowess. George Creel was a newspaper reporter from the Midwest when, upon the outbreak of World War I, President Woodrow Wilson named him the head of the Committee on Public Information. With much of the American public skeptical about the decision to commit troops to the bloody conflict raging in Europe, Wilson deemed it important to persuade the American masses that the cause of the war was just and victory required the unquestioned support of the entire population. Creel approached the task of disseminating information to the masses in the same manner as a general thought about deploying force on a battlefield, and just as a military professional used all the combat weapons available to triumph over the enemy, the information professional had to use all the media tools available to reach as many members of the population as possible. The following quote captures well how Creel saw information dissemination as another "front" within the larger war:

> There was no part of the great war machinery that we did not touch, no medium of appeal that we did not employ. The printed word, the spoken word, the motion picture, the telegraph, the cable, the wireless, the poster, the sign-board—all these were used in our campaign to make our own people and all other peoples understand the causes that compelled America to take up arms.[21]

Stated another way, what Creel expresses here is the weaponization of information and entertainment. In the struggle to emerge triumphant in World War I, little distinguished the battle for territory and the battle for hearts and minds.

Creel and the Committee on Public Information's efforts to use media as weapon of war alongside the implements of violence in World War I was but one waypoint in a larger historical process that saw platforms of information and entertainment become as important for the construction and maintenance of imperial power as the weapons of war. This book seeks to give the fullest account available of how this fundamental transformation in the nature of international politics took place and the role of the United States in bringing about this transformation in pursuit of a new kind of totalizing power that makes the challenges of managing global affairs more efficient and palatable. By understanding the central place of media technologies and entertainment in the larger global apparatus of power, one discovers the claim that the United States is an empire relies not on rhetorical hyperbole, but on solid historical evidence. Intriguingly, the story of the rise of the American media power also clues one in on the spaces and opportunities where the absent resistance to American power might find opportunities and spaces to froth. While it is true, as this book will explore, that the American apparatus of spectacle has dissolved much of the resistance to an American-led world order, the disruptions and uprisings of the last few years may yet point the critical observer toward the still hidden wellsprings of resistance and the tools they can use to challenge the American arsenal of entertainment.

With this in mind, this book begins its analysis by looking at some of the early innovations in communications technology of the British Empire and how Great Britain's experience with these technologies provided important lessons for the United States. The first chapter argues that the success of Great Britain in creating the largest empire in the world during the nineteenth century was due, in part, to its ability to direct entertaining propaganda through new media technologies to key audiences. During the rise of British power between 1815 and 1857, the rise of mass circulation newspapers and mass exhibitions tapping into the ideas of humanitarianism and liberal free trade allowed the architects of imperial power to present British power in an appealing manner that neutralized much working class dissent within Great Britain and some foreign dissent outside the country. During the maturity of the British Empire between 1857 and 1902, new forms of populist journalism and music hall entertainment stirred the passions of nationalism and demonized the perceived barbarism of native populations to justify expansions of British power in Asia and Africa. During the crisis and decline of the British Empire between 1902 and 1945, the British discovered the need to make more universal appeals to audiences beyond the homeland and the imperial sphere using early radio broadcasting and film technologies. The chapter concludes, however, that despite all these innovations, the British Empire could never fully exploit these innovations in communications technology due to several factors, including an inadequate global communications infrastructure, racist ideologies, and a model of imperialism that placed coercive force and formal rule at the heart of its approach to empire. Nevertheless, on those occasions when Britain was able to fully exploit the communications media of the day and disseminate an entertaining and compelling narrative to a targeted audience, its power enjoyed less formal resistance and provided a model the United States could emulate and improve.

Chapter 2 of this book shows how the United States between 1898 and 1945 applied the lessons of the previous era while also making important discoveries of their own. Like Great Britain during the early part of the nineteenth century, the United States used entertaining discourses of nationalism to create domestic cohesion among a socially and geographically diverse population. Unlike Great Britain, however, discourses of American exceptionalism were more entertaining—even if they did often suffer from the same toxic forms of racial and civilizational superiority that created an obstacle to making effective appeals to audiences around the world. The first part of the chapter looks at how the new technology of film augmented the power of newspapers to legitimize the Spanish-American War between 1898 and 1902. The second part of the chapter looks at how the medium of film played a crucial role in overcoming isolationism and stirred the moral sensibilities of American audiences toward an obligation to spread democracy around the world during World War I between 1914 and 1918. Finally, film combined with newly arrived radio technologies legitimized the leading position the United States took during World War II between 1930 and 1945 and laid the groundwork for the assertion of American hegemony after the war.

The third chapter focuses on the maturity of the American Empire between 1945 and 1968—a period where the United States consolidated its newly won power after the war and constructed a system of global governance through which it managed world affairs. This chapter begins by examining the American international radio broadcasting efforts between 1945 and 1949 that attempted to justify the new international development institutions (such as the World Bank and IMF) to a global audience skeptical of liberal economic principles and American leadership. The chapter then focuses on television and the power of this new visual medium to both harm and enhance the discourse of American power as demonstrated during the period of the McCarthy anticommunist purges between 1949 and 1959. The chapter also examines the renewed rise of international fairs and exhibitions that were a location of superpower propaganda and the attempts by the United States to use the 1964 World's Fair as an opportunity to showcase to the world the virtues of capitalist inspired consumerism.

The period between 1968 and 1989, the focus of chapter 4, was one of the most volatile in the history of the American Empire, and part of this volatility was due to the reorganization of the American economy toward knowledge and service industries and away from manufacturing. This gave information and knowledge a much higher value in the global economy than in previous eras. The chapter begins with an examination of the brief period of revolts against the liberal assemblages of power both within the United States as expressed by student protestors, woman's right campaigners, and African-American activists of the era, as well as outside the United

States by Viet Cong insurgents during the Tet Offensive. These dissenters discovered the power of *detournément*—or the ability to turn the power of the media against those who normally control the messaging of mainstream media outlets.[22] However, as time passed and the Watergate Scandal unfurled in 1973, it was neoconservative activists who discovered the new potential of media networks and combined the platforms of print, broadcast, and other technical innovations to create an apparatus of partisan entertainment that splintered the liberal postwar consensus in the Western world. The result was the election of Ronald Reagan on a neoliberal platform that enabled the generation of unprecedented amounts of investment capital that poured into multinational corporations, including international multimedia companies. Flushed with cash and easy credit, these companies created an array of global entertainment products like blockbuster films and slick television series that sought the widest possible global audience. It was these kinds of entertainment weapons that brought the Cold War to an end alongside the military and strategic weapons of the era.

After the Cold War, the conventional wisdom held that the United States would oversee an era of perpetual peace and prosperity as all its geographic and ideological rivals had been vanquished. Much of the world accepted this conventional wisdom in part because at the heart of the entertaining spectacles of the post–Cold War world was the message that there was no alternative to the neoliberal world order. However, events like the September 11, 2001, attacks, the wars in Iraq and Afghanistan, and the financial crisis of 2008 have undermined this narrative. Moreover, new digital media technologies that emphasize decentralized organization and horizontal collaboration have facilitated the creation of global networks of resistance against American-sponsored neoliberalism. With these developments in mind, the book concludes by acknowledging that the propaganda of spectacle and entertainment has been the most effective weapon utilized by the United States in maintaining its power in the face of several challenges over the past century. However, in making this assessment, the conclusion of the book also suggests that proponents of the current status quo have been slower to understand and appropriate the potential of digital media technologies of the twenty-first century, leaving open the possibility that the most entertaining spectacle of all might be the sight of a new form of global resistance to the American Empire.

Legitimacy through Popular Entertainment: Bringing the British Empire to Life (1815–1945)

Introduction

Despite the restoration of hereditary aristocratic rule at the Congress of Vienna, the beginning of the nineteenth century was a time of social turbulence and political change. The Industrial Revolution was moving Europe away from an agricultural economy lorded over by nobility and toward a machine economy presided over by manufacturers, merchants, and financiers. This shift in the location of social power accompanied the rise of new political ideologies and value systems like utilitarianism and nationalism. Concrete expressions of such novel ideas were visible in 1830 as popular revolts took place in France, Belgium, Poland, and Switzerland, and then again in 1848 when widespread nationalism brought an even larger outbreak of revolt to the aforementioned states plus principalities in what is today Italy, Germany, Denmark, and Hungary. Toward the end of the century, in 1870, the Paris Commune represented yet another attempt by disenfranchised and exploited urban poor to take over the ruling institutions of France.[1]

Curiously, however, Great Britain managed to avoid much of this revolutionary activity—a rather unexpected development since Great Britain was the birthplace of industrial production and few states were more deeply impacted by the effects of industrialization. To be sure, there was much social strife in Great Britain as aristocrats with their traditions of paternalism and sovereign right confronted a bourgeoisie bearing the marks of utilitarian thought and republican reforms while a mass working class demanding full enfranchisement and labor rights also joined the fray. However, by 1848, when the rest of Europe was ablaze with nationalist fervor, the bourgeoisie of Britain enjoyed a largely uncontested hegemony. Their control over British political institutions enabled the rapid and extensive expansion of the British Empire around the world with only moderate domestic social dissent. Even in later years, when the British Empire began to wither and collapse, this loss of power took place, at least domestically, without catastrophic social unrest.[2]

Why did Great Britain endure the tribulations of industrialization with so much more poise? Conventional explanations argue that activist movements, including those calling for the abolition of slavery, the reform of Parliament, and universal suffrage, and most especially nonconformist religious principles, created a more democratic Britain that cooled the forces of revolutionary change in British society.[3] Other explanations point to the wealth and prosperity unleashed by a rapidly liberalizing economy. Once the growing pains of early marketization were removed, including the enclosure of the commons and the removal of protectionist trade barriers erected to promote the interests of landed nobility, an abundance of cheap food and other goods flowed into the country to alleviate the poverty and hunger of the masses.[4] Still others suggest that as the century wore on, a more interventionist government that pursued policies of mass literacy, universal education, and the provision of certain welfare services created a social safety net that removed the precariousness of working-class life and dulled the impulse to revolt.[5] All these explanations no doubt tell an important part of the story, but they also overlook other factors that are only now getting a more thorough examination.

Chapter 1 provides just such an examination to one of these variables—the rise of mass communications technologies and their ability to inform, persuade, and ultimately, entertain the masses of Great Britain. Beginning with early forms of broadsheets and newspapers like *The Times* and *The Guardian*, running through the era of music hall performances and early motion pictures, and ending with the development of the broadcasting capabilities managed by British Broadcasting Corporation (BBC), this chapter examines how Great Britain and those social groups that controlled or influenced its political institutions utilized ever-more advanced forms of communications technology to shape the popular narrative of British public life, capture the imaginations of the national (and later global) audience, and eventually, co-opt or neutralize much (but by no means all) of the dissent to British rule at home and abroad. The evidence for this account comes from taking a long historical view of the British Empire and identifying key stages in the rise and fall of British power where new information capabilities combined with shifting justifications and legitimizing discourses for British rule confront the various domestic and foreign challengers to British power.

This chapter will detail three stages—the rise of British imperial power between the defeat of Napoleon in 1815 and the opening of the outbreak of the Indian Rebellion in 1857, the maturity of the British Empire between 1857 and the end of the South African War in 1902, and the decline of British imperial power from 1902 to the end of World War II in 1945. During the first phase of British power between 1815 and 1857, the key innovations in media capabilities included the widespread use of broadsheets, periodicals, and public exhibition. The application of these technologies began with the publicity campaigns advocating the abolition of slavery before showcasing the abundance of British industry at the Great Exhibition and other subsequent "world's fairs." In the latter half of the nineteenth century amid the mature phase of British imperial power, innovations in printing such as the tabloid newspaper and the staged music hall performance shifted some of the focus of British media away from activist spectacle to mass entertainment with a more nationalist tone. This included using newspapers to glorify the heroism of British military officers during the crisis in Egypt and Sudan and capturing the emotions of the populations through multiple forms of music hall reviews during the crisis and war in South Africa. The final part of the chapter examines how the state becomes the primary organizer and innovator of information technologies that assisted in allowing Great Britain to survive World War I through the organization of overseas media campaigns, the utilization of film technology to encourage consumer spending before and during the Great Depression, and the use of innovations in radio technology to keep the British Empire together long enough to defeat Nazi Germany.

After examining this rich history of communications technology and its connection to fluctuating levels of British imperial power, the importance of media spectacle and entertainment as a form of power begins to surface. The ability of British propaganda to not just persuade its domestic population (and at times, a significant foreign audience) of the virtues of British rule but also provide a moderately entertaining media product for the disinterested enabled the British Empire to neutralize and co-opt many of the challengers to British dominance.

In the end, however, the ugly side of imperial rule—racism, colonial occupation, and peripheral underdevelopment—negated the positive benefits of British power celebrated in sympathetic media outlets. No amount of compelling stories or patriotic songs could overcome the fact that a state claiming to be a defender of civilization and human rights was a habitual violator of these same standards. Nevertheless, the stirring narratives disseminated to an ever-growing mass audience enabled the British Empire to sustain its legitimacy for a longer period of time than it might otherwise have done—especially considering the challenges posed by its European rivals in the late nineteenth and early twentieth centuries. More importantly, the lessons revealed by Britain's mastery of print and early broadcasting technologies revealed an approach to exercising power at the global level that the United States would later show enormous interest in when it would take Britain's place as the world's most powerful empire after World War II.

From Activism to Spectacle: Printing and Exhibition amid the Rise of the British Empire (1815–1857)

The existence of simple printed text on unbound paper produced and distributed to a wide readership for a particular issue or cause goes back to at least the twelfth century in Europe.[6] Since those early days, pamphlets, handbills, newsletters, and other print ephemera were a common sight in cities or towns where a modest literate population resided, especially during times of political crisis, such as the English Civil War and the Glorious Revolution of 1688. As the struggles between elite factions in society subsided after the establishment of Great Britain in 1707, British politics shifted toward the acquisition and maintenance of overseas colonies and the struggle to protect these colonies and their bounty from European rivals. This meant protecting Britain's lucrative Caribbean plantations, the shipments of sugar and other agricultural consumer products cultivated on them, and most controversially, the cargoes of African slaves sent to work on them. On this issue of slavery and their transport, the tradition of mass printing through pamphlets and other reading material reached an important moment when, "amid flatbed presses, wooden trays of type, and large sheets of freshly printed book pages, [there began] one of the most ambitious and brilliantly organized citizens' movements of all time."[7]

The movement to abolish slavery in Great Britain was a central tenet of much religious agitation in the aftermath of the Restoration and the Act of Union. By the late eighteenth century, the movement began to gather genuine momentum thanks in large part to a clever publicity drive organized by a small group of antislavery campaigners meeting in a small house in London.[8] In 1807, they succeeded in persuading Parliament to ban slave trading within the British Empire. However, slave trafficking continued throughout much of the world by other states and rogue British merchants while slaves in British colonies remained in bondage. Seeing the act of Parliament as only a partial victory, William Wilberforce, the movement's most famous figure insisted,

> Never will we desist, till we have wiped away this scandal from the Christian name; till we have released from the load of guilt under which we at present labor; and till we have extinguished every trace of this bloody traffic, which our posterity, looking back to the history of these enlightened times, will scarcely believe to have been suffered to exist so long, a disgrace and a dishonor to our country.[9]

These fiery words were dramatic in their resolve to see the barbarity of the slave trade end throughout the world and served as a call to arms that would rally public support toward the cause.

In 1807, however, the British population had its gaze transfixed on the emerging threat from France and the successes of Napoleon in his bid to conquer the continent. For the likes of William Wilberforce and his fellow abolitionists like Zachary Macaulay and Henry Thornton, the effort to win the support of the public to persuade the British state to actively intervene in the Atlantic slave trade had to wait until more pressing problems in Europe were neutralized.

In the meantime, abolitionists began using all the means of publicity available to them to communicate their abhorrence with the institution of slavery. A multitude of journals, pamphlets, and newssheets were printed in small presses throughout Britain and tacked up on public walls, read at abolitionist meetings, and discussed in local coffee and tobacco shops. For example, between 1807 and 1833, the British Anti-Slavery Society published almost three million copies of newssheets and pamphlets.[10] The most important of these publications was *The Anti-Slavery Reporter*. Begun in 1825 by Zachary Macaulay, it became the primary medium through which the struggle for emancipation found a public audience. The journal's primary function was publishing the minutes of the meetings as well as the activities of the members of the British Anti-Slavery Society in order to keep large numbers of sympathetic readers across Britain informed of the activities of the organization. *The Anti-Slavery Reporter* also served as a precursor to the kind of online chat forums familiar to the Internet age in its role as a platform where approaches to dealing with the problems of enacting abolition could be debated and the critiques of abolition's opponents could be rejoined.[11]

Printed material was not the only medium available to antislavery activists. Many among the abolitionist movement or those sympathetic to it sought to express their sentiments through artistic platforms. Antislavery poems like Thomas Day's *The Dying Negro* or Hannah More's *Slavery* were representative of an outpouring of material designed to raise the awareness of the practice.[12] In addition to textual material, small drawings and images were widely produced to serve as logos for the movement. The most famous of these was Josiah Wedgewood's sketch of a kneeling African slave surrounded by the by phrase, "Am I Not a Man and a Brother?" So popular and powerful was the image that the present-day American historian Adam Hochschild concludes, "Wedgewood's kneeling African…was probably the first widespread use of a logo design for a political cause."[13] In the succeeding years after the prohibition of the slave trade, these words and pictures made a return appearance in the effort to effect total abolition.[14]

Hinting at a future time when visual images would overtake text as the preferred platform of propagandistic messages, numerous painted and drawn pictures played a role in the antislavery campaign as well. Drawings and etchings were a central part of the campaign to eliminate the slave trade, especially those depicting the nightmarishly cramped conditions on slave ships. Indeed, these visual images were perhaps the most effective pieces of propaganda in that they depicted in a brutally honest manner the realities of the slave industry, and would hint at the power of visual images to arouse popular outrage to justify aggressive imperial activities. Around the time of emancipation in 1833, these simple drawings were accompanied by full-sized paintings, with several works taking their place among the best works of art of their time. The French painter Auguste Biard enjoyed the greatest notoriety, with works painted in the 1830s titled *Scene on the African Coast* and *The Slave Trade*, the latter of which was bought and displayed in the home of famous antislave crusader Thomas Fowell Buxton. British painters made their mark on this subject when J. M. W. Turner debuted his haunting *Slave Ship: Slavers Throwing Overboard the Dead and Dying, Typhon Coming On*. In that same year, 1840, Benjamin Robert Haydon attempted to glamorize the antislavery movement with a depiction of a famous antislavery meeting titled *The Anti-Slavery Society*, though the latter work pales in artistic quality with the former.[15]

As the layout of newssheets grew from a single broad page to multiple pages, arrangements were made with sympathetic journal publishers to have antislavery pamphlets, such as Macaulay's famous pamphlet *Negro Slavery*, inserted between these pages. This tactic was also utilized to spread material to the rural parts of Great Britain as well.[16] At one critical point in the campaign when an initial measure to abolish slavery was being debated before Parliament in 1823, "material went out to 38 counties in England as well as Edinburgh and Glasgow, Dublin and Belfast, and Neath in South Wales."[17] A handful of mainstream journals also made space available for the publication of antislavery material. Both the *Edinburgh Review* and the *Westminster Review* published stories and opinions supporting the abolitionist cause and thus allowing the issue of antislavery to become intertwined with other causes of political change, including the reform of Parliament and the repeal of the Corn Laws.[18]

It is impossible to know with any empirical certainty how influential the proliferation of this material was in raising the awareness of the abolitionist cause. However, the fact that antislavery sentiment crossed class lines in an era when class distinctions were being exacerbated suggested the information was having a mass appeal. Indeed, abolitionists found fervent support from the expanding assemblages of working-class Britons who saw the cause of antislavery harmonious with the demands of exploited laborers in Great Britain's factory towns. From 1789 onward, slavery was linked with "conscription and flogging in the military, the agricultural poor, debtors, domestic animals, the Celtic poor of Scotland and Ireland, the forced emigration of Highlanders, [and] the unrepresentative House of Commons"[19] Thus, it is of little surprise that many prominent working-class advocates that drove the Chartist movement in the 1830s and 1840s in pursuit of workers' rights got their start in political activism in the campaigns to abolish slavery.[20] Their main publications, including *Poor Man's Guardian* and *Northern Star*, often featured stories praising antislavery activities and editorializing in favor of antislavery causes.

As a result, antislavery was quickly becoming one of the first national and international human rights *cause célèbre* in the early nineteenth-century Britain. The abundance of antislavery literature suggests a strong popular demand for the opinions and commentary of the movement not so much for the purpose of freeing slaves but for satisfying a desire to consume information related to the cause. This trend intensified as the publication of information about the suffering of beleaguered slaves moved toward a focus on the efforts at slave interdiction. Dramatic stories filling the periodicals of Britain depicting the Royal Navy chasing slavers off the coast of Africa began to provide a compelling narrative that not only boosted the sales of newspapers, but also made the costs and repercussions of empire more palatable across a broad social spectrum.

Great Britain made the decision to actively thwart the trading of human cargoes after the passage of the Anti-Slave Trade Act in 1807, but it was not until after the end of the Napoleonic Wars that naval resources became available for such interdiction activities. Once these operations began in earnest, however, the stories and articles from the front lines of slave interdiction proved to be extremely popular among a wide spectrum of the reading audience. In these stories of daring-do on the high seas, few figures were more popular than Thomas Fowell Buxton was. Indeed, if one had to associate a single individual with antislave campaigning in Africa in the early nineteenth century, that individual would be Buxton. In 1839, he wrote the highly influential tract *The Slave Trade in Africa*, which served as the informal blueprint of British antislaving policy in the region for decades.

Buxton begins his book by asking, "How...shall we undeceive our [African] chiefs, and convince them, that it is for their interest that the Slave Trade should cease?"[21] This was a central question for many abolitionists at the time, as they pondered the moral obligation of Great Britain in redeeming itself for its past transgressions when it was a participant in the slave trade. Buxton's answer was quite clear: "This we *must* do for Africa: we must elevate the minds of her people, and call forth the capabilities of her soil."[22] Here, Buxton insisted that the British government take an active role in the eradication of slavery by supporting efforts to destroy slavery at its origins in Africa and replace it with a viable local agricultural industry with which it could develop and prosper. This sentiment defied much of the conventional thinking about British colonial policy at the time, where the prevailing thought was to disentangle the empire from foreign commitments, rather than make new and ambitious ones to the better part of an entire continent. Nevertheless, Buxton's powerful words and wide distribution of *The Slave Trade in Africa* meant that many in Great Britain were persuaded to pursue a policy of military, economic, and social intervention in Africa.

Even before the publication of Buxton's blueprint, British efforts at disrupting the slave trade were moving in a more interventionist direction that attracted a great deal of attention and interest back home. In 1807, the Royal Navy deployed a single slavery interdiction squadron off the coast of West Africa that bore the entirety of the burden for interdicting slavers along an immense three-thousand-mile long coastline stretching from Cape Verde just north of Gambia, through the continental coastal bend of Sierra Leone, across to the south-facing coastline of the Bight of Benin, and south across the equator to the mouth of the River Congo.[23] Needless to say, such a small force stood little chance of making any significant impact in reducing the traffic of slave ships, evidenced by the fact that the number of slaves transported across the Atlantic during this period actually rose.[24] After 1832, however, more squadrons combined with other nations embracing the cause of slave trade interdiction meant Britain's humanitarian efforts were starting to bear fruit. Between 1835 and 1842, the number of slaves exported to Cuba and Brazil, the primary destination for slave ships, dropped significantly.[25]

As these interdiction events transpired, resulting in the spectacular capture of slaving vessels and their human cargo, abolitionist and missionary journals back in Great Britain enthusiastically updated the fight of antislavery beyond the home shores to its readers. To take one example, the *Missionary Herald*, published by the Birmingham Missionary Society, became an influential alternative source of news during events directly related to abolition, including the Jamaican slave rebellion in 1831 when mainstream news reports were lacking detail.[26] Other religious periodicals soon published dispatches from their own missionaries spread across the world. West Africa provided the dateline for many of the stories, but other dispatches came from missionaries as far flung as East Africa, India, and China. As the British Navy began patrolling for slave ships off the coast of Africa, the *Missionary Herald* began to report their activities as a kind of episodic military campaign, tantalizing its eager readers with pages filled with maps of the African coast and "engravings of 'Greegree' men of West Africa"[27] For British readers of these adventures, antislavery was increasingly becoming as much a form of entertainment as a humanitarian cause.

These cumulative efforts to destroy the slave trade started to have interesting effects. They not only neutralized some of the imperial skepticism that existed in the British homeland during the first half of the nineteenth century, but were stirring similar movements in other nations as well. British successes in stemming the flow of slaves to the Western hemisphere helped spur the abolition movement in the United States, while in France, meetings among European abolitionists often featured formal speeches of praise for the British efforts at smashing the slave trade.[28] Some British activists, such as the Reverend Edward Bickersteth, even allowed themselves to imagine the kind of heroic reputation Great Britain was making for itself among the African populations who were suffering under slavery: "The name *Englishman* is already, through the African continent, becoming a simple passport of safety. If a white missionary visits a black tribe, they ask only one question, does he belong to the people who liberated our children from slavery?" (emphasis original).[29]

Even when certain members of Parliament objected to the cost of slave interdiction or pointed out that more and more nations had outlawed the practice of slave transport for their merchant ships, popular support remained sufficiently strong so that no action was taken on these proposals until long after the abolition of slavery in 1833.[30] Indeed, the effort to destroy slavery meant having to maintain a presence in West African colonies that many were eager to ignore or get rid of entirely. As Ronald Robinson and John Gallagher suggest, many British ruling elites found the possession of African colonies "miserable enough. But the British government had to go on dragging these burdens because public opinion would not give up these symbols of the fight against the slave trade."[31]

The popularity of antislavery activities remained a popular theme in British society for decades to come, but around 1833, the power of these stories to entertain and entice began to wane. This can be attributed to three reasons. First, the year 1833 saw the British Parliament outlaw slavery throughout the empire giving the impression that the battle to free the slaves was more or less at an end. Second, the passage of the Great Reform Bill in 1832, while enfranchising much of the upper echelons of the bourgeoisie, left the rest of British society disenfranchised and still unable to participate in organized politics. Finally, the dire conditions of the impoverished masses resulting from the social effects of industrialization and economic depression undermined the legitimacy of the bourgeois ruling coalition and fostered radical protest movements, most notably in the form of a Chartist movement that sought universal suffrage. Nationalist revolt in Europe taking place in the early 1830s only exacerbated the fears among the bourgeoisie that they were losing control of the nation's institutions. Such fears came at an inopportune time as the British Empire found itself deploying ever-more resources overseas, including attempts to open closed markets to British manufacturing in South America and Asia. These events prompted the search for new discourses of legitimacy to maintain the bourgeoisie's fragile hold on power and permit the expansion of British power around the world without recourse to expensive options of violence and coercion.

During the turbulence of the 1830s and 1840s, the focus of the British Empire turned inward to address the social challenges of industrialism. The media weapons and techniques of capturing the mass imagination that had worked so well in publicizing the antislavery campaigns now targeted the working classes in the hopes of winning their support in bringing about the liberal reforms. Newspapers, magazines, and an array of other printed material from utilitarian advocates as well as activists of Chartism inundated British society with a flood of propaganda material.[32] In 1846, an improving economy and the repeal of the Corn Laws pacified much of this upheaval, but the flirtation with open revolt in Great Britain alongside the outbreak of nationalist revolution in Europe in 1848 once again compelled important leaders in British society to contemplate ways of neutralizing dissent without the need for physical force.[33] In 1851, they revealed the result of these reflections—the Great Exhibition.

The Great Exhibition grew out of the perception that the best argument for the benefits of liberalism (understood here as the free movement of goods and services across state boundaries) came not from upper-class bourgeoisie lecturing their working-class countrymen, but through a hands-on demonstration of what liberalism produced. Hand in hand with this belief was the idea of cultivating a spirit of internationalism and human prosperity that would win the hearts and minds of foreign peoples. Though many newspapers and other print materials of the time were beginning to circulate internationally, something more spectacular was required. Thus, the idea for the Great Exhibition took shape. Here, the trend toward symbolic and image-based propaganda broke new ground with a dazzling array of manufactured products, exotic items from overseas, and cutting-edge technologies designed to capture the imagination of individuals not only from different classes, but also from different continents. However, the exhibition was also to be the site of the British Empire's future challenges and contradictions, as the attempt to dramatize the prosperity and power of Great Britain could not fully expunge the more self-aggrandizing elements of British nationalism. As people gathered under the high roof of the Crystal Palace, the material abundance on display sent a message not just of British ingenuity, but also of British superiority.

Local fairs and exhibitions were a common sight in the growing towns of Great Britain prior to 1846. Though popular as an attraction for local townspeople, the true intention of these exhibitions was to recruit apprentices and raise funds for still fledgling industries. With no mass educational apparatus in existence in Great Britain at the time, entrepreneurs and manufacturers were responsible for providing to prospective employees the technical training necessary to maintain their machines and support their businesses.[34] With the national economy completing a transition from agricultural production to industrial production, however, proponents of free trade and industrialization began demanding more national perspectives on industrial education and the cultivation of artistic taste among the aggregate population. The prime advocacy group for this movement was the Society of Arts, which had been responsible for many of the smaller exhibitions in the past. But with the arrival of Prince Albert, the husband of Queen Victoria, as the head of the society in 1845, plans were soon hatched for a national exhibition that would showcase the vast array and volume of industrial output and their role in fostering a national prosperity.[35]

In the wake of the bitter conflict over the repeal of the Corn Laws, however, much of the British populace still needed to be persuaded about the truth of free trade. As fortune would have it, Richard Cobden, the most vocal advocate for free trade anywhere in Great Britain, was also a member of the Society of Arts and helped hatch the idea of a Great Exhibition as a way of inviting the British public to expand the horizons of their imagination by showcasing the tangible products a world built on principles of free trade would bring. If the attendees found the world represented at the Great Exhibition sufficiently attractive, they would support the larger agenda of a world completely free of barriers for free exchange of goods. The established liberal view had undergone some nationalist refurbishment amid the context of the European revolutions three years prior to incorporating the opinion that a strong British nation required its economy to be unrestrained by unnecessary tariffs and taxes on its international trade and manufacture. Even with this addendum, however, the prevailing sentiment still retained its universalist core—the virtues of free trade were not to be treated as a state secret to be guarded, but as universal principles available to all nations. Now, it was an advantage to Britain that it be a leader in bringing this liberating philosophy to the world. As explained by Prince Albert as the event was in the planning stages,

> It was a question whether this Exhibition should be exclusively limited to British Industry. It was considered that, whilst it appears an error to fix a limitation to the Production of Machinery, Science and Taste which are of no country but belong as a whole to the civilized world, particular advantage to British Industry might be derived from placing it in fair competition with that of other Nations.[36]

Such statements reflected the Cobdenite philosophy that free ingenuity, investment, and trade with other nations would create a mass prosperity and abundance for the whole of the British state as well as the other peoples of the world.

A special building dubbed the Crystal Palace was built especially to house the Great Exhibition's displays. The effect of the architecture of the Crystal Palace itself served as a billboard to the promise of liberal development.[37] Constructed primarily out of highly refined building materials such as iron and glass, the edifice was "a third of a mile long, a hundred yards wide, and three stories high."[38] Completion of the structure brought widespread praise from a cross section of public opinion, being hailed as magnificent, novel, and perhaps most importantly, functional.[39] Its designers thought of it as a sort of utilitarian cathedral that would serve a similar function as the Gothic originals—only instead of venerating the majesty of God, it venerated the majesty of manufacture.[40] The items on display inside played their role in wooing the visitor into new ways of conceptualizing their lives in the age of industrialism and global trade.[41] Half of the Crystal Palace was reserved for displays from Great Britain while the other half was for British colonies and sovereign nations. In all, 32 countries were represented in the international half of the Crystal Palace, bearing the samples of the natural resources and manufacturing prowess of their respective nations. Visitors could gaze at "Egyptian carpets, Turkish embroidery, Roman mosaics, German porcelain, Russian furs, and India rubber."[42]

The message promulgated from the Great Exhibition was so seductive that print media sources provided a wealth of free and complementary publicity.[43] *The Economist* predicted, "Every future improvement in society will radiate in some unknown or known way from the Great Exhibition."[44] *The Times* declared the opening of the exhibition as "the first morning since the creation of the world that all peoples have assembled from all parts of the world and done a common act."[45] Implied in all these exhortations was the fact that many of the impressive innovations in manufacture and design were of British origin, and required national economic mobilization to bring such visions to reality.

Though the planners at the Society of Arts had hoped to avoid overtly nationalist sentiments, appeals to a more populist pride that celebrated

Great Britain less in its industrial innovations and productive capacities and more on its alleged superiority to other nations were also on display at the Great Exhibition. These views reflected a lingering aristocratic view of the British Empire in the world that held British interests abroad had to be vigorously protected and extended through the use of military force. Success in this endeavor required a strong British state with a powerful military and an often-disparaging conception of international political rivals.[46]

Many of the exhibits at Crystal Palace featured manufactured objects laden with more traditional representations of British nationalism. Housewares such as plates, cups, tea sets, and pieces of furniture were often decorated with profiles of famous British war heroes or symbols of British power. Other presentations showcased works of art deep in allegorical meaning and symbolism, such as intricately ornamented vases with full-bodied carvings of "Nelson, Wellington, Milton, Shakespeare, Newton, and Watt being crowned with laurel wreaths."[47] Of particular note was the "Sportsman's Knife" that featured 80 individual blades etched with images ranging from Windsor Castle to the then famous railway bridge over the Menai Straits in Wales. Manufactured by the firm Joseph Rodgers and Sons from Sheffield, the knife epitomized the tension underlying two differing strands of nationalism on display at the Crystal Palace. On the one hand, such a multibladed knife embodied the attempt at efficiency and instrumentality of the utilitarian approach with a single tool that has the ability to perform multiple tasks. On the other hand, the knife was utterly useless as its "gold inlaying, etching and engraving" made the "Sportsman's Knife" a tool "that no sportsman would ever handle."[48]

In addition to the formal displays, the exhibition was also a scene of furious publishing and pamphleteering. Writers were wandering the grounds, soliciting attendees to purchase their small tracts for a shilling apiece. The most popular of these small works were commemorative poems and musings on the power and majesty of Great Britain represented in the Great Exhibition. These ranged from simple anonymously written verses to more eloquent offerings by established writers. One example of the latter was the poem "Recollections and Tales of the Crystal Palace" by Caroline Gascoyne:

> Away with chains!—Britannia's flag unfurled,
> Speaks Peace and Freedom to th'assembled world!
> Where'er her banner floats—or sounds her name,
> Distant or near, her power is still the same—
> The power of Justice, Liberty, and Right,
> Calm in their force, majestic in their might![49]

The complimentary themes of technological advancement combined with patriotism implicit in many of the demonstrations allowed the exhibition to appeal to a wide cross section of British society.[50]

There were also noticeable racial, ethnic, and class tensions detectable among many publications covering the exhibition, especially those oriented toward workers. With a large segment of industrial workers upset at the increasing power of commercial and industrial interests after the repeal of the Corn Laws, events like the Great Exhibition were sometimes attacked by many of the cheaper newssheets and journals like *Punch*. In these attacks, nationalist sentiments were quite popular with readers, and attacks on internationalism and free trade were common.[51] Such commentaries and cartoons suggested that though most of British society found the world on display at the Great Exhibition interesting and novel, there was no guarantee these groups were fully persuaded by its promises.

That said, the Great Exhibition was a stunning success. Large audiences from around the world visited the Crystal Palace experienced a show unlike anything that had ever been put on in the history of the world up to that point in time. Yet, for all the diverse crowds the exhibition attracted, the event itself was an anomaly for the mid-nineteenth century. For the vast majority of the world's people who lived under the rule of the British Empire, the experience of subjugation was one of hierarchically imposed orders enforced with coercive force. The Great Exhibition opened up the possibility that a new and less abrasive form of imperial dominance was possible—one where material goods and entertaining spectacle could make the day-to-day experience of life under foreign domination more palatable and perhaps even pleasing. However, as British domination continued in the latter part of the nineteenth century, the internationalist example of the Great Exhibition did not leave a very lasting impact. Instead, the more nationalist flavor of the exhibition persisted as several overseas crises erupted in the British Empire.

Missed Opportunities to Entertain Overseas: Tabloid Journalism and Music Hall Spectacle (1857–1902)

The spectacle of the Great Exhibition and its success in captivating the imaginations of both local Britons and foreign visitors provided a potential means for Great Britain to manage and maintain its dominant position in the world as the British Empire entered a mature phase of development. As the imperative to eradicate slavery, expand free trade, and grow the material output of the British economy persisted in the middle part of the nineteenth century, the likelihood of greater conflicts with local inhabitants promised to increase. Also contributing to these pressures was the continued rise of nationalist sentiment in Europe, which often manifested itself with expansionist movements among rival nations to challenge British hegemony. Nevertheless, between 1857 and 1902, the preference among British leaders was to avoid direct confrontation whenever possible.[52] Given this outlook, one might expect the British Empire to apply some of the insights of the effectiveness of mass persuasion demonstrated at the Great Exhibition to good use in conflict zones around the world.

However, this was rarely the case. The nationalism that had erupted in Europe in the early 1830s and that swept away many old aristocratic regimes in 1848 was used as a means to consolidate bourgeois control of British society in the face of a growing middle class that demanded greater political freedom and material security. Stirred by the images of the Great Exhibition, many of these middle-class fortune seekers sought their own opportunities for wealth in the imperial hinterlands of Great Britain. They were far less interested in the humanitarian ideas of the previous decades and when their schemes were threatened by local resistance, they demanded strong and powerful state assistance in the form of military intervention.[53] Rather than acting as a means to soften the blow of an expanding British imperial footprint, new innovations in media technology, which included the tactics of sensational journalism and staged entertainment, celebrated these coercive steps of imperial expansion and legitimized a policy of more aggressive foreign interventions among the domestic population. Rarely was this technology directed overseas in an effort to pacify indigenous groups who increasingly turned to violence to resist British expansion, and when it was tried, as in the case of Charles Gordon's trip to Sudan discussed below, the result were inauspicious. The lessons of the Great Exhibition appeared to be lost.

This section looks at two examples of this phenomenon. The first took place during the European race to colonize Africa when Great Britain used coercive force to shore up its control over Egypt by putting down a revolt deep in the interior of Sudan. As previously suggested, the original hope of Great Britain was to avoid a long and protracted military campaign in a distant and inhospitable region and rely on the soft power of skilled diplomatic emissaries—in this case General Charles Gordon, a veteran of British colonial administration around the world. However, Gordon's mission took place amid the backdrop of the "tabloidization" of the British press, which saw colonial conflict as eye-catching fodder for sensationalist newspaper stories. Indeed, much of the British colonial policy toward Egypt and Sudan during the later nineteenth century came about in large part due to tabloid newspapers arousing intense populist agitation that often compelled the British government to act in ways it would have otherwise not preferred. The other example, focusing on the outbreak of war in South Africa between 1899 and 1902, features not only the role of the tabloid press in whipping up a frenzy among the masses, but also the role of a newly politicized medium of entertainment—the music hall. As throngs of working men and women gathered at the local pubs and theaters for an evening's merrymaking, patriotic songs and nationalist theatricality facilitated Great Britain's entry into an ill-conceived war with Boer farmers in the interior of South Africa. Though the Boers were of European extraction and could plausibly be moved to conform to British colonial interests had Britain's primitive arsenal of entertainment been directed at them, Britain instead invaded the country with military force and nearly lost a vital strategic colony in the process. This jarring experience triggered ominous warning signs about the future of the British Empire and the best means to protect it.

Indeed, many of the warning signs of an empire beginning to slip away were starting to emerge even in the afterglow of the Great Exhibition. In 1857, a massive revolt took place in India where relations between locals and agents of British power had been relatively peaceful. The revolt began when Indian soldiers enrolled in the British army killed their commanding officers and took control of several key towns in central India. Britain responded with a brutal and bloody counterrevolutionary effort that saw atrocities committed on both sides. By 1859, almost all the rebels had been dispatched and stability slowly returned to the colony.[54] In the succeeding years after the rebellion, the British government abolished the East India Company and turned over the administrative responsibilities of India to the Colonial Office of the British government. This action had a slight ring of irony given that Britain was at the height of its infatuation with liberal free trade economics and informal approaches to imperial governance. Had a more potent international-communications infrastructure been in place, it is possible Britain may have granted some degree of autonomy to India in a similar way the United States in the present era seeks to grant some form of pseudosovereignty after it has pacified local resistance to the influx of external economic and cultural forces associated with globalization. Instead, the absence of such an infrastructure meant the establishment of India as a crown colony and the expansion of Britain's bureaucratic and military presence in the country.

The Indian Revolt served not only as a harbinger of things to come for Great Britain, but also an example of what can happen when there are no soft power assets available to make imperial rule and dominance palatable to local populations. Yet with a global media apparatus still in a primitive stage, the ability for Great Britain to use platforms of spectacle and engagement to avoid such uses of violence was limited. In the decades after the revolt, however, this slowly began to change with the introduction of the tabloid press. Amid the rebellion in India, many newspapers still catered to a limited class-based demographic with little attempt to combine readerships of varying social backgrounds into a more aggregate whole. Technology and education, however, began to undermine the limitations that existed to mass readership. The years between 1860 and 1900 saw a number of technological advances, including the development of the telephone, typewriter, and better methods of processing and printing drawings and illustrations, the latter of which resulted in the creation of new illustrated journals, such as *Graphic* and *Black and White*.[55] More importantly, the British government passed the Education Act in 1870, mandating the entire population attend school and acquire basic reading and writing skills. By 1900, 97 percent of the British population was considered functionally literate.[56]

With the better part of the British population having access to and the ability to read the information contained in the nation's print media, the stage was set to create information outlets that attempted to appeal to the entirety of the British reading public. Sunday newspapers had been the first to exploit this trend at the end of the period of radical agitation in the 1840s. Publications like *Lloyd's Weekly News* and *Reynold's News* had gained circulation numbers in the hundreds of thousands. After tumults abroad, including the Crimean War and the Indian Rebellion, raised the profile of the British Empire in the wider world, halfpenny newspapers created in the early 1880s (e.g., the *Daily Mail* and *Daily Express*), achieved circulations in excess of one million issues and enjoyed some cross-class appeal by tapping into the increasingly educated public's interest in news from abroad.[57]

This most effective conjunction of imperial politics, colonial insurrection, and sensationalist newspapers began with the *Pall Mall Gazette*. It was the *Pall Mall Gazette*, under the leadership of W. T. Stead that truly achieved one of the largest circulations in the late nineteenth-century Britain. The paper had shrewdly tailored its news and editorial content to emphasize issues susceptible to sensationalism and fear, such as the price of housing, crime, and sports.[58] As the politics of imperialism in Egypt began to heat up after 1869, it pushed its human-interest material to the back pages and placed colonial policy in Africa at the front and center of its news coverage. The large audiences that the paper had accumulated through dramatizing the plight of the poor and homeless were easily retained when the topic shifted to the plight of heroic British soldiers fighting for their lives in a hostile territory. For the government, the ability of the *Pall Mall Gazette* to mobilize such a large amount of public opinion for a conflict located on a forgotten periphery of the British Empire was both surprising and unnerving. Such papers had the ability to direct populist sentiment into certain directions that might not have been in the interests of the government, especially in the development of its imperial policies.

The popularity enjoyed by the *Pall Mall Gazette* stemmed from the paper's great journalistic innovation of eschewing the perceived duty to report the news in a generic and matter-of-fact way and instead write stories that actively appealed to the interests of the random reader. This innovation was the brainchild of the newspaper's famous founder, W. T. Stead. The problem with the traditional newspaper, especially those based in London, according to Stead, was that it was a "mere news-sheet, without weight, influence, or representative character."[59] It did not provide adequate representation to those outside the halls of power and more often than not reflected the interests of the bourgeois owners and publishers. As a result, the obligation of a journalism professional, no matter how badly this might offend the traditional sensibilities, was to publish material that would actually interest the publications readers:

> The editor must keep touch with his readers. He must interest, or he ceases to read. He must therefore, often sorely against his will, write on topics about which he cares nothing, because if he does not, the public will desert him

for his rival across the street. This, which in one sense is a degrading side of journalism, is in another a means of preservation and safety.[60]

Such devotion to reader interest did not mean a complete abandonment of attention toward important political issues of the day. On the contrary, adherents of this "new journalism" aggressively directed the attention of their readers to the most current controversies and pushed for appropriate measures to address them. Like parliamentary ministers or the queen herself, newspapers were a part of the government that had the honor and responsibility to advocate for the people. Quoting the prophet Ezekiel from the Bible, Stead suggested,

> The duty of a journalist is the duty of a watchman. "If the watchman see the sword come, and blow not the trumpet, and the people be not warned, if the sword came and take any person from among them, he is taken away in his iniquity; but his blood will I require at the watchman's hand."[61]

From this perspective, journalism that actively sought to change government policy was not only accepted, but also encouraged.

The kind of journalism Stead advocated was about appealing to the wants and desires of the masses as opposed to attempting to persuade them to adopt certain principles for their own good. High circulation numbers were still the ultimate goal—not emancipation of an oppressed or marginalized group as seen in the antislavery print material. Because of this, the use of sensationalism was not considered taboo: "Sensationalism in journalism is justifiable up to the point that it is necessary to arrest the eye of the public and compel them to admit the necessity of action."[62] Consequently, publications that adopted this style of journalism were noticeably different from their traditional competitors. Staid reports and editorials about issues being debated in Parliament were interspersed with more tabloid stories about gruesome murders and other obscene crimes, social gossip among the rich and famous, and the latest scores and news from popular British sports, including cricket, rugby, and football—the latter of which was exploding in popularity.[63] One can read in this the ethos of the tidal wave of tabloid journalism yet to come, from the yellow journalism that helped arouse the war fever of the Spanish-American War to the graphic-laden cable television news and sports broadcasts of the present day.

Another of Stead's great innovations in this regard was the frequent use of interview. Through this device, Stead could intimately introduce the heroes of the empire to the great reading masses of Great Britain. Formal interviews of important or famous newsmakers had yet to enter the canon of conventional journalism. Traditional newspapers obviously quoted individuals for their stories as well as publishing whole speeches of ministers on the floor of Parliament, but the notion of publishing a lengthy conversation between a reporter and a newsmaker despite the fact that there might not be a pending story that would justify such close journalistic scrutiny had yet to enter the editorial mainstream. Stead, on the other hand, was highly fond of the practice. It fit very well within the methodology of his new brand of journalism by dissolving the distance and aloofness of preeminent political and social figures and reduced them to a level approachable by the average reader.[64] Unfortunately, Stead never thought to use the interview or other pioneering aspects of the new journalism to attract foreign audiences or lionize foreign figures for the British reading public.

The tragedy of General Charles Gordon serves as an illustrative example of the new journalism affecting imperial policy. When rioting in Egypt threatened British and French investments as well as the security of the recently completed Suez Canal, political pressure was placed on Prime Minister William Gladstone to intervene. Related to this unrest was the rise of Islamist rebellion in the unincorporated hinterlands of Sudan that were under the nominal rule of Egypt. It became apparent that to deal with the unrest in Egypt also meant dealing with the rebellious lands of Sudan. Many leaders in the British ruling class made their recommendations known, but it was a long letter from noted imperial adventurer and explorer Sir Samuel Baker published in *The Times* that recommended that General Charles Gordon be sent to Sudan to quell the rebellion and reestablish order under British auspices.[65]

General Gordon's reputation as an imperial warrior and hero was well known throughout the British public. He had first served with distinction during the Crimean War, but came into true prominence with his campaign that successfully put down the Taiping Rebellion in China in 1864 with a "small, motley army" of Chinese soldiers.[66] The success of this campaign brought much media attention and led to his being dubbed "Chinese Gordon" in the British press. He then served as a provincial official in Egypt in the 1870s where he again gained notoriety for his efforts to quash the robust slave trade among local tribes and end some of the corruption rampant among Egyptian administrators.[67] By all accounts, General Gordon was the type of imperial hero whose story would trigger an outpouring of popular support for the protection of British interests in Egypt and Sudan and reverse what were seen as the submissive policies of Gladstone. All that was left was for someone to present this narrative to the masses in an engaging and entertaining way—a job perfectly suited for W. T. Stead.

As befitting a newspaper that practiced the new tabloid journalism, Stead's *Pall Mall Gazette* reported frequent updates on the fate of British forces in colonial lands, including the defeat of General Hick's Egyptian force in the deserts of Sudan in 1883. With a headline in the November 22, 1883, edition of the Gazette reading, "The Catastrophe in the Soudan," the paper published an article by the aforementioned Sir Samuel Baker that called for swift and deliberate action by an experienced colonial warrior: "Not an hour should be lost in deciding upon the plan of operations, which should be under the control of the only one responsible individual, who should be unfettered in his action. That person should be an Englishman."[68] Despite the attention, however, the public's interest in the crisis showed signs of waning after the initial shock of the first report of Hick's defeat. Moreover, Stead learned that Gordon, despite the recommendation given by Baker in *The Times* for service in Sudan, had accepted a position in the Congo region of Africa, for which he would soon depart from Great Britain.[69] Fearing the direction of colonial policy was moving away from that of an honorable and necessary intervention in Sudan, Stead decided to use the personality of Charles Gordon to bring the issue back into the public limelight and steer government decision making in the proper direction.

With little time to spare, Stead sprang into action. In the January 5, 1884, edition of the *Pall Mall Gazette*, Stead asked, in regard to Gordon's new job, "Is it not a pity at a time when so much other work is urgently wanting to be done in Egypt and elsewhere, the ablest leader of irregular forces England has produced should be told off to the service...amid the swamps of the Congo?"[70] With that question hanging in the air, Stead then proceeded to arrange an interview with the fabled general himself. The two men spoke at length about Gordon's previous experience in the region and the challenges of projecting power in an area where both the land and the people were seen as inhospitable. Stead then sought Gordon's advice on how the government should proceed, which Gordon refused to provide in any great detail as he wished to avoid publicly criticizing the government. However, he did conclude the interview by declaring, "If I can do anything for them [the Sudanese] I shall be only too glad."[71]

The interview appeared in the January 9, 1884, edition of the *Pall Mall Gazette*. A day later, it was reprinted in countless London and provincial papers accompanied by editorials insisting any future intervention in Sudan required the leadership and character of General Gordon.[72] In a matter of days, administrative and parliamentary gridlock on how best to proceed in the face of the problems facing British influence along the Nile evaporated and by January 19, 1884, the War Office announced that it would be sending a "special mission" to Khartoum under the leadership of General C. B. Gordon.[73] Stead wasted no time in celebrating the announcement: "The whole Egyptian question has been revolutionized in an hour. At yesterday's informal meeting of the Ministers at the War Office there was taken one of those decisive steps that make or mar the destinies of empires."[74] For the first time ever, a newspaper had played a fundamental role in the selection of a general for an imperial campaign.

To label the new journalism as pro-imperialism would be a bit hasty. Stead and some of his contemporaries were often critical of expansionist aspects of British foreign policy and were downright opposed to the Boer War in South Africa that broke out in 1899, a stance that earned him a Nobel Peace Prize nomination.[75] However, as this and subsequent examples of British overseas involvement show, mass audiences were especially drawn to articles and reports about wars and conflicts abroad, and with the expansion of the British Empire to even more remote areas like Sudan and the rise of competing empires vying with Great Britain for control of these exotic locales, the publications of tabloid journalism found themselves with a multitude of opportunities to give the people what they apparently wanted. However, in giving the people what they wanted and directly affecting the outcome of British policy overseas, newspapers that trafficked in the stories of imperial heroism and daring-do brought about tragic consequences for both the imperial idols they worshipped and for the local indigenous communities, which saw these individuals not as heroes but as foes.

Such a scenario transpired, as the crisis in Egypt and Sudan worsened and the superhuman powers bestowed on General Gordon by papers like the *Pall Mall Gazette* were shown to be illusory. After arriving in Khartoum, Gordon was unable to quell the Mahdi rebellion in Sudan as Great Britain assumed greater control over the internal affairs of the Egyptian government despite Prime Minister William Gladstone's desire to reduce the presence of the British Empire in the region. Meanwhile, the tabloid newspapers that helped send General Gordon to Sudan in the first place abandoned the story in search of fresh scandals at home and new heroes to lionize abroad. The Mahdi rebels, however, did not forget about Gordon, and at the end of January 1885, launched an assault on Khartoum that saw the rebels take control of the city and General Gordon killed in battle. The techniques of tabloid journalism, which with a little bit of tinkering could have been useful as a tool to legitimize British intervention among the Egyptian people, instead drove British power deeper into the region resulting in the death of one of its celebrated heroes.

The saga of General Gordon was perhaps the most stirring and tragic episode of Great Britain's imperial presence in Africa. In the wake of the tragedy, however, British magazines and newspapers, both cheap and traditional, continued to report on the stories of Britain's imperial activities in Africa to the delight and entertainment of an increasingly literate and prosperous British mass public. Thus, as the scramble for colonies around the world continued, newspapers continued to twist and refresh the themes of nationalism, racial superiority, and heroism as the century came to a close. However, by the end of the nineteenth century, more potent and entertaining platforms of mass appeal emerged to make themes of patriotism more powerful than they could ever hope to be on the printed page.

This was due to the British music hall emerging at the center of British cultural life in the late nineteenth century. Featured at the music hall was an endless stream of patriotic songs, farcical staged productions of past imperial events, and celebrations of the courage and bravery of Britain's military heroes. These music hall productions whipped their audiences into a patriotic frenzy that J. A. Hobson labeled as jingoism—a heightened emotional state of nationalism that combined racist attitudes, lionization of British culture, and a lust for the destruction of any group that questioned the right of Great Britain to rule the world. In jingoism, politically themed entertainment aroused the masses to support a war that did not promise to benefit them in any way in favor of the interests of a narrow set of industrial, financial, and government elites.

The war that broke out in South Africa in 1899 was an interesting example of the missed opportunity to use entertainment and amusement disseminated through a media capability that now had global dimensions. The war took place due to the discovery of gold deposits in the recently independent Boer (white South African settlers of Dutch and German extraction) republics of Orange Free State and Transvaal. When these Boer republics refused to cooperate with British mining companies to arrange for the extraction of the gold, leading members of the mining interests like Cecil Rhodes persuaded their British colleagues in the government to use coercive force to reclaim the republics and thereby give the miners access to the gold. What makes this case interesting is that, on the surface, the problems of insufficient technological advancement (a problem that was clearly present in India and Sudan) to wage a noncoercive media campaign against the intransigent Boers were not present. Telegraph links existed between Cape Town and London and much of the population in South Africa was Anglophone and read copies of London-based newspapers. With the arrival of the music hall as one of the primary means of leisure time activity, an enticing form of entertainment could have been deployed to either propagandize the message of Great Britain through music and song or, at the very least, neutralize some of the dissent building among local inhabitants against the prospect of British intervention in South Africa.

As with the tabloid press, the power of the music hall was a function of an increasingly literate and prosperous British middle class. Many important reforms had taken place in Great Britain in the last few decades that made this social group a power broker as the century came to an end. In 1867, Parliament passed a second reform act, granting the franchise to a larger segment of Britain's adult male population. In 1871, trade unions were legalized allowing members of the working class to organize and provide themselves some measure of protection against an economy still vulnerable to boom and bust cycles of financial speculation. In 1884, one year before news reached Britain of Gordon's death, a third reform act granted full suffrage to Britain's males. Perhaps most impactful of all was the Labor Party coming into existence and changing the face of British politics forever. However, the increasing power of the working classes was a challenge to the leadership of Great Britain as the scramble for Africa began to wind down and the continent almost completely carved up among the imperial powers.

As Vladimir Lenin argued in his famous pamphlet *Imperialism: The Last Stage of Capitalism*, the decline in unclaimed territory in places like Africa spawned conflicts between European states seeking to grab the last vestiges of land and protect those colonies already under their respective control. This increase in imperial rivalry required substantial material investment that may not have been available if powerful working-class organizations used their power to divert state resources toward domestic social welfare programs. However, as thinkers like Sigmund Freud and Hans Morgenthau pointed out in later years, the dynamics of mass psychology were such that certain ideologies like nationalism could channel the aggressive instincts of individuals toward mass support for policies they might not otherwise support. For Great Britain facing an extended era of imperial rivalry, keeping the fires of nationalism raging guaranteed the increased power of the working classes would not be used to interfere with interventionist policies.[76]

For the British Empire at the turn of the century, music hall entertainment was the gasoline that ignited one of the most intense forms of nationalism yet seen—jingoism. According to J. A. Hobson, jingoism is "a coarse patriotism, fed by the wildest rumors and the most violent appeals to hate and the animal lust of blood...the passion of the spectator, the inciter, the backer, not of the fighter."[77] In a later work, Hobson further elaborates, "Jingoism is merely the lust of the spectator, unpurged by any personal effort, risk, or sacrifice, gloating over the perils, pains, and slaughter of fellow-men whom he does not know, but whose destruction he desires in a blind and artificially stimulated passion of hatred and revenge."[78] This jingoistic passion gripped British society at the beginning of the South African War, allowing expansionist interests in British society and the government to pursue their interests with the enthusiastic backing of public opinion and virtually no organized dissent.

According to Hobson, these expansionist interests were "certain definite business and professional interests feeding upon imperialistic expenditure...and, instinctively feeling their way to one another, are found united in strong sympathy to support every new imperialist exploit."[79] These "business and professional interests" varied depending on the region of the world and the industry in question. In South Africa, the chief industry was diamond and gold mining, with several large firms entering the country with the discovery of these precious resources in 1884 (especially with the discovery of large gold reserves in the Witwatersrand area in Transvaal). The most famous of the mining companies active in South Africa was the DeBeers Mining Company and its aggressively expansionist leader, Cecil Rhodes. In a memorable line from one of his speeches, Rhodes claimed, "Having read the histories of other countries, I saw that expansion was everything, and that the world's surface being limited, the great object of the present humanity should be to take as much of the world as it possibly could."[80] After the discovery of gold in South Africa, however, recently independent Boer republics were posing significant obstacles to his efforts to fully exploit the region.

Elements of the British government shared Rhodes's affinity for expansion, but for different reasons. One of the most prominent of these sympathetic forces was the Colonial Office under the leadership of Joseph Chamberlain. Having assumed the office of colonial secretary in 1885, Chamberlain sought to bring the two breakaway Boer republics of Transvaal and Orange Free State back under the authority of the British crown in a unified South African colony. Such a union would solidify British control over a crucial region of the world and prevent interference from other colonial powers that were meandering around on the fringes of South Africa. In addition, Chamberlain, being a Liberal and opposed to political disenfranchisement, saw British intervention in South Africa as a means to alleviate unfair constraints on the political power of the Uitlanders (residents of Transvaal of British origin who did not have voting rights). A potential war in South Africa would be as much about "defense of principles" according to Chamberlain as it would be about securing resource-rich territory for British exploitation. With this harmony of material and ideological interests, the stage was set for armed intervention in Boer-controlled areas of South Africa.[81] The only wild card would be public opinion—how to persuade Britain's rising middle and working classes to support or be indifferent to war. Fortunately for Rhodes, Chamberlain, and a host of others who were eager for war, the British public was already being properly groomed for the coming conflict.

The reason for this good fortune stemmed from a new powerful force in British culture that was hitting its apogee at this time, contributing to a public obsession with the events in South Africa that greatly eclipsed anything seen before in British society. This new force was the music hall—a generic term that encompasses a wide variety of establishments mixing the traditional features of the pub with some sort of stage entertainment. Music halls themselves usually consisted of an audience seated at benches (sometimes with tables as well) facing a stage where a singer or group of singers performed songs, often encouraging the audience to join in if the song was familiar. Other popular forms of music hall–style entertainment, however, included the pub "free and easy" (pubs without licenses to book performances), saloons, and variety and melodrama theaters.[82]

Staged entertainment may seem like an odd place to locate the origins of a potent sociological force like jingoism, but as John MacKenzie argues,

> Its [the music hall's] phenomenal growth in the 1870s represented the first great entertainment boom. It seemed, moreover, to appeal to all social classes, offering the same performers, often working class in origin, in a great range of theatres with a wide spectrum of ticket prices. Above all, it reflected the dominant imperial ethos of the day in topical and chauvinistic songs, royal fervor, and patriotic tableaux.[83]

Indeed, it was the music hall that gave the world the term "jingoism." As the Russian army approached Constantinople during the Russo-Turkish War in 1878, Great Britain began mobilizing for war in the event it had to intervene to defend the Turks and maintain the European balance of power. With tensions mounting, a popular song written by G. W. Hunt and featured in a music hall owned by the noted theater owner G. H. MacDermott began being played repeatedly on stages throughout Great Britain. Heaped in the language of extreme patriotism and military self-confidence, the song's key line exclaimed,

> We don't want to fight,
> But, by Jingo, if we do,
> We've got the men,
> We've got the ships,
> We've got the money too.

The song then concluded with the rousing declaration, "The Russians shall not have Constantinople."[84] Though the conflict that inspired this song ended in a negotiated peace and Britain never had to intervene militarily, the enormous popularity of the song and the fervor with which it aroused the passions of the throngs of working classes in relation with complicated issues of British statecraft left an indelible mark on British social critics. J. A. Hobson, perhaps the music hall's fiercest detractor of the day, insisted, "The music hall, and the re-creative public houses into which it shades off by imperceptible degrees, are a more potent educator than the church, the school, the political meeting, or even the press."[85]

The music hall was successful in capturing the imagination of the British working classes for several reasons. First, songs and crude military stagecraft reconstructed the news of the day in an appealing and invigorating way. Men who had spent the week laboring hard in workhouses or factories and did not have the desire, energy, or ability to read up on the latest news from overseas could have the key events conveyed to them through song, dance, or dramatic recreation.[86] Second, music hall productions were not mere news bulletins disguised as entertainment, but also morality plays that harkened back to a time when genuine humanitarianism dominated British imperial propaganda during the heady days of antislavery activism. As the conflict between Boers and Britons became increasingly intractable, songs and plays that portrayed previous colonial conflicts in India and Southeast Asia as struggles between good and evil with the British forces on the side of virtue and their foes on the side of vice provided a framework for understanding this next big conflict in South Africa.[87] Finally, the music hall became the first place where the use of film was introduced to a mass audience. Though the quality of the film was low by present-day standards, the opportunity to put faces with the names of famous individuals proved a source of great delight. As Steve Attridge writes, "pageant, the novelty of film, and the excitement of seeing Buller [a key British general in the early days of the South African war] himself could provide a vicarious sense of being part of the embarkation for the war."[88] The introduction of film would also be important as the medium would be a prime means of enticing American audiences to go to war with Spain in the Spanish-American War and with Germany in World War I.

As the conflict between the Boers and the British became intractable and hostilities were imminent, the British public became primed to support the cause of their nation in southern Africa. Newspapers sold many copies of their dailies by predicting the upcoming conflict would be a "teatime war" and end with Britain victorious and in charge of the entirety of South Africa.[89] One leading figure in the British government, Lord Milner, sensed this when he claimed in a letter to a colleague, "The times are very exciting. Public opinion has been stirred on Imperial questions as it never yet has been in my lifetime, and it is impossible to say what may come out of it."[90] Milner's observation was shared by British writer George Sturt, who commented upon witnessing a nearby shop full of men eager for the latest war news: "For so long they had been waiting about, with nothing to do, expectant of the stimulus, and desiring something truly stirring. They would like a bloody battle twice a day, so that breakfast and supper might have a relish, and ennui be chased away."[91] Sturt's comment captures perfectly the ends of a well-functioning arsenal of entertainment, and at the height of the South African War, Britain's media force was delivering a devastating barrage of imagery and spectacle even before the real guns started firing.

So potent was this jingoistic spirit that even leading figures among the working classes were either supporting the cause for war in South Africa or fearful of dissenting against it. Robert Blatchford, editor of the socialist newspaper *The Clarion* remarked, "My whole heart is with the British troops, when England is at war I'm English. I have no politics and no party. I am English."[92] Another notable radical, Leslie Stephen, observed when asked to make a statement opposing the war, "I confess that it seems to me to be not only useless but mischievous to protest against the war now! The thing is horrible—it distracts and torments me—but it has got to me; and we must, in my opinion, keep what we have to say for a better time."[93] For the few newspapers that took editorial stands against the war and the overarching British policy toward Transvaal, the consequences for this dissent were crippling. The *Manchester Guardian* nearly shuttered when its contrarian view cost it most of its readers. Another paper, the *Daily Chronicle*, switched its editorial position from antiwar to pro-war when a new editor realized the paper would not survive without retaining its dwindling readership by echoing the popular sentiment.

After war was declared, the tabloid press assumed its familiar place as a source of both news and entertainment. Ironically, part of the nature of the war in South Africa—consisting of numerous sieges of British-controlled towns by Boer armies—began to blur the distinction between real life and fictionalized entertainment. As Paula Krebs explains, "a siege makes for good long-term drama for a newspaper, almost as good as serial fiction for winning reader loyalty. It takes no great military mind to follow the details of a siege, and the situation itself—dwindling supplies and ammunition, no relief in sight—inspires concern."[94] In 1900, the *Daily Mail*'s circulation broke the one-million-copy mark—the first daily newspaper to reach such a milestone.[95] Such a gigantic audience provided the opportunity for these newspapers to broaden and deepen the jingoistic sentiments that buttressed support for the war during these early defeats and keep the reading public eager for more news.

As the sieges wore on, however, news from the beleaguered towns began to dry up. Journals and magazines of all types sent correspondents to South Africa to increase the flow of information and attempted to make contact with individuals already in the besieged towns. However, a combination of cut telegraph lines, unreliable dispatches sent via heliograph, and an aggressive censorship policy implemented by the British military made getting access to reliable information difficult. In these conditions, correspondents, mindful that their editors wanted stories that would appeal to the emotions of the average worker's sense of patriotism, often combined rumor, speculation, and jingoistic pronouncements to fill pages and keep circulation numbers high.[96]

Eventually, the sieges were lifted (including the infamous siege at Mafeking that triggered a wild night of street celebration and merriment in several British cities) and superior numbers of British forces were brought to bear that resulted in the defeat of the Boer armies. However, in the immediate aftermath of the conflict, Great Britain found itself unable to deploy the necessary military forces necessary to keep its scattered colonies and spheres of influence secure. This realization required Britain to enter into a strategic alliance with Japan in 1902 in which the Japanese military assumed hegemony over the waters of the Eastern Pacific Ocean. Such an arrangement was a tacit acknowledgment that Great Britain could no longer take sole responsibility for the maintenance of world order and that its status as the globe's leading nation was in serious doubt. All the patriotic fervor contained in catchy music hall songs and jingoistic performances in London could not hide the fact that the British Empire was in a state of decline and that its people were oblivious to this fact in large part because the newspapers and music halls had kept them so well entertained.

Britain Overexposed: State Propaganda, Film, Radio, and the Decline of the British Empire (1902–1945)

Nationalism, in its differing variations, sustained popular support for the numerous expansions of the British Empire throughout the second half of the nineteenth century. In an era when the increasing power of domestic working classes and international imperial rivalry put unprecedented pressure on British power, potent narratives of nationalism dramatized in cheap newspapers and on the stages of music halls ensured that the British Empire kept a leading position in the world. However, the tone of this media output that was doing such a fine job of keeping the masses entertained began to change after the seemingly omnipotent military forces of the British Empire nearly fell to defeat on the *veld* of South Africa. Discourses that demonized foreign populations or deified British leaders were increasingly out of congruence with the reality of Britain's vulnerabilities. As Great Britain relied more heavily on the peoples of its empire to confront the new challenges of the early twentieth century, the universalist themes of Britain's antislavery campaigns and Great Exhibition wove themselves more deeply into the narratives of British media. On top of this, the development of pivotal new communications technologies, including film and radio, served as crucial tools in disseminating this new and more inclusive legacy to the world.

The imperative to develop a more conciliatory theme of imperial communications stemmed from the stark reality that Britain was entering a new phase in its imperial epic—that of decline and possible collapse. During this phase, the past political and economic innovations of an empire became increasingly antiquated as rival powers introduced new ideas and new technologies that laid the foundation for new assemblages of global power. Few developments represented the rise of a new echelon of power and the decline of British world order better than the shift in the center of world industrial production from Great Britain to other industrial centers. Benefiting from the innovations of Henry Ford and Frederick Taylor in factory organization and worker's rights, the United States established a leading position in the world's industrial output.[97] On the European continent, a fully unified Germany brought together through an ambitious industrial policy and a package of welfare benefits introduced by Otto von Bismarck, surpassed British industrial output, dealing a further blow to British power and prestige.[98] Meanwhile, back in Britain, much of British wealth remained in financial investments that were beginning to dry up as the race for colonies ended and the ability to exploit new markets declined. The need to ensure that the areas under the control of Great Britain remained as productive and supportive as possible to the imperial homeland meant that media products that denigrated or diminished the position of colonies, allies, or lower classes, while not abandoned, diminished significantly. It also meant that any new communications technology that made the exchange of information between far-flung peripheries more efficient was to be exploited to the fullest extent.

Thus, this section examines how new innovations in image management and control, such as government information ministries, films and newsreels, and state radio outlets were essential steps to mitigate the decline of British power in the military and economic sector and rally international support to the cause of the preservation of the British Empire. They provided a model that future powers like the United States adapted to build up their own imperial frameworks without resorting to the formal structures of hierarchical rule that were now proving to be a liability to British power. For Great Britain, however, these appeals to progressive values were actually a sign of Britain's weakened state. Britain no longer had the military or economic capacity to restrain powers like Germany alone nor the ability to force colonies eager for independence to remain in the empire. In this sense, the use of progressive rhetoric was a desperate attempt to keep the key components of the British Empire together through global events that were driving the empire apart. During World War I, the development of state propaganda agencies rallied many current and former colonies of the empire to support their mother nation, but in Ireland, resistors to British rule used their own innovative methods of propaganda to revolt against British power in 1916. In the 1930s, attempts to cultivate imperial unity through film and newsreels struggled to gain traction amid the shrewd use of media and imagery by dissidents like Gandhi in India. In the days preceding the outbreak of World War II, international radio broadcasting managed to push world opinion to support the allies, but this task was made far more difficult by the ability of the propaganda machine of the Nazis to use Britain's imperial history to portray it in a negative light.

However, if all these innovations were successful in contributing to the building of a coalition to confront totalitarianism and depression, they also took the entertainment value out of the British Empire. Appealing media content during the early twentieth century centered on attracting the eyes and ears of overseas audiences as much as that of the domestic population, which meant the most entertaining discourses of the past rooted in nationalism and imperial exceptionalism were abandoned. This struggle to universalize entertainment for a global audience amid intense global tensions provided an interesting opportunity to observe similarities and differences for the present prospects of American power immersed in the trying times of the early twenty-first century, when economic recession, the arrival of new great powers, revolutions in client states, and an inability to properly apply new media technologies may be indicative of an imperial power in a state of decay. Though Britain could not sustain itself amid the contradictions of democracy and imperial rule, it did discover effective ways for manipulating the minds of large groups of people to allow it to survive the challenge of German aggression and economic depression. These innovations went on to become indispensable to the United States in the twentieth and early twenty-first centuries as it faced similar challenges of legitimizing its expansion after World War II.

The idea of an "overexposed" Britain began to reveal itself as the state became more heavily involved in wartime propaganda. Upon the outbreak of World War I, the British government established the War Propaganda Bureau (known more informally as Wellington House in reference to the name of the building where its offices were located). During its wartime activities, Wellington House relied heavily on imperial imagery and text to stoke the patriotic passions of Britons and encourage support of British troops on the front lines. It also, however, invoked discourses that emphasized the fact that British armies included ranks from all corners of the empire.[99] According to Philip Taylor, Wellington House had secretly produced, by 1915, 2.5 million pieces of propaganda in 17 languages as well as circulating 6 illustrated newspapers and publishing 4,000 photographs a week.[100]

Wellington House also authorized and bankrolled propaganda films, newsreels, and other visual propaganda media that took advantage of the advancing technology of motion pictures. As mentioned in the previous section and will be discussed more fully in chapter 2, crude short films were available at the turn of the century and were a useful tool in boosting jingoistic or nationalist sentiments. However, these films, while contributing to the overall patriotic timbre of the time, were more curious novelties and played second fiddle to the staged productions of the music halls. By 1914, the technology advanced considerably and feature motion pictures were major productions that required extensive planning and coordination. Wellington House films ran the gambit from preparedness documentaries that were produced primarily for local consumption such as *Britain Prepared* to large spectacles that sought to entertain a wide international audience such as the *Battle of Somme*.[101]

For all its success, Wellington House did have two drawbacks that worked against a nation trying to cultivate a notion of self-determination and greater self-governance among its colonies and allies. For one, Wellington House operated in almost total secrecy in the belief that audiences would react negatively if they knew the item of information they were pondering was the product of propagandists. Indeed, much of the Wellington House propaganda directed at the United States was done in ways to disguise its point of origin in London. This fear of negative blowback bore out when postwar revelations about Wellington House's activities in the United States showed how much of the news and information in American newspapers originated from Wellington House. Much of the American public was outraged, including the famous muckraking journalist Upton Sinclair, who included himself as "one of the hundred and ten million suckers who swallowed the hook of British official propaganda."[102] The second problem was Wellington House's focus on cultivating elite opinion instead of popular sentiment. This disposition prompted severe criticism from the likes of Lord Northcliffe—the press lord who ran Britain's largest newspapers at the time and whose experience as a populist newspaper publisher allowed him to see the error of such an approach in an age of Fordist production and mass military conscription. For this reason, Wellington House's activities were pared down once Northcliffe's political ally David Lloyd George became prime minister in 1916.[103]

Lloyd George favored a more open approach to information management and set about establishing a more transparent propaganda apparatus with the creation of the Ministry of Information (MOI) in 1917.[104] Upon its establishment, the MOI took over most of the duties of Wellington House and reoriented itself toward making appeals to the masses—such a change was more in the spirit of a nation that was ostensibly fighting for democracy and self-determination and not preservation of a paternalist empire. The MOI went on to produce a sizable heap of propaganda material, including more films, newsreels, and prewritten newspaper stories. But by 1917, the primary target of this propaganda—British skeptics, colonial holdouts, and isolationist Americans—had by and large been persuaded to join the cause. The task that remained for the rest of the war was to use propaganda to undermine the power of the enemy.[105]

The effort to direct propaganda against Britain's enemies took place at Crewe House in London. For this task, the British government turned to its master tabloid newspaperman, Lord Northcliffe, to lead the operation against neutrals and enemies. Such a project took on greater importance as the alliance structure of the Triple Entente went through upheaval with the loss of Russia to internal revolution and the United States not yet joining the fight. Upon assuming his position of leadership, Northcliffe found that a great deal of confusion existed among Britain's leadership about the moral aim of the war. Sure, the survival of Britain and its empire were at stake, but that message would not persuade the soldiers of the Triple Alliance to question their orders and refuse to fight. The task for Northcliffe and the propagandists at Crewe House was to find something broadly appealing that transcended nationality, but not to make promises that would not be honored. One worker at Crewe House, R. W. Setson-Watson, insisted it was important not to raise "false hopes" that Britain had "no intention of assisting."[106]

The impasse was solved not by British politicians and propagandists, but by the arrival of the United States and the articulation by Woodrow Wilson of the Fourteen Points. Of particular relevance in this document were the numerous calls for the readjustment of European boundaries in accordance with the locations of various national groups—in essence an acknowledgment by Wilson of the right for national self-determination. Members of Crewe House took the Fourteen Points to be ideal content matter for their propaganda output, and before long were churning out millions of leaflets and newspapers celebrating the idea of ethnic groups having the right to rule their own state and determine their own future.[107] One of the first targets for this campaign was Austria-Hungary. No belligerent in the war was more troubled with ethnic and cultural infighting than the teetering Habsburg Empire, and with British propaganda rousing nationalist groups to seek their independence, the internal pressure was more than the monarchy could bear. The last year of the war saw "60 million copies of 643 different leaflets in 8 languages, and some 10 million copies of 112 different newspapers in four languages, distributed to Austria-Hungary."[108] By October 1918, Slavic soldiers in the Austrio-Hungarian army deserted en masse and the state ceased to field an effective fighting force.

The development of an effective state-run propaganda apparatus articulating a progressive message of self-determination allowed British influence to extend beyond its own empire and into the hearts and minds of individuals who were not in any way connected with British politics or culture. The successful use of propaganda against Austria-Hungary echoed the lessons of the Great Exhibition of the previous century and demonstrated how information could be a tool for not just imperial manipulation, but also global manipulation. However, the propaganda that allowed Britain to undermine the power of its enemies was also being deployed to neutralize its own power by exposing the hypocrisies and contradictions of its newfound progressivism. Indeed, one reason why Setson-Watson and other staff members of Crewe House were uneasy about making specific promises to sympathetic populations in rival nations was because the events of the Easter Uprising in Ireland still lingered in the collective consciousness of Britain. In 1916, Irish nationalists calling for home rule (another way of saying self-determination) attempted to take control of the city of Dublin and stir a mass uprising against British rule. After gaining control of a handful of key buildings, the nationalists were defeated a week later when British reinforcements entered the city to support the local police and militias. Though the rebellion was unsuccessful in the short term, it nevertheless sparked the revival of direct action by Irish nationalists that eventually led to civil war after the end of World War I. From the perspective of British propaganda, however, the Irish rebellion represented a major perception crisis that threatened to undermine the messages of commonwealth and democracy being directed elsewhere in the world.

Propagandists in Ireland were well aware of the precarious position Great Britain was in during World War I and went out of their way to exploit this weakness. The frightful losses of men and material in the trenches meant Britain relied heavily on troops from its colonies. Ireland was no exception, and British recruitment campaigns attempted to stir the feelings of unity in the face of German atrocities like the sinking of the Lusitania to encourage reluctant Irish men to fight under the British flag. Irish nationalists, however, were swift in bringing up Britain's own history of humanitarian abuses in their rule over Ireland, and given the frequent brutality of the tactics police and soldiers used to suppress nationalist demonstrations, contradictions between image and reality were never far from view. Indeed, just ten days before the start of the war, British soldiers opened fire on a nationalist crowd gathered in Dublin, giving Irish opinion makers a fresh example of British tyranny to neutralize calls for supporting the British war effort on humanitarian grounds.[109]

Throughout the war, Irish printers and pamphleteers buried Dublin and other major Irish cities in a blizzard of anti-British print material that made the antislavery campaigners of the previous century turn green with envy. Nationalist newspapers like the *Irish Volunteer* and *Nationality* published bits of poetry and ran serialized tabloid stories in the tradition or W. T. Stead and Lord Northcliffe.[110] When self-determination became a common theme in British propaganda as well as in British imperial politics, newspapers ran stories, editorials (and in one case, a cartoon depicting racists caricatures of Westernized African tribesmen) that evoked the contradiction of celebrating the virtue of people ruling themselves in Eastern Europe, Oceania, and Africa, but explicitly denying it in Ireland. If Britain's violent put down of the Easter Rebellion reignited the nationalist fervor that had lain dormant in Irish society for many years, the proliferation of anti-British propaganda that mocked British claims of benevolence and respect for democracy certainly sustained that fervor through battles that eventually led to conditional Irish independence in 1921.[111]

News of the uprising also did no favors for Britain within its own empire or cultural and linguistic community. The Irish-American newspapers like the *Gaelic American* delighted in pointing out 13 million square miles of the earth's surface and 444 million people were subject to British control while in Britain itself, 2.5 percent of the population controlled 98 percent of the wealth. Given these figures, the claim that Britain was fighting for democracy "was a sick joke."[112] In other parts of the empire, the Easter Rebellion stirred condemnation and undermined colonial unity for the home country in its hour of greatest need.[113] Rumors and allegations that the Irish rebels were secretly being helped by Germany prevented the damage from being much worse, but the fact remains that Britain's harsh treatment of its Irish colony and its reluctance to make the same promises to it as were being made to enemies like Austria-Hungary dealt a severe blow to an empire that was struggling to fight off the effects of decline and decadence.

Nevertheless, with the victory of Britain and its allies at the end of the war, the empire appeared to have survived its greatest challenge. This triumph was brought about in no small way by the ability of British bureaucrats and media masters like Lord Northcliffe to create a state-based propaganda apparatus that rallied support for Great Britain both within the empire and from sympathetic allies overseas. But in ensuring that this potent propaganda machine made the greatest impact on both friend and foe, a refrain of commonwealth, self-determination, and democracy had to take center stage despite their obvious antagonism toward the ruling structures of the British Empire. With the Irish Rebellion in 1916, this antagonism was exposed for the world to see, and undermined the legitimacy of the British cause. However, the bad publicity associated with the Easter Uprising would not be the rhetorical deathblow to the British Empire. Britain was only now beginning to unlock the true power of media technology not only to consolidate its population, but also to attract a larger numbers of allies and adherents beyond its own imperial boundaries.

As the postwar euphoria gave way to depression in the late 1920s and 1930s, the need to cultivate new technologies like film, newsreel, and radio were of paramount importance to craft new and compelling messages for audiences around the world. Ireland was just the first of many potential contradictions that could bring down the empire if overexposed. Few understood this threat better than John Grierson did. After serving in World War I and attending college, the Scotsman went to the United States to study propaganda and mass communications. The aftermath of the war resulted in an increasing interest in the study of mass media, with prominent philosophers like Bertrand Russell and Harold Laswell expressing their fear that propaganda techniques developed during the war would continue to be used for nefarious ends in peacetime.[114] Grierson thought differently. He insisted that mass media and persuasion could bring about positive ends that could facilitate a common national identity and overcome economic and social differences. This process of engaging a mass audience in a positive way to bring about some sort of shared social perception or belief later came to be known as public relations, and Grierson was among its first British practitioners.[115]

Advances in technology were a big part of Grierson's vision. World War I demonstrated the effectiveness of the motion picture and news-reel in capturing the attention and imagination of audiences around the world. More importantly, just because the war was over did not mean the task of consolidating public opinion was any less important, and if new motion picture technologies could be utilized to great effect during wartime, there was nothing preventing this same technology from being put to similar purposes in peacetime as well. Grierson was among one of the early advocates of using films to educate mass audiences on the important issues of the day and "impart important information to the electorate."[116] While studying at the University of Chicago, Grierson began to explore the potential for cinema to "bridge the gap between citizen and his community" and become a powerful force for public education.[117] One of his more interesting theories was the possibility of creating a special type of film that would be "representative of reality but with more creative input than a fly-on-the-wall actuality film."[118] In essence, this new form of film would both educate *and* entertain. In 1926, he began using the term "documentary" to describe such projects, and upon his arrival back in Great Britain, sought opportunities to begin making and distributing this new kind of film.[119] It was not long before his first big opportunity arrived.

The Empire Marketing Board (EMB), established by the government in 1926, was the primary institution in British society that kept an increasingly faltering empire fresh in the minds of the British public. Rather than focus on a military or political relationship between Great Britain and its colonies, the EMB sought to raise awareness of imperial issues through commercial publicity and advertising campaigns encouraging British citizens to buy consumer products from colonial possessions. As envisioned by one of its founding members, W. S. Crawford, the EMB was to create an "Empire-conscious people," who would make "empire buying a national habit."[120] In pursuing this objective, "the EMB used almost every conceivable form of publicity—posters print advertisements, Christmas cards, postcards, leaflets, lectures, radio broadcasts, film screenings, Empire shopping weeks and exhibitions."[121] It was here at the EMB where Grierson would begin his work with documentary filmmaking and help give the embattled empire a much-needed public face-lift.

Grierson arrived at the EMB shortly after its founding and quickly began work on producing short films about various colonial industries and the products these industries produced that were available for purchase in British stores. The first of these films, titled *Drifters*, focused on British herring fishermen and despite its rather pedestrian subject matter, garnered a significant amount of attention both inside and outside the government and led to the EMB forming its own film division.[122] This move was a milestone of sorts in the history of media in Great Britain, for it marked the first occasion when a formal government entity produced its own publicity material outside of a wartime situation. More short documentary-style films were made by the EMB, including *One Family*, "a story designed to reveal some of the riches of the Empire by sending a boy in a shopping expedition around the world gathering ingredients for a King's Empire Christmas pudding."[123] Thereafter, other films by other directors were made and screened in local movie houses, including *The Country Comes to Town* (London's food and milk supplies), *Cargo from Jamaica* (bananas), *Shadow in the Mountain* (pasture experiments in Wales), *Windmill in Barbados* (sugar), and *Industrial Britain*.[124]

The EMB, however, served not only as an entertaining publicity machine for colonial industries, but also in changing the British imperial "brand." Earlier expressions of British hegemony were rife with images of military strength, economic prosperity, and moral virtue. These images were directed at a narrower upper-class audience that saw the prowess of Great Britain as an extension of their own God-given prerogatives. As British society became more enfranchised and democratized, images of strength and power were transformed into jingoistic messages that catered to larger audiences within the nation as a whole. Yet, in the wake of the devastation of the Great War, these themes were no longer effective and contradicted the discourse of commonwealth and trusteeship Britain hoped would help keep its empire from cracking to pieces. Instead, images of cooperation between motherland and colony and peace and prosperity through mutual understanding were the dominant themes. As observed by John MacKenzie, "the Empire being developed by this co-operative effort was a force for international peace. Traditional late nineteenth century imperial images of jingoism and military conquest, the iconography of battle, were significantly avoided."[125] In emphasizing images of cooperation over conflict, the EMB was echoing the new priorities in international politics where weakened imperial powers attempted to regrip the colonies that were slowly slipping away from their grasp.

However, neither could the EMB obscure every image of repressive imperial rule amid economic hardship nor could it counter the more compelling narratives emerging from the colonies as imperial subjects demanded the right to be free of British imperialism. Few things are more entertaining to a mass audience than the depiction of an underdog challenging and triumphing over a bully—and in India, Mahatma Gandhi was providing just such a narrative. Indeed, Gandhi demonstrated that colonial dissidents often times understood the power of media images better than the state technocrats in London did as he embarked upon a campaign to expose the contradictions of British rule through Britain's own print and visual media. While much attention has been directed at the normative and spiritual dimensions of Gandhi's nonviolent tactics, the motivation for the use of such tactics also stems from a realization that images of unarmed and peaceful protestors being manhandled by agents of the empire would direct the world's sympathy toward the cause of the dissenters and expose the brutality of the imperial regime. In essence, Gandhi's success came not (only) from his political philosophies but from his media savvy.

As Eric Louw suggests, "Gandhi was 'a televisual performer' before television existed."[126] Gandhi was keenly aware of what images would make the biggest impressions on audiences in Britain and the rest of the world sympathetic to the cause of colonial emancipation and sought to put himself and his followers in positions that would create those images:

> Gandhi's performances were magnificent—scripted around a brilliant visual gimmick of a half-naked little man in a dhoti (white shawl), holding a bamboo stave who looked like a victim rather than a skilled political operator...Gandhi invented symbols (e.g. the spinning wheel) and staged performances to embarrass India's British rulers, and provoke them into arresting him, thus making themselves look like heavy-handed villains.[127]

In newspaper and newsreels around the world, these images captivated audiences and transformed Gandhi and his cause into a focal point of international sympathy. Indeed, Gandhi's effectiveness at exposing the nature of imperial rule revealed an effective weapon of resistance applicable to all formations of power that could not disguise the gaps between their progressive rhetoric and their repressive realities. Later years saw Martin Luther King and Archbishop Desmond Tutu use similar strategies of counterspectacle to undermine the legitimacy of the regimes that ruled each of them. Back in London, imperial administrators were unable to counter the negative imagery coming out of India and other colonies agitating for independence. As the Great Depression continued to devastate the economy of Great Britain, groups from across British society, including trade unions, liberal bourgeoisie, and university intellectuals demanded an end to British rule in India.[128]

The fate of India, however, soon took a back seat to more pressing problems closer to the British home shores. With the dark clouds of totalitarianism beginning to gather by the early 1930s, learning how to appeal not just to subjected peoples in the empire, but the entirety of the global population became of paramount importance. Agencies like the British Council, first founded in 1934, focused more on spreading British culture and lifestyle rather than on a specific political or economic message. With offices in multiple locations around the world, the British Council offered programs such as English language instruction, productions of staged plays in English, and the maintenance of English libraries in foreign countries.[129] Though outfits like the British Council neither prevented the emergence of fascism nor undid the bad publicity of the British Empire in places like India, they did provide a foreign platform to counter local misperceptions and revealed how information presented in an intriguing and entertaining manner had the potential to stir sympathies with local populations. However, it was not only Great Britain that was learning this lesson, but also Nazi Germany and republican North America were starting to pay attention to Britain's grappling with the power of media, information, and entertainment.

As the threat of Nazi Germany became more apparent, Great Britain widened the scope of its rhetoric about the need to protect democracy, civilization, and human rights knowing that it could not defeat Hitler's growing war machine by itself. As Winston Churchill stated in a speech in 1938, "Civilization will not last, freedom will not survive, peace will not be kept, unless a very large majority of mankind unite together to defend them and show themselves possessed of a constabulary power before which barbaric and atavistic forces will stand in awe."[130] Yet for all the stirring words Churchill and his contemporaries gave in their efforts to arouse the nations around the world to form a grand alliance to fight the barbarism of the Nazis, key nations like the United States were slow to heed the calls. Thus, the challenge for British propaganda in the days leading up to the outbreak of World War II was a rather straightforward one—tell the truth in a compelling manner about the nature of Nazi power and let Germany's own misdeeds speak for themselves.

To accomplish this, however, the coy use of the latest communications technologies would be necessary, and fortunately for Great Britain, in 1896, it had welcomed a young Italian inventor who was in the process of perfecting just such a device. Guglielmo Marconi did not find much support for his crude and bulky radio transmitter in Italy. However, his fortunes turned when he arrived in Great Britain, and before long, his invention brought him worldwide attention and commercial success. Agents of the government, including a little-known politician from Scotland named John Reith, soon became interested in the potential applications of radio for the British government, envisioning some kind of information service that could broadcast to the entire nation as well as to audiences overseas. In 1922, Reith's arguments for the benefits of radio garnered enough support in the government to launch the BBC.[131]

Reith's early support for state involvement in radio broadcasting resulted in his being named the BBC's first director. Reith also published an influential book on the role of radio in British society entitled *Broadcasting Britain*, where he outlined the vision for the application of the new wireless medium. Reith was disgusted by the way cinematic media had devolved from a tool of education to a tool of entertainment, and sought to avoid a similar fate with radio.[132] Reith believed radio broadcasts should be made compelling by "carry[ing] into the greatest possible number of homes everything that is best in every human department and endeavor and achievement, and to avoid things which are, or may be, hurtful."[133] To Reith, this meant broadcasting "the classics" when it came to music and literature readings accompanied by intellectual commentary and lectures. The programming was very much in the Victorian tradition of giving the population that which was best for them and not that which they (the audience) actually wanted.[134] In this sense, the radio was to be a force for stability and the status quo, and this conception extended to its representation of the empire and its broadcasts overseas.

A look at the programs broadcasted by the BBC intended for imperial audiences reveals how well Great Britain understood the power of information and its effectiveness to keep the empire from unraveling in the days before World War II. Content for programs echoed that of the EMB and the themes of its documentary films, namely, "internationalism and economic harmony."[135] National holidays proved especially potent as content for the broadcasting platform. Among the most important days on the imperial calendar after World War I were Empire Day, Armistice Day, and Christmas Day. Each of these occasions marked a special schedule of musical and spoken-word programming, including speeches by members of the royal family, "nonpartisan" speeches by prominent politicians, poetry reading by famous British authors including Rudyard Kipling, and the playing of orchestral music by notable British composers like Edward Elgar.[136] The BBC radio broadcasts also provided opportunities for the colonies to have a voice, albeit in a way that always flattered their imperial masters. A program run in the 1940s titled *The Empire Speaks* allowed the premiers of the various colonial dominions to record a message for broadcast throughout the BBC media's network.[137] Such programming allowed the leadership to participate in the process of creating positive publicity for the empire and project what appeared to be a strong and unified imperial consensus to both British citizens and subjects.

As World War II approached, however, concerns with the withdrawal of Germany from the League of Nations accompanied by the rise of Hitler brought the BBC into closer contact with the Britain's foreign policy apparatus. Broadcasting to the colonies messages of imperial unity quickly shifted toward news updates on the succession of European political crises triggered by the Nazi program of German expansion.[138] In focusing on the threat posed by the Nazis, the BBC widened its broadcasting ambitions to include the entire world. As with World War I, much of this international effort began with programs directed toward the United States through a series of programs with the informal label of "Hands across the Sea." These shows focused on the common civilization the United States and Great Britain shared and featured everything from listener participation shows like *Trans-Atlantic Call* and *Listening Post*, which discussed the content of German propaganda.[139] In those parts of the world where the presence of the BBC was limited, representatives for the organization produced indigenous language stories played on local broadcasting outlets. By the height of World War II, 500 different broadcasting outlets representing 19 different languages broad-casted BBC produced content.[140]

For all the regional and linguistic variations of BBC radio content, how-ever, the anchor remained the same—honest and open news and informa-tion without any hint of sensationalism or fabrication. One BBC official made the reason for this disciplined approach to programming clear when he stated,

> Of course there has to be denial of certain mis-statements, but the best pro-paganda must be positive: we must get in first, and put the enemy on the defensive. A prompt and regular supply of significant news will be far more effective at home and overseas than the desperate effort to contradict every false story from Germany.[141]

This "tell it straight" method of news reporting started to pay substan-tial dividends in the battle for hearts and minds when German aircraft began their relentless bombing of British cities during the Battle of Britain in 1940. News reports of London under attack riveted American audi-ences who could hear updates not only from BBC broadcasts but also from Edward R. Murrow's live Columbia Broadcasting System (CBS) broadcasts introduced with the famous phrase "This is London." The vivid sounds of bombs falling, buildings collapsing, and victims grieving accompanied by the no-nonsense narration of a radio reporter had the effect of portraying the Germans as destroyers of civilization without recourse to any sensation-alistic deviousness on the part of the BBC or other allied broadcasters.[142]

Without a doubt, the BBC represented a remarkable and audacious inno-vation in media technology and its use for political ends. With Nazi propa-ganda taking a far more aggressive approach to information dissemination, the temptation to replicate the methods of Nazi propaganda master Joseph Goebbels, especially when the early days of World War II brought little good news to Great Britain, was enormous. Nevertheless, the legacy of John Reith, who left the BBC in 1938, remained strong as the BBC manag-ers resisted the temptation to turn toward more entertainment program-ming and stuck with content focusing on education and the cultivation of high cultural taste. But other elements in Britain's propaganda bureaucracy were not above indulging in a few examples of "black" propaganda aimed at foreign audiences (especially those in enemy territory).[143] For this type of operation to be successful, an alternative way of using radio was developed that might be offensive to the likes of Reith, but would nevertheless gain the mass audiences who might not have access to BBC transmissions or found them turgid and unappealing. Into this breech was inserted Radio Luxembourg (RTL).

Begun by British entrepreneurs with American financial backing, RTL transmitted in multiple languages but spent much of its day broadcasting in English. The original idea was to use RTL to broadcast commercial programming back into Great Britain and break the monopoly of the BBC. What made RTL unique was its transmissions of popular music to gather large audiences combined with time blocked off for advertising and other commercial activities.[144] Naturally, Reith and the BBC detested the station, and were none too happy by the reports of RTL's popularity throughout Great Britain.[145] After a change in ownership in the mid-1930s, however, RTL suddenly demonstrated a decidedly pro-British orientation in its programming and seemed to be curiously on the cutting edge of major stories dealing with British politics in Europe at the time of the rise of German fascism. During the Munich Conference in 1938, which saw European leaders gather in Germany to prevent the outbreak of war by appeasing Hitler's demand for the Sudetenland in Czechoslovakia, RTL managed to broadcast key speeches and statements of British prime minister Neville Chamberlain and US president Franklin Roosevelt (who did not attend but did issue statements on the direction of the negotiations) at a time when such transmissions were rare and difficult. About the same time, the ability of RTL to broadcast worldwide via shortwave transmission suddenly came online.[146]

What was happening was the skillful behind-the-scenes manipulation of RTL by the hidden propaganda agents of Great Britain. Rather than fuss about the vulgar programming and commercial advertising for which the station was famous, elements within the British government saw RTL as a tantalizing opportunity to broadcast messages friendly to British interests on a non-British platform that garnered a significant international audience due to its entertaining playlists of popular music. By 1940, the spread of the Nazi scourge into the Low Countries forced the station to cease operations but Germany never did find out the truth about RTL and its informal control from London.[147]

Even though it went off the air, however, the approach of RTL in gathering and building large audiences was having enormous impacts in how radio and other platforms of communications were deployed throughout the war. Managers at the BBC, raised under the tutelage of John Reith, nevertheless found themselves bucking the dogma of no-frills objective news and pulling subtle but effective gimmicks to increase the dramatic content of their transmissions. For example, many of the live broadcasts made by BBC and CBS reporters were done in a way to coincide with Nazi air raids. Furthermore, as German bombing became more frequent and regularized, BBC producers scheduled live entertainment shows to be broadcast with the sounds of the air raids taking place in the background. While the hope here was to show the resilience of the British people who continued to go on with normal life despite the barbarity of the German air force, the effect was to mix together live news updates with entertainment into a package from which one could not pull one's ear away.[148]

Indeed, the experience of RTL was not lost on the information managers from the United States and other Western nations of the post–World War

II occupation who set up many ostensibly commercial radio and television stations that relied on popular culture to hide a more pointed political message to a large audience. A hint of this was present in the waning days of the war when General Eisenhower requested that British war planners devise a way to destroy the German will to resist through psychological and informational measures. Eisenhower revealed himself to be an advocate of propaganda and information as part of a larger war strategy when he said "that the expenditure of men and money in wielding the spoken and written word was an important contributing factor in undermining the enemy's will to resist."[149] In essence, what Eisenhower wanted was an information assault that would persuade, convince, deceive, or otherwise compel German soldiers and the German population to surrender and avoid the final bloody battles that would be necessary to bring the war to a full conclusion. While little in the way of tangible results came of Eisenhower's order, it was significant as a preview not only of the coming American Empire that did not reveal itself fully until after World War II, but also the way the United States saw information as means for creating compliance and neutralizing resistance.

The struggle of protecting civilization from Nazism constituted the last episode of Britain's long imperial epic (though a host of postimperial epilogues transpired in the subsequent decades). The primary themes of democracy and civilization that Britain deployed during the period were sufficiently powerful to stir a massive international effort to resist and eventually destroy the forces of totalitarianism. Indeed, Britain's greatest media coup—RTL—demonstrated how Great Britain had finally learned the most profound lesson of the Great Exhibition of 1851 regarding the power of entertainment media to not only enhance the material power of an empire, but also to make it palatable to the rest of the world who would have to abide by its rules. The lesson, however, was learned far too late. Its appeals for assistance in protecting freedom, democracy, and human rights were a symbolic surrender of its ability to legitimize the continuation of its empire by contrary appeals to racial superiority or strategic necessity. With the myth of Britain's fitness to hierarchically rule its colonies discredited and beyond the ability of the most entertaining media content to contain, nationalist movements overseas as well as anticolonial impulses within the halls of imperial power in London oversaw Britain's relinquishment of its colonies in India, Jordan, Burma, and a host of African territories after the war.

Conclusion

At the height of British power in the late nineteenth century, the propaganda themes based on nationalist bravado and patriotic fervor aroused the British masses to support numerous deployments of military force to protect and sustain the British Empire. The need to win the hearts and minds of colonial peoples or populations outside the British Empire was less of a priority because of crude communications technology, blindness to the lessons of the Great Exhibition, and the reality that any dissent could be stifled through brute force or imperial prestige. Beginning in the twentieth century, however, with advances in communication technology, more competent information warriors assuming positions of power in the government, and more entertaining programming, the ability to communicate to audiences both within and beyond the borders of the empire gained paramount importance. As a result, a new imperial narrative emerged based on the broad ideal of democracy and the need to safeguard it from political and economic threats. This drama played out on new forms of communications technology like film and radio and became centrally organized to ensure mass dissemination around the world. As a result, Great Britain succeeded in sounding the alarm about the true nature of Nazi Germany and was able to build a strong Allied coalition around its resistance of Hitler's expansionist vision.

The success of Britain to rally the world to its cause was due in part to the application of the lessons it had slowly learned over the course of the past century and a half when it sought a way to manage world affairs without the expense of constant deployments of military force. The first clues that such arrangements were possible came after the defeat of Napoleon, when antislavery reformers and free trade advocates used newspapers, magazines, and other print ephemera to build cross-class coalitions in support of their causes. Captivating accounts of successful interdictions of slave cargoes in emancipation journals moved a potent segment of the British population to support additional deployments of British military assets off the coast of Africa. For advocates of free trade, print matter was not sufficient to publicize their cause, especially if they hoped to reach a more global audience. With this in mind, leading liberal members of the British elite organized a Great Exhibition to be held in London. Under the heights of the Crystal Palace, audiences from around the world marveled at the material abundance produced by the industrial capacity of British industry and were invited to imagine similar harvests should they conform to the leadership of the British Empire.

The Great Exhibition, taking place amid the eruptions of nationalism in Europe in the middle of nineteenth century, also revealed how information and entertainment, when used to promote narratives of exclusivity and racism, increased the amount of resistance and dissent in the empire. Two examples of this took place in the latter part of nineteenth century in Sudan and South Africa. In the first example, the development of a tabloid press that could garner readerships in the millions stoked the fires of nationalism and hero worship by demanding the British colonial warrior Charles Gordon be sent to put down an indigenous uprising in the remote interiors of Africa. This expedition ended in tragedy when Gordon was killed shortly after his arrival and a war that would go on to kill thousands over the next decade began. The other example saw the incorporation of music hall entertainment as a political weapon to arouse the jingoism of the British masses. With no discernible dissent in British society to oppose a war of choice in South Africa to protect the mineral holdings of British mining companies, the British Empire nearly fell into disarray as pugnacious Boer farmers nearly defeated the armies of the queen. During these overseas wars and conflicts, the powerful British media apparatus and its tools of entertainment were rarely deployed overseas, resulting in a missed opportunity to maintain its empire without recourse to violent instruments.

The weakness of the British military revealed in South Africa meant that Britain had to make a more universal appeal for its leadership role in the world. As rival European states vied to compete with Great Britain for imperial grandeur, Britain finally began to apply the lessons of the Great Exhibition. This began in World War I when the need to find allies to fight alongside it against the Triple Alliance prompted Britain to form propaganda agencies that created interesting and compelling material to persuade neutral nations like the United States to join the war and enemy nations like Austria-Hungary to surrender. The state's involvement in information dissemination continued during the Great Depression as the application of film technologies sought to bolster the imperial economy. Finally, the approach of totalitarianism saw Great Britain use radio in an innovative way to capture the imaginations of people around the world through solemn news reporting, popular music, and entertainment programming that contributed to the building of the grand allied coalition that defeated the Nazis in World War II. Yet, once the war was over and an incalculable sacrifice had been made to preserve the values of democracy and civilization, the contradiction present throughout the run of the British Empire in the nineteenth and early twentieth century—that a democratic state could rule much of the world undemocratically—could no longer be sustained.

The end of the British Empire as a major player in international politics, however, did not mean that the lessons learned by them in their attempt to preserve their empire were lost on other nations vying for control of the globe in the wake of the collapse of British hegemony. As the next chapter will show, the United States was already constructing its own media apparatus in the hopes of forging a world that would conform to American interests. The media weapons deployed by the United States built upon the innovations Great Britain pioneered during its imperial heyday, including centralized state information agencies, heavy deployments of film, and an elaborate radio broadcasting capacity that would serve as a foundation for a much more potent television apparatus yet to come. Seeing the successes of Britain's experience with these platforms, the United States was eager to build upon them as they assumed an imperial stature of their own.

At the core of the American Empire, however, was something more assuming the leadership role abandoned by Great Britain. While not explicitly acknowledged (or perhaps even understood) at the time, the focus on new technologies and entertainment programming was part of a larger project for new vision of empire. This new imperial framework was built upon noncoercive or quasicoercive institutions like the United Nations, the

Marshall Plan, and the North Atlantic Treaty Organization. Military force would no longer necessarily be the first option in keeping subordinate territories in line and confronting hinterlands outside of the area of American influence. In time, even the fundamental factors of economic production would shift, unleashing a wave of social unrest and the reconsolidation of power in forms outside the sovereign authority of the nation-state. The American Empire would be an empire without colonies—and information, communications technology, and the need to entertain hearts and minds would be among its most important elements.

2

Overcoming Isolationism: Film, Radio, and the Rise of the American Empire (1898–1945)

Introduction

The British experience with changing media technologies demonstrated an increasing capacity for governments to bring about political goals with less recourse to physical coercion. By creating attractive content distributed over platforms capable of ever-growing dispersion, decisions and policies made by Britain's ruling assemblage of power could be rendered palpable to a mass audience that might otherwise have been skeptical or hostile. Due in part to these innovations, the British Empire endured the trials and tribulations of expansion more effectively than its European rival—even if the ability of these media technologies was insufficient to prevent the collapse of the empire by 1945. Despite this outcome, however, the popularity of using the techniques and tools of soft power to entrance and capture the minds of larger and more antagonistic populations grew substantially among the other belligerents and raised the possibility, as Dwight Eisenhower hoped toward the end of World War II, that deployment of potent weapons of information would minimize the amount of coercive force needed to end the war.[1]

However, while the idea and practice of "weaponizing" mass communication capabilities first emerged in early nineteenth-century Great Britain, the idea was no less popular in the United States before World War II and the arrival of American hegemony. As with key members of British leadership during the early days of its rise to global domination, advocates for broadening American power like John Fiske, Josiah Strong, John W. Burgess, and Alfred T. Mahan had the task of overcoming popular distaste for foreign intervention and local impulses toward isolation throughout the American population in the days when the United States began its rise to prominence.[2] Unlike Great Britain, however, the United States was not bound to centuries-old social traditions or technological limitations that might prevent it from fully comprehending or implementing the advantages new communications platforms provided. Indeed, with the rise of the American Empire in the time between the Spanish-American War in 1898 to the end of World War II in 1945, the full potential of information technologies as weapons of mass persuasion were revealing themselves as more profound than anyone in the nineteenth century could have imagined.

This chapter explores how the advanced media technologies of the early twentieth century contributed to the birth and early rise of the American Empire. It argues that the need to overcome a legacy of isolationism required the building of a popular narrative of American exceptionalism (sometimes tinged with themes of omnipotence, but at other times tinged with themes of humanitarianism and democracy) to make the prospect of a more adventurous foreign policy more palatable to the American public. In bringing this transformation about, mass communications platforms with an ability to disseminate information and imagery across a vast continent (and eventually across oceans) were an essential component. They would transmit stirring images and compelling rhetoric of American uniqueness and greatness that ensured popular support for three key events that took place between 1898 and 1945: the Spanish-American War and its aftermath between 1898 and 1913, the outbreak of World War I in 1914 through the armistice in 1918, and finally the Great Depression and World War II between 1919 and 1945.

While all major media platforms of the era will be discussed, the chapter is particularly interested in the exploitation of technologies new to the scene in the early twentieth century, especially the medium of cinema. Early developments in the invention of film predate the Spanish-American War by several years, with the first celluloid motion pictures in the United States being attributed to the invention of the kinetoscope by Thomas Edison in 1894.[3] By 1898, the medium had advanced to a point where public exhibitions of motion pictures (usually at vaudeville theaters) were a familiar sight in cities like New York, Boston, and New Orleans while a burgeoning film industry produced hundreds of relatively short films for exhibition.[4] The technology associated with this medium, however, advanced rapidly from these rudimentary origins, ensuring that film was a central platform that appealed to both private and public advocates of American imperial expansion. Indeed, motion pictures became so intrinsically linked with American power that famous film director D. W. Griffith said in 1919 that the cinema "is the only truly American art that is seen and understood by every race on earth," and thus the cinema has the ability to "Americanize the world."[5]

In terms of using this enticing new medium to drum up support for the Spanish-American War, the timing could not have been better. Indeed, while almost any high school student knows from his history lessons that the sensationalist yellow press played a pivotal role in drumming up war fever in 1898, what is not so widely known is the crucial role early motion picture technology played in advocating for war in certain American cities. This chapter will shed some additional light on this history and give film its due in stirring the war fever of the United States during this crucial episode of American history. By 1914, two important developments had taken place that would allow film technology to help push the United States toward participating in a bigger and more devastating war in Europe in 1917. The first was the growth over the first decade and a half of the twentieth century of a fully developed motion picture industry complete with a complex of studios, a network of theaters, and a list of international film stars. The second development did not come about until the American entry into World War I—the creation of a centralized government propaganda apparatus called the Committee on Public Information (CPI). Led by George Creel, the CPI produced an avalanche of war-related media content and distributed this material through every communication platform available at the time. This chapter will take special interest in the motion picture division of the CPI and argue that this component of the organization was among its most effective. Finally, motion pictures—now with sound—would be called on to rally not only American audiences, but foreign audiences as well to the cause of anti-Nazism during World War II when American state-run information agencies, much like their British counterparts, once again took the lead in Allied propaganda activities.

The focus on film in this chapter stems from the unique new capability it provided that was different from other media of the time. Film had the ability to capture and manipulate moving imagery (and eventually sounds as well) and thus could more easily stir the imaginations of audiences coming from different ethnic and social backgrounds throughout the nation. However, as Great Britain learned with the Great Exhibition, sensationalist presses and its bustling music hall scene, the arousing of powerful emotions and reveries among the population could go beyond the ability of anyone to control them. Information and images designed to groom audiences into embracing the "progressive" values of a brave new world where the United States projected its power overseas could also drive them toward coarse patriotism and racial prejudices. Such complexities were on display at the cinema in the early twentieth century as the desire to persuade the American people to abandon their provincialism and distrust of outsiders often came at the cost of conjuring up the demons of jingoism and racial superiority. Would the American experience using entertainment as a weapon of imperial expansion result in the same contradictions as the British experience or would a package of more liberal ideas and more capable technologies result in more favorable results for American power?

Tearing down the Spanish Flag: Early Motion Pictures and the Spanish-American War (1898–1914)

On the surface, there was no obvious reason for a farmer in Kansas, a factory worker in Massachusetts, or a shopkeeper in New York to passionately support an ideology of expansionism as the nineteenth century came to a close. In the tumultuous days and months leading up to the sinking of the battleship *Maine*, however, such attitudes became a reality.[6] What accounts for this popular enthusiasm and how did the advanced media technologies of the day make this change in attitude possible? This section answers this question by first examining the changing foreign policy priorities of the United States and its turn away from its past ostensible commitment to isolationism and toward an impulse to expand. After this, the section briefly explores some of the various soft power mechanisms designed to glamorize, sensationalize, and rationalize this new turn toward a more assertive US foreign policy before going into a more lengthy discussion of the power and influence of early motion pictures during the Spanish-American War.

In the wake of the Civil War, the locus of power in the United States moved from an agricultural hegemony toward an industrial one. Much wealth was generated by industrial financiers in New York and concession-wielding bureaucrats in Washington in the massive effort to reconstruct the South. As these investments became stagnant, capitalists redirected their money toward the ever-expanding Western frontier, helping to settle and develop what many saw (however incorrectly) as a *terra nullius*. As dusk began to settle on the nineteenth century, however, the rate of profit began to fall and new investment opportunities became increasingly scarce. From the perspective of many financial elites and bureaucrats, the only option left was to go overseas. As Walter LaFeber points out, American political and financial interests already had a substantial presence abroad as represented by "a reinvigorated Monroe Doctrine, participation in an increasing number of international conferences, and a magnificent battleship fleet [making] explicit America's world-wide political commitments."[7] The United States saw itself becoming more deeply involved in the race with other European powers to extract as much treasure as possible from China as well as annexing the independent island chain of Hawaii for both economic and strategic reasons. The efforts to streamline trade and render greater returns on investment also directed American expansionists' eyes toward the Caribbean Sea and the possibility of building a shipping canal across one of the narrow points of Central America.[8] There appeared to be few places in the world where the United States did not see economic opportunity or strategic risk—and few political and military measures were ruled out to protect it.

Though these changes were wrought by a complex of American industrial and banking elites, zealous politicians, and military careerists, their impact reverberated down to the bottom of the American social ladder. The aforementioned farmer in Kansas, factory worker in Massachusetts, or shopkeeper in New York enjoyed a comforting stability in their daily routines that may not have led to vast wealth, but did provide the foundation for what they believed was wholesome moral living. Industrialization, with its powerful corporations, activist labor unions, immigration, and harsh business cycles of boom and bust had a way of disrupting these calm, if not entirely lucrative lives. The frontier had provided a convenient place with which to displace the social conflicts of the industrial portions of the country, but now the frontier was closed and some other mechanism was necessary to incubate the industrial elites from the social strife and economic disparities of urban society.

With European colonial powers repeatedly coming in contact with American strategic and economic interests in places like China and Hawaii, those with a direct stake in protecting overseas interests became increasingly aware that the United States would have to shed its apparent devotion to isolation and embrace a new international role that would combine the same values that spawned American continental expansion and propel the nation to a place of strength and dominance in the world. This philosophy of American expansion first found purchase with the general public as well as prominent politicians in the pages of various periodical magazines and journals of widespread circulation. Social Darwinist John Fiske's article "Manifest Destiny," first published in *Harper's Magazine*, featured a thesis that the racial superiority of the American white majority served as a rationalization for foreign intervention. This article soon formed the foundation of a series of lectures enjoying numerous public engagements throughout the country.[9] Naval strategist Alfred T. Mahan, arguing for the construction of a large battle fleet, not only wrote several articles published primarily in *The Atlantic Monthly*, but he also enjoyed exposure in *Forum*, *North American Review*, *Harper's Magazine*, and *McClure's Magazine*.[10] Religious periodicals added their own voice to the chorus of calls for American expansion, arguing American interventionism would provide "a supreme missionary opportunity" to legions of young proselytizers yearning for the chance to convert exotic heathens.[11] This body of thought, however, merely provided the ideological foundation up which a carnival of spectacular and jingoistic media would spring forth like a jack-in-the-box at just the right moment. In early 1898, when news arrived from Cuba that the American battleship *Maine* had mysteriously exploded in Havana harbor, that moment arrived.

As the landmark studies by Marcus M. Wilkerson and Joseph E. Wizan show, "coverage" of the insurgent uprisings in Cuba prior to 1898 by the New York press presented an impassioned (if lopsided) view of the conflict in which the Spanish were portrayed as vile and depraved oppressors of an innocent and vulnerable island people.[12] As the continuous reporting of the conflict took root in the public consciousness, an army of correspondents, illustrators, artists, poets, and other such "observers" poured into Cuba to cover the numerous alleged Spanish atrocities being committed on the island, thus feeding the tabloid monster back in New York—especially the two biggest heads of that monster, Joseph Pulitzer's *World* and William Randolph Hearst's *Journal*.[13] Many cities bought the news services of these papers, giving the rest of the country the same sensationalist flavor that was available everywhere in New York City.[14] When the *Maine* exploded, this intense saturation of coverage of the events in Cuba reached a fever pitch and before long the United States declared war on Spain.

Though at first skeptical of a possible war with Spain, the business community warmed up to the notion of imperialism once American victory appeared likely.[15] Financially oriented newspapers such as the *Wall Street Journal* marveled at some of the economic prospects of a free Cuba, as well as the subsequent acquisitions of Puerto Rico and the Virgin Islands.[16] Looking toward the Philippines, prospects were not seen quite so rosy, but the islands' strategic location to China, which was seen as a gold mine of profits for the businessmen and a purgatory of heathen souls for missionaries, convinced American policy makers to annex it. In this situation, as in others to come in the future, prominent newspapers provided both the explanations and justifications for such acts of intervention. In addition to the usual patriotic rancor of the Hearst and Pulitzer tabloids, New York publications such as the *Times* and *Sun* provided timely articles and editorials ranging from the alleged inferiority of the Filipinos for self-government to dismissing reports of American atrocities to questioning the loyalty of anti-imperialist activists in the United States.[17]

For those who found the adventurism of short newspaper articles insufficient to satiate their jingoistic reveries, prolific author Edward Stratemeyer, most famous for his *Hardy Boys* and *Nancy Drew* books for younger readers, provided novel-length representations of Americans gaining glory overseas. Between 1896 and 1909, Stratemeyer wrote several series of historical fictions that depicted young and spirited Americans participating in many of the historical events that brought several overseas territories under American sovereignty.[18] For example, the titles of Stratemeyer's Old Glory Series included the books *Under Dewey at Manila*, which depicted in epic terms the capture of Manila Bay in the Philippines by Commodore George Dewey on May 1, 1898, and *A Young Volunteer in Cuba*, which told a similar story of heroism and adventure—this time with Theodore Roosevelt in Cuba. The third volume of this series, titled *Fighting in Cuban Waters*, in the model of the first two books, told of the naval battle at Santiago Bay where yet another Spanish fleet was destroyed by the Americans.[19] Like with the music halls and tabloid press in Great Britain, the effort to legitimize and justify overseas intervention in the United States relied heavily on mass media output that blended jingoistic sentiment with entertaining content. However, by 1898, a new technology had arrived with secrets the United States was more adept at discovering than Great Britain—motion pictures.

The fusion of film technology and the promotion of American war aims stemmed from the penchant that already existed within American media culture for the audiovisual. For example, Frederic Remington, an illustrator for the New York *Journal* as well as the magazine *Harper's*, gained international recognition for his drawings and paintings that capture images of American soldiers fighting their way to victory on the hills of Cuba.[20] Remington himself was "a close friend of Theodore Roosevelt and helped create the legend of Roosevelt as a soldier by painting the Rough Riders going into action with Roosevelt at their head."[21] Other illustrators enjoying widespread publication included William Glackens of *McClure's Magazine* and Howard Chandler Christy illustrating for *Harper's* and *Leslie's Weekly*.[22] Songs also proliferated throughout the country at the time (usually in the form of sheet music, given that the development of radio was still several years off) that commemorated the sailors that were killed on the American battleship *Maine* and remained in the public consciousness well after the end of the war.[23] American poets, though not as famous or as skilled as the ones in Great Britain, wrote and recited their odes to commemorate American victories throughout the course of conflict with Spain to great applause.[24] Finally in the world of sculpture, David Martin Reynolds remarks, "The Spanish-American War of 1898–1902 and the subsequent Philippine Insurrection not only established the United States as a world power and expanded its territories to include Puerto Rico, Guam, and the Philippine Islands, but it also produced a new icon of the American infantrymen, the [statue] *The Hiker*."[25]

No medium of the time, however, showed as much potential power to capture and transfix the hearts and minds of audiences both domestically and overseas than the motion picture. The technology to project moving pictures was still in its very early infancy by the time the war broke out in 1898, but nevertheless, keen and innovative entrepreneurs were aware of the technology's ability to bring in large audiences and potentially rake in sizeable profits. Two who paved the way were Albert Smith and J. Stuart Blackton. Smith, fittingly enough, was a stage hypnotist and showman (a "mentalist" in today's parlance) who plied his trade in Great Britain before coming to the United States and teaming up with his fellow expatriate J. Stuart Blackton in the purchase of one of the first Vitascope—Thomas Edison's new and improved motion picture projector.[26] In 1897, the two men founded the American Vitagraph Company, began producing short films (including early attempts at animation), and showed them at vaudeville theaters and public halls around New York.[27] The big break for the men, however, came with the destruction of the *Maine* and the public's sudden appetite for war-related films.

One of Smith and Blackton's earliest efforts at producing entertaining war propaganda was titled *Tearing down the Spanish Flag*. The film was very short—about two-minutes long in total—and the picture quality was extremely poor. The narrative of the film was also quite crude. A flagpole is pictured innocently flying a Spanish flag when suddenly, a pair of hands enters the screen and ferociously lowers the flag from its previous height and brutally rips it off the pole. The film then depicts these same hands attaching an American flag to the pole and raising it to the same height the Spanish flag once occupied—the yellow and red (or at least the shades of grey that passed for yellow and red on the black and white print) that represented Spanish tyranny were replaced by the red, white, and blue of American freedom and might. Despite the fact the graininess of the film made the action hard to follow at times, throngs of New Yorkers, already brimming with outrage toward Spain and its alleged mistreatment of Cuban freedom fighters as reported in the tabloid newspapers, fled to theaters exhibiting the film to experience for themselves this two-minute orgy of jingoism. The film was so successful that Smith and Blackton immediately set to making several more like it.[28] In doing so, however, they captured both the power of film to tap into the public imagination and the difficulty of controlling the consequences of this power once unleashed.

The first example of this tension came in the production of a film titled *The Battle at Santiago Bay*. Produced by Smith and Blackton's American Vitagraph Company, the film purported to be actual footage of the decisive battle between the American and Spanish fleets off the coast of Cuba. Almost immediately, however, the film's fakery was obvious as the ships depicted in the film appeared to be little more than crudely assembled models and the blue horizon of the Caribbean Sea seemed strangely static and artificial. Shortly after the release of the film, Smith and Blackton admitted that the film was a hoax and that the purpose of the picture was to create a patriotic simulation of the battle rather than provide an objective documentary account of the event.[29] Nevertheless, the film was wildly successful and was shown throughout the New York and Boston area.

The second example of entertainment, propaganda, and reality becoming blurred came from Smith and Blackton's claim that they had traveled to Cuba with American soldiers and had filmed Theodore Roosevelt's famous charge up San Juan Hill. According to newsreel historian Raymond Fielding, the footage they recorded was released as a film titled *Fighting with Our Boys in Cuba* and despite the fact that the footage reveals the charge up San Juan Hill to be a much slower and less glamorous event than described in the newspapers or depicted in drawings, the film enjoyed much popularity.[30] There is, however, a debate over whether the men actually made it to Cuba and that—in a similar way as the phony film *Battle of Santiago Bay*—the footage of the Rough Riders taking San Juan Hill is also fiction. Louis Pizzitola, while citing a soldier's diary's firsthand account of seeing Blackton's presence in Cuba, also points out that no copyright of a film with the title *Fighting with Our Boys in Cuba* exists and the only visual evidence of the film are a few pictures of film frames in the trade publication *Image* dating from the 1920s.[31] If the film does exist and is authentic, it would represent some of the earliest battle footage ever recorded. Moreover, while there is no evidence that the charge up San Juan Hill took place for the benefit of motion picture cameras that may or may not have been present, the idea that such an event was even partially staged is not that preposterous an idea given the present-day revelations about the activities of the Rendon Group during the liberation of Kuwait or the orchestrated toppling of the bronze statue of Saddam Hussein in Baghdad's Firdos Square in 2003.[32] Smith and Blackton may simply have been ahead of their time.

Nor were they alone in their endeavors. After inventing the kinetoscope and vitagraph, Thomas Edison started a film production company titled Edison Manufacturing Company that produced scores of films during the Spanish-American War. Unlike Smith and Blackton and the mystery surrounding their travels to Cuba, a clear filmography of 23 pictures exists that were recorded in the Caribbean region by the Edison firm.[33] Most of these films were shot by freelance cameraman William Paley who also received money and material support from tabloid publisher William Randolph Hearst.[34] One of Paley's most famous films that caused the largest stupor of war-related sentimentality was titled *Burial of the "Maine" Victims*. Like *Tearing down the Spanish Flag*, it was short—just over two minutes—and featured "the procession of horse-drawn hearses bearing the remains of some of the 266 sailors lost in the *Maine* disaster."[35] Another of Paley's films, echoing some of the slave interdiction material of Great Britain, focused more on the humanitarian dimensions of American power projection—*Cuba Refugees Waiting for Rations* shows "a line of listless Cubans, tin cups in hand, waiting for relief from the United States."[36] Other films shot by Paley included *Morro Castle* and *Havana Harbor*.[37] A rival production company, Biograph, also sent photographers to Cuba to record yet more footage of the *Maine*'s wreckage as well as anything else that was remotely nautical and martial. Indeed, the fascination with these images was so great that at one point, Biograph cameramen were filming generic shots of American battleships sitting in American harbors and still drawing large crowds when these pictures were released.[38]

The low quality of the images in early motion pictures combined with the banal or phony nature of the film's content would likely fail to move the moviegoer of the twenty-first century. However, it must be kept in mind that this film technology, however primitive, had a similar mass effect on the audiences of the late nineteenth and early twentieth century as the biggest special effects laden summer blockbuster of the twenty-first century. Data on ticket sales and audience numbers from this time is largely unavailable, but strong evidence exists that these war films were both persuasive and entertaining. In Washington, DC, for example, the operators of the Columbia Theater took over a neighboring lecture hall and used the space to screen war-related motion pictures around the clock.[39] In Chicago, a city that had only recently received its first motion picture projector at Hopkins Theater, the screening of the Biograph film *Battleships "Maine" and "Iowa"* (it turned out the *Maine* was actually the *Massachusetts*, but the filmmakers conveniently overlooked this error) caused an incredible stir. According to an article by the *New York World*, when the film began playing, "there was fifteen minutes of terrific shouting...when the battleships *Maine* and *Iowa* were shown in the biograph maneuvering off Fortress Monroe. The audience arose, cheered and cheered again, and the climax was reached when a picture of Uncle Sam under the flag was thrown on the canvas."[40]

During the height of this patriotic fervor, each screening of a war-related film released a small public revelry akin to that seen in Great Britain on a mass scale during "Mafeking Night" during the South African War. Indeed, the same principles of jingoism that Hobson observed taking place in Great Britain during the South African War were present in the theaters and screening halls of the United States. However, in Great Britain, the original Mafeking Night came about due to an actual event—the lifting of the siege of the town of Mafeking in South Africa where British troops had been trapped by the Boer Army. In the United States, the most electric outbursts of jingoism took place any time an audience gathered to watch the latest film on the status of the war regardless if the images on the screen were actual footage of real events, elaborate recreations of real events, or outright fakery. When American war fever was nearing its climax, the *New York Tribune* wrote, "There is no other place where it is so easy to get the people of New York together as in a theater...So it is naturally to the theaters that one turns to find public sentiment expressed."[41] After commenting on the various ways the theater aroused the patriotic passions of the audience, the article observes, "The determination seems to have been to stir the audience with the sight of the flag or the sound of a tune at every possible or impossible opportunity."[42]

The popularity and eager consumption of the entire panoply of audiovisual material related to the Spanish-American War by a public that had until recently been content with the nation's isolationist approach to foreign policy testified to the power of platforms like motion pictures to transform attitudes and values. Yet as seen in the previous examples, the effectiveness of such conduits of information stemmed less from their power of persuasion and more from their ability to stir emotions and enrapture imaginations. Beyond the yellow journalism of the New York tabloids, music and motion pictures served as an essential component of wooing the hearts and minds of Americans toward war and imperial expansion. Albert Smith spoke to this when, while in court settling a legal dispute with Thomas Edison, described himself and his partner J. Stuart Blackton as being "in business as entertainers prior to July 1898. He [Blackton] was a cartoonist and I was an impersonator and ventriloquist."[43] It is telling that the first great film propagandists in history were not evil politicians, greedy film studio executives, or war mongering generals, but rather simple street-level showmen.

More importantly, even at this very early stage of production, there were indications that film had a power to transgress class, social, and national divides despite the extreme particularism of the content. In the case of the era of the Spanish-American War, while the initial audience for motion pictures was largely confined to middle-class audiences before the outbreak of war, the production and screening of war-related films marks the beginning of the era when the working class took to the cinemas. It also represents a time when certain cities in the North like New York, Boston, and Chicago saw large ethnic and racial enclaves rise up with mass immigration of Irish and Italians from Europe and mass migration of African-Americans from the South. They too would compose large segments of the audience for motion pictures.[44] Indeed, in the case of the latter, the Edison Manufacturing Company made two films where African-Americans were the "stars" of the show—*Colored Troops Disembarking* and *Steamer "Mascotte" Arriving at Tampa*.[45] This influence did not necessarily end at American shores. After Cuba fell into American possession, motion pictures were a central part of a package of foreign influences that burrowed into the daily lives of locals and began to transform the island nation's culture. As Frank Nikovitch observes, in the years after the Spanish-American War, "English became a second language (in Cuba)," and "Cubans adopted American movies, drove American cars, played baseball with a passion, and absorbed American radio broadcasts."[46]

It should be stated that film was not some magic medium that obliterated the social tensions of the era and that somehow equality and justice could be found in the darkness of a movie theater. Very real tensions existed in American society and the policy of going to war with Spain for what amounted to imperial expansion was not unilaterally applauded in the country. As the crowds packed into the theaters to see the latest patriotic motion picture extravaganza, prominent Americans like Mark Twain, Andrew Carnegie, and Jane Addams formed the Anti-Imperialist League to drum up public opposition to the United States' new interest in overseas expansion.[47] The league deployed an active (but limited) informational campaign decrying the war and motivations through the deployment of tens of thousands of pamphlets, letters, and leaflets. The league also published a compendium of poems that criticized and mocked the jingoistic spirit of the time that included Mark Twain's *To the Person Sitting in the Darkness*. Despite the league's presence, however, there were no films made during this time that celebrated isolationism or accused the United States of imperialism.[48]

In the end, even the most principled anti-imperial sermonizing could not withstand the mass appeal of jingoistic cinema. The more audiovisual nature of the motion picture technologies combined with more focus on entertainment and amusement rather than the overt moralizing of a particular attitude or worldview meant that the content of motion pictures could capture the imaginations of much larger swaths of the population. If viewing the films of William Paley or Smith and Blackton actually persuaded a portion of the American public of the virtues of expansionist ideals, this was merely icing on the cake. The real power of film and other media platforms was both the unique experience of going to the movies and the fun and entertaining product that was drawing in audiences by the thousands. Much like the mass American consumers of the present day who struggle to identify on a map the part of the world where the latest deployment of American troops is taking place, the people who attended the cinema during the Spanish-American War were less interested in policy debates and more interested in having a good time. Nevertheless, this desire for distraction and amusement had political consequences. A mass public enthralled with the sights and sounds of foreign intervention and war served the interests of those who sought to legitimize the expansion of American power overseas during the Spanish-American War.

As with the explosion of jingoism during Great Britain during the South African War, however, the delirium of American war fever during the Spanish-American War eventually gave way to a harsh crash and bitter hangover. While Cuba was granted tentative independence after the defeat of Spain and the end of the war, political stability never fully returned to the island until (for better or worse) Castro launched his revolution in 1959. Things were less volatile in Puerto Rico, where the local inhabitants more or less accepted American sovereignty and commercial investment from the moment Spanish rule ended.[49] The biggest "headache" for the United States in the aftermath of its end-of-century adventurism was the Philippines. Here, the United States, after annexing the islands, engaged in a long counterinsurgency campaign that attempted to combine military occupation and antiguerilla activity with "soft power" initiatives such as the construction of schools, hospitals, and missions.[50] None of these activities however, was the subject of new films for the major motion picture producers. Once hostilities ended between the United States and Spain, the wellspring of patriotic material dried up and the film producers sought content from other places. Even if motion picture cameras were present in places like the Philippines once the United States took possession of the islands, it is possible that their film would have captured the very unpleasant activities of the counterinsurgency campaigns that took place there for the next decade—a campaign that included torture, forced relocation, and humanitarian atrocities committed on both sides of the struggle.[51]

Even if the war had gone on and the public's bellicose spirit persisted, the nature of their experience with the motion picture would have likely changed. Shortly after the end of the Spanish-American War, the film production process went through significant changes. Small independent producers of film like the Edison Manufacturing Company and Smith and Blackton's Vitagraph Company were soon eclipsed by the large movie studios taking root in Southern California. Film became less of a medium that entertained through the recording of reality to a medium that produced and recorded its own reality.[52] As these studios grew in power, they began to transform the medium just in time to be put in service again for another American overseas adventure a little more than a decade on the horizon. For the time being, however, motion pictures (as well as the multitude of other media of the time) succeeded in legitimizing a dramatic shift in American foreign policy away from isolationism and toward overseas expansion. It is perhaps appropriate that the first major explosion of unvarnished antipodean imperialism in American history should rely so heavily on film technology for its justification. Both American expansion and film technology were very new developments in world politics and as time unfolded both phenomena would become intertwined.

"Fighting with Films": Movie Studios, the CPI, and World War I (1914–1918)

Despite the fact that certain segments of the American ruling class (epitomized by war hero Theodore Roosevelt) sought in the aftermath of the Spanish-American War to make military readiness for foreign activity permanent through a "preparedness movement," most Americans fell back into provincial thinking once the war ended. Moreover, mass media platforms like tabloid newspapers and motion pictures largely ended their dissemination of entertaining mixtures of American exceptionalism and overseas adventurism when troops returned home.[53] American society and its political class appeared content with its newly won status as a regional power. Indeed, by 1914, the news of mass mobilizations from across the Atlantic tended not to arouse much concern or consternation in the United States outside of specific immigrant communities. Yet in a matter of months, this perception changed dramatically. President Woodrow Wilson, who had won reelection in 1916 by boasting of his ability to keep the nation out of a distant European war, was now demanding unconditional support from the masses for an American Expeditionary Force setting sail for the battle trenches of France in order to make the world safe for democracy.

This section examines how the medium of silent cinema and the institutions that arose to produce and distribute these films facilitated the entry of the United States into World War I. Thanks to advancing film technologies, motion pictures helped to successfully neutralize resistance to the most ambitious and entangling foreign deployment of American power to date. While the description of American foreign policy as "isolationism" has always been problematic, one thing that had always been true was the refusal of the United States to become directly involved in the power politics of Europe.[54] Now, with Wilson demanding the deployment of American military into the heart of a malevolent European fratricide on the side of the Triple Entente, the United States was renouncing forever its claim to a national identity uninterested in getting involved in the decadent politics of Europe. As with the Spanish-American War, multiple media platforms, including newspaper, periodicals, and staged production played important roles in promoting American entry into the war. Yet once again, the contribution of film technology looms especially large and will be a focal point of analysis. Moreover, what makes the period between 1902 and 1918 unique in the history of communications is the transformation of motion pictures from a novel form of news and entertainment to a central component in the mental life of the American (and increasingly global) population. During the Spanish-American War, film was an experimental weapon of mass enticement still in a prototype stage of development. During World War I, films were mass produced and took their place on the front lines in the battle for ideas.

Two fundamentally important developments in this process of "weaponizing" motion pictures were the growth of a large and powerful film industry (located primarily in Southern California) and the creation of a governmental propaganda apparatus by the United States upon its entry into World War I. In the first case, film studios like Fox Pictures, Metro, United Artists, and Universal cultivated the feature-length motion picture complete with epic storylines, grand set designs, and internationally recognizable film stars. Such developments represented a quantum leap in the quality and entertainment value of film compared with the cruder versions of the medium on display during the Spanish-American War. These innovations were never more apparent than when the American movie entertainment complex began making films on the topic of the war in Europe and the need for the United States to involve itself in this war. The development of a state-run propaganda agency in the United States was no less significant. Begun in 1917, the CPI represented the unprecedented moment when the American state constructed its own media industrial complex—a remarkable development for a nation that believed in the principles of limited government. Under the leadership of former news reporter George Creel, the CPI produced, distributed, and screened pro-war material in every conceivable medium available at the time. Despite this ambition to appropriate the entire spectrum of communications, however, film was a focal point of the CPI's propaganda strategy.

Together, the film industry and the CPI were not just improving the means of mass information dispersion, they were planting the idea in the public imagination of a bolder and more aggressive United States on the world stage. Motion pictures continued to be produced in the name of entertainment and amusement, but the need to legitimize the American entry in to World War I added a moralizing dimension to this process. Like the Great Exhibition in London or the music hall shows of the 1899 South African War, the film output of the day was meant to change minds while amusing them. As a result, the idea of American exceptionalism matured from the crude and ribald jingoism on display during the Spanish-American War to a more sophisticated notion of the obligations and responsibilities of the United States as both a republican state committed to protecting democracy around the world and a great power with a need to partake in the management of global affairs. These ideas would slowly make both the American and the world population more comfortable with the idea of the United States as a world power (and eventually) an empire.

Such grand political trajectories were likely far from the mind of the entrepreneurs who moved to California to start new film ventures beginning in 1908. Because of efforts by Edison Manufacturing Corporation, Vitagraph, and a handful of other motion picture companies to create a monopolistic trust in New York, independent producers had to seek other locations if they wished to make films free of interference. The area around Los Angeles offered several advantages to upstart movie makers that were difficult to find elsewhere—pleasant weather, diverse topography (for film backdrops), cheap labor, and perhaps most important of all: a location that "was only a hop-skip-and-jump to the Mexican border and escape from injunction and subpoenas" from the preestablished film trusts.[55] By 1913, an area just outside of Los Angeles called Hollywood had more or less become the home not only of dozens of fledgling film production companies, but also of many of the older members of the New York monopoly. As the first shots of World War I were fired in Europe, Hollywood, California became the nerve center of the American film industry.[56]

Once ensconced in California, a genuine film industry quickly took root and sprouted robustly. At the heart of this growth was the transformation of the single motion picture corporation that handled production, distribution, and exhibition to multiple firms that developed a division of labor among these functions within the larger filmmaking environment. Thus, companies like Edison Manufacturing Corporation, Vitagraph, and Biograph that in the past had to handle not only the making of a film, but also the distribution and screening of a film, could now cast off the roles of screening and distribution to other companies and focus on production. This led to the birth of new film production studios like Fox Film Corporation, Metro Pictures Corporation, and Universal Film Manufacturing Company that joined Edison, Vitagraph, Biograph, and others in an environment that was bursting with competition and creativity. At the same time, the practice of exhibiting films went through a dramatic and necessary metamorphosis considering how effectively studios were churning out hundreds of different films for screening. The first step in this process was the development of film exchanges to ensure all the content produced by the studios made the rounds among the various exhibition platforms, including fairs and other public exhibitions. Beginning in 1905, however, the nickelodeon rose to promise as the preferred venue to watch a film, and before long, the film exchange networks had a consistent roster of customers for the films they sought to distribute.[57]

As the popularity of moviegoing spiked in the years prior to World War I (some nickelodeon theaters were open from 8 in the morning until 12 at night), the intense competition pushed movie makers to innovate new ways of attracting audiences to the theaters to see their films.[58] This environment had two major consequences in terms of turning film into a medium that had universal appeal and could serve a political end on the international stage. The first was the development of the story-based feature film. As seen in the motion pictures made during the Spanish-American War, films tended to be rather short and often featured documentary footage of real events or re-creations of actual events. Shortly after the war, however, the focus of filmmaking began to shift to drama and storytelling. One of the earliest American (story-based filmmaking had already begun in Europe a few years prior) motion pictures to tell a fictional story was *The Great*

Train Robbery.[59] Made in 1903, the film featured 14 separate scenes that together told a complete story about a band of desperados who hold up a train only to be hunted down and eliminated in an elaborate gun fight by a posse of townsfolk. The film was a smash hit at the nickelodeons around the country and set the tone for the kind of motion picture entertainment that became standard in the succeeding years.[60]

The second important consequence of the creation of a large film industry was the rise of the so-called star system. Early films did not identify their actors or actresses and film producers set on churning out reel after reel of product saw performers as little more than a factor of production to manage along with sets, lighting equipment, and cameras. However, a few enterprising staff found that audiences often enquired to local theater staff on the identities of particular members of the film's cast. At first, the performers were identified through nicknames derived from their on-screen characters like "Little Mary" or "Broncho [*sic*] Billy," but eventually, as the practice became more common, producers displayed cast members' names at the end of the film.[61] As studios learned which performers were the most popular, they began to feature the identities of these players in promotions, advertisements, and the branding of the studio itself. Thus, the actress "Little Mary" was identified as the now legendary Mary Pickford, whose picture would appear on the movie posters pasted around town before a premier. Many of the more successful actors or actresses tended to be hired by a particular studio on a permanent basis, thus Mary Pickford who starred in films made by the Biograph film corporation became intrinsically linked with this studio. To be a fan of Mary Pickford was to be a loyal patron of Biograph films.[62]

The rise of the film star had important impacts not only for the development of American cinema, but also for the culture of global filmmaking. With the onset of World War I, the vibrant overseas film industries that were growing independently of Hollywood, especially in countries like France and Italy, began to wither as resources moved toward the logistics of war. In 1914, about half the world's films were made in the United States; by 1917, this percentage approached 100 percent.[63] As Lewis Jacobs observed in 1939, "for American producers the European disaster was a stroke of fortune, since it gave them a virtual monopoly of the world movie market."[64] As American movies became the only option in the nickelodeons and movie houses of the world, the stories and stars of the United States enjoyed unfettered access to the imaginations of the world's population. American film stars became beloved by audiences in Europe and Latin America while the preferences and tastes of the American movie audience replicated themselves in communities far away from the American mainland.

World War I did not just eliminate the competition for the American film industry in the early part of the twentieth century, it also served as an opportunity for creativity and innovation in the development of the cinematic art. Film directors who would later become legends of American cinema, like Cecil B. Demille and Frank Capra, all got their start making pro-war propaganda films in the prelude to World War I.[65] Other more well-established directors also made their contributions, such as J. Stuart Blackton, who by now was the grand patriarch of propagandistic filmmaking due to his work during the Spanish-American War. Blackton directed in 1915 *The Battle Cry for Peace*, a film that enjoyed popular acclaim in both Great Britain and the United States, earned the endorsement of Theodore Roosevelt, and was considered an essential piece of the rhetorical effort to popularize American participation in World War I.[66] Charlie Chaplin's film *Shoulder Arms* was one of the few comedic works within the greater body of war-related films and according to Gerald Herman it is "the most-enduring film of this period."[67]

Charlie Chaplin represents perhaps the best example of what made American motion pictures so enticing. Coming to the United States from Britain in 1914, Chaplin quickly became famous for his unique comedic styles drawn from his experience as a vaudeville performer and refashioned them for the cinema screen in the form of a character dubbed "The Little Tramp." With his now famous "baggy pants, cane, derby hat, oversized shoes, tiny jacket, and moustache," Chaplin's Little Tramp spoke to themes that went over well with American and international audiences.[68] These included "always being the little guy, an easy target for the bullies of the world, but also agile, quick-witted and ingenuous at always being able to fend them off. Through struggle after struggle 'the Little Tramp' was able to survive in a mean, cruel world, drawing on the audience's empathy."[69] As Emily Rosenberg points out, Chaplin's films were a hit with both the diverse population of the United States increasingly flush with immigrants as well as with overseas audiences. "American films were perfectly suited for a world market," Rosenberg says, because they were "designed to entertain a diverse multi-ethnic patronage at home" and because "silent films present no language barrier, and the humor and appeal of stars like Charlie Chaplin...were truly universal."[70]

However, this power to speak to universal audiences had an unanticipated dark side captured by perhaps the most notorious film in the history of American cinema: D. W. Griffith's *Birth of a Nation*. On its outermost surface, the film is a Civil War epic that depicts the fate of two families (one from the North and one from the South) not only through the events of the war but also during the period of reconstruction in the South. The film makes clear from its first scene, however, that the source of division in American society was the presence of black slaves who were recklessly freed by Northern abolitionist radicals, thereby threatening the proud culture of the South and the delicate reunion of the two belligerent sides after the war. Thus, the South, which had fought gallantly but unsuccessfully to retain its independence during the formal Civil War must fight a second informal battle against a mob of black and mulatto former slaves intent on seizing the institutions of the state and destroying white "civilization." The film resolves this conflict by showing how Southern Civil War veterans

formed the Ku Klux Klan to engage the horde of former slaves and ultimately restore white power in Southern society.[71]

The film remains a landmark in the history of cinema and captures what
made motion pictures the most seductive medium of its time. Everything
about the film was epic—cast (in the thousands), costumes, sets, use of
cameras, musical score (coming in the form of a live in-theater piano or
orchestral accompaniment), and an elaborate film choreography (including
several minutes of recreated Civil War battles reminiscent of Smith and
Blackton's work during the Spanish-American War). In an era when motion
pictures were made cheap and had relatively short running times, *Birth of
a Nation* clocked in at just over three hours and required a special admission price of $2.00 to recoup a production cost in the hundreds of thou-
sands.[72] Yet despite the special price, the film was a smash. In an era when
great fortunes could still be measured within six figures, *Birth of a Nation*
made millions of dollars and captured the imagination of the American
public. Indeed, President Woodrow Wilson saw the movie privately at the
White House and commented that the film "was like writing history in
lightning"—perhaps due to the fact that a few lines from Wilson's book,
History of the American People, were quoted in some of the film's inter-
title cards.[73] With the American film industry increasingly becoming the
only viable mass producer of motion pictures in the world as European
cinema lagged during the Great War, *Birth of a Nation* circulated beyond
the domestic market to audiences overseas. Empirical data on total viewers
is difficult to pin down with any accuracy, but some estimate that between
1915 and 1946 over two hundred million people around the world viewed
the film, with most of that audience accounted for in the first four years
after it premiered in early 1915.[74]

Because of all this, *Birth of a Nation* "signaled the advent of the motion
picture as an art form, political statement and major cultural event."[75] Yet
in the discovery with *Birth of a Nation* of how a motion picture could be
a powerful weapon to stir the minds and spirits of mass audiences, a fresh
problem arose. With its undisguised racist story, *Birth of a Nation* stirred
as much social division and antagonism as nationalist pride or amused
passivity. Social unrest, especially among African-American communities,
was common in most major American cities where the film was screened
with protestors demonstrating outside theaters or in large public spaces.
Indeed, the activism surrounding the effort to publicly condemn the racism of *Birth of a Nation* helped to galvanize the National Association for
the Advancement of Colored People and propel it into one of the most visible African-American pressure groups in the United States.[76] The backlash
against the film in the African-American community also foretold a similar reaction overseas when seen by foreign audiences—the *New York Age*
wrote in 1919 that "no more sinister emissary of anti-Negro propaganda
could be sent across the waters."[77]

While the controversy over the release of *Birth of a Nation* continued to
stew in 1915, Wilson suddenly found himself facing a more profound crisis.

On May 7, 1915, a German U-boat sank the passenger liner *Lusitania* killing 1,195 passengers, of which 128 were American. This event, combined with Lord Northcliffe's coy pro-British propaganda campaign among the American population, resulted in the United States going to war with the Triple Alliance in 1917. The decision to go to war presented several challenges to Wilson and his administration. The most obvious of these was the operational and logistical tasks of training and moving hundreds of thousands of American troops from North America to Europe. Beyond this, however, was the joining of the battle in the mental environment of the world's collective consciousness. America's entry into the Great War meant the government had to reorient the minds of its citizens away from their traditional and narrow provincial idylls to an expanded and engaged international mindset. Moreover, other nations that had only limited exposure to the culture of the United States would need an orientation in the sensibilities, motivations, and values of the American nation and its people who, in the form of American doughboys, would be showing up in foreign cities and towns.

Such a gargantuan task required the United States government, for the first time in its history, to get involved in the creation and dissemination of information in order to quell the possibility of mass dissent and arouse what George Creel would call the "war-will" of the population at large.[78] Like Great Britain before 1914, the United States had little experience running an agency that would regulate information—the sacred nature of the First Amendment saw to it that the American government minimized press interference, to say nothing of actually producing its own original content. With the country in the midst of a war, however, the priorities shifted and the state foresaw a need to govern information. Without governmental coordination, private media outlets—city newspapers, newsreel makers, and the shiny new studios of California—could not, "weld the people of the United States into one white-hot mass instinct with fraternity, devotion, courage, and deathless determination."[79]

This crucial task fell on the newly formed CPI. Under the direction of George Creel, the CPI was the first formal American experiment in the tactics and strategy of information management. As a former newspaperman sympathetic with the meritocratic conception of democracy of the then popular progressive movement, George Creel was an ideal candidate to persuade the American people of the righteousness and necessity of participating in the war in Europe. The challenge, as he saw it, was to recognize that the struggle to win the public imagination was but one battlefront among many in a global war:

> It was in this recognition of Public Opinion as a major force that the Great War differed most essentially from all previous conflicts. The trial of strength was not only between massed bodies of armed men, but between opposed ideals, and moral verdicts took in all the value of military decisions.[80]

On top of this was Creel's conception of the various media platforms of the day as weapons in their own right. To be successful in fighting an informational war, one had to deploy all the weapons of communication available. Thus, the CPI sought to harness the power of "the printed word, the spoken word, the motion picture, the telegraph, the cable, the wireless, the poster, (and) the sign-board"[81]

The key to winning this battle was the proper harnessing and blending of two elements: objectivity and salesmanship. In the case of the former, Creel recognized that coercively silencing voices of dissent and limiting official information in a style that was common in the propaganda and information management techniques in other belligerent countries in Europe was undesirable. Instead, Creel insisted, "our job...was to present the facts without the slightest trace of color or bias, either in the selection of news or the manner in which it was presented."[82] As media outlets in the United States (as well as around the world) were buried in an avalanche of "facts" put out by the CPI, the hope was that false reports put out by hostile agents or critical journalist would be neutralized and the government would be seen as the only credible source of American news about the war.[83] In this way, the CPI pioneered an information deployment model that would later be picked up by communications entities like the British Broadcasting Corporation (BBC) and made permanent.

Creel, however, understood that a daily dose of objective facts were insufficient to win the hearts and minds of global populations—a lesson the BBC took much longer to learn. Laced within those facts needed to be a subtle element that enticed and tempted the audience to come back for more. To accomplish this part of the task, Creel sought to harness the emerging art of advertising to supplement its news releases and stir the patriotic passions of the average American. Creel himself declared the CPI as "a vast enterprise in salesmanship, the world's greatest adventure in advertising," and in his study of the effects of the CPI on American society, Stephen Vaughn points out, "The CPI enlisted some of the best advertising men in America to stimulate the country's patriotism."[84] In tapping into these novel techniques of advertising and public relations, Creel was not only aligning the new techniques of information management with the needs of the nation, but also with the early stages of consumer capitalism. With the output of factory production outpacing the narrow demand of wealthy elites buying the multitude of manufactured goods, private business interests saw the still nascent American middle classes as the solution to their problem of declining profit margins. As a result, the time period surrounding the world wars began an era of "things" in which agents in the private as well as the public sector actively sought to create mass markets for material goods by providing "objective" information on the benefits of a particular product.[85] Practical-minded consumers, upon seeing these advertisements, would then go out and buy the product. All the CPI was doing was providing the objective benefits of going to war and raising the international profile of the United States. The techniques used by the CPI to stir the population toward the idea of going to war would be used in later decades to stir the population to go to the mall and shop. They would also be taken up by the American government after the terrorist attacks of September 11, 2001, but with less auspicious results.[86]

In delivering the objective information of the war in a way that "sold" the product of American power and prestige, the CPI utilized every medium available to it. This began with the newspaper. Indeed, in many ways, World War I represented the apotheosis of the newspaper as the main vehicle of information about world events, and the high prominence of these publications in the CPI underscored this fact. Because of George Creel's weariness of official censorship, other tactics of information management were devised in order to guarantee that the proper messages of American virtue captured the eyes of the citizenry. As previously emphasized, "facts" were "the life-blood of the CPI," and the CPI's Division of News voraciously sought them "from the front, from training camps, from the White House, from farms and factories, from worker's homes, from every place that had a story to tell regarding American people in the war."[87] These mountains of information were compiled around the clock by CPI personnel who conveyed them as stories in the *Official Bulletin*, the country's first government-issued national newspaper, or as official news releases in the *Official War Digest*, which gave easily accessible war information to the thousands of rural dailies that subscribed to the service.[88]

The CPI also drew from the lessons of the Great Exhibition and the grand international fairs that continued to be popular in the early twentieth century. Creel understood perfectly what made for a good exhibition: "The all attraction of a circus and all the seriousness of a sermon."[89] The traveling exhibitions of the CPI certainly fit this bill, with the objectivity of informational displays focusing on the rationale for intervention, the belligerent nations, and the military capability of American forces in Europe combined with staged battles that "aroused the assembled thousands to the highest pitch of enthusiasm."[90] By the end of the war, the CPI's exhibitions made visits to 21 cities for a total viewership of 10 million people.[91] One can see in these activities and their success not just the legacy of the Great Exhibition, but also the audience-pleasing spectacle of the early filmmakers of the Spanish-American War.

If one did not live in a city visited by the touring exhibition, abundant opportunities still existed to experience the virtues of the war extolled in an entertaining manner. Most likely, this would take the form of a speech given by a live orator. The Speakers Division of the CPI kept a card catalogue of ten thousand speakers around the country who could be called upon to give a rousing address in their local community.[92] Among the most effective of these speakers was a traveling troupe of orators dubbed the "Four Minute Men." These specially selected speakers would go to public gathering places and give short four-minute speeches that argued for the cause of the war and encouraged audience support for the endeavor. According to Creel, the corps of four-minute men numbered 75,000 and gave over 7 million speeches in front of an estimated 130 million people.[93] Eventually, professional singers accompanied the four-minute speakers and the singing of patriotic songs became part of a four-minute speech.[94] Like in much of his descriptions of the CPI's other activities, Creel described the work of the four-minute men in a heavily militarized language of arms and weaponry: "And let it be borne in mind that these were no haphazard talks by nondescripts, but the careful, studied, and rehearsed efforts of the *best* men in each community, each speech aimed as a rifle is aimed, and the driving to its mark with the precision of a bullet."[95] The CPI was no less eager to tap the potential of other media. Newspaper and magazine advertisements, picture posters, cartoons, and ephemera (small toys, cigarette cards, and other trinkets) all had their own division within the CPI.[96]

Few media, however, got Creel more excited than that of motion pictures—indeed, Creel was far ahead of his time in understanding the power of film and the crucial role the medium would play in the development and expansion of the American Empire. The comedic films of Charlie Chaplin and the epic films of D. W. Griffith had already demonstrated the weaponized potential of motion picture as a means to conquer the minds of the masses. Yet like the jingoist films of the Spanish-American War or Griffith's *Birth of a Nation*, these weapons of spectacle ran the risk of limiting their effectiveness to domestic audiences (or in the case of *Birth of a Nation*, certain racial segments of that audience). The films produced by the CPI represented an important innovation in the development of effective imperial propaganda in that they were designed to appeal to audiences both domestic *and* overseas. Creel's real genius as head of the CPI was his understanding that it was not enough to stir the passions of the domestic American aggregate—one also had to create compelling and persuasive media content for foreign audiences who might find themselves subject to American power.

This began by avoiding the problems represented by *Birth of a Nation*. Creel testified to this when he said after the war, "What we wanted to get into foreign countries were pictures that presented the wholesome life of America, giving fair ideas of our people and our institutions. What we wanted to keep out of world circulation was the 'thrillers,' that gave entirely false impressions of American life and morals."[97] Instead, films screened by the CPI, much like its printed material, were rooted in objective fact. Early on, the CPI determined that some of the best footage of war-related events came from the raw documentary film stock of cameras operated by the Army Signal Corps. The CPI secured access to this stock footage and began splicing it into its own newsreels and feature presentations or loaning it to private film producers. Thus, newsreels could give visual corroboration of the events they were presenting and fictionalized films would have an air of authenticity and legitimacy. Before long, "a steady output, ranging from one-reel subjects to seven-reel features, and covering every detail of American life, endeavor, and purpose, carried the call of the country to every community in the land, and then, captioned in all the various languages, went over the seas to inform and enthuse the peoples of Allied and neutral nations."[98]

Indeed, it was in the presentation of CPI films outside the United States where the motion picture as weapon of mass entertainment came into its own and signaled how this medium was to be used in the future. Overseas agents of the CPI exhausted every means available to ensure the screening of their films. Theaters were rented out, exhibitors were paid above-market rates to distribute CPI films, and in some cases, CPI agents put "a projector on an automobile and traveled from village to village, delighting the rustic populace with 'the wonders of America.'"[99] Yet this focus on truth and authenticity, while important to establish the credibility of the CPI's film output, was not by itself sufficient to truly win the hearts and minds of worldwide audiences. As Creel read the reports of his committee's work overseas, he discovered that "upon investigation we found that it [newsreels] did not go far enough. *What the war-weary foreigners liked and demanded was American comedy and dramatic films*. They had to have their Mary Pickford and Douglas Fairbanks and Charlie Chaplin and Norma Talmadge."[100] Creel suggests here that so long as foreign audiences were properly entertained by American media content, the United States would enjoy at minimum indifference to its overseas activities and at maximum enthusiastic support for its war aims and larger grand strategic goals. As in other cases from this era, good foreign audience data on the viewership of American media output is difficult to track, but Creel references one screening of the CPI produced film *America's Answer* in The Hague, "where the police had to stop [the] performance... owing to the great pro-American demonstrations that it aroused."[101]

By almost any measure, the CPI, with assistance from the burgeoning American film industry, did its job well. Public support for American participation in the Great War, while wavering a bit at the beginning, eventually became hearty and vigorous.[102] Some of this enthusiasm might be chalked up to the relatively short length of time of the United States' participation in the conflict and the distance of the homeland from the frontlines that prevented the American masses from experiencing the hardship of war. However, there is no denying the impact the CPI had in overcoming the isolationist impulses of the American public through its effective exploitation of print media, public oratory, and motion picture technology.

Nevertheless, the use of these powerful weapons of mass entertainment did result in some postwar "collateral damage." Outrage and curiosity over the state's foray into the uncharted realms of centralized information creation and dissemination greatly interested researchers of social psychology and sociology. Landmark studies on the techniques and methods of war propaganda (in both Great Britain and the United States) by such luminaries as Bertrand Russell, Harold Lasswell, and José Ortega y Gasset revealed the extent to which information resources and technologies could tap into a heretofore scientifically unrecognized "herd instinct" that could manipulate the passions of the whole populations through the spread of misinformation.[103] Most researchers greeted this discovery with disquiet and dread, emphasizing, on the one hand, the importance of public education to create a free-thinking individual that could resist the reptilian appeal of enticing spectacle and propaganda, while on the other hand, not expressing a great deal of confidence in the ability of education to perform this important task.[104]

These concerns resulted in much hostile castigation for Creel and his agency once the war had ended. Indeed, the irony of the criticism leveled at Creel stemmed not from the fact that he did his job poorly and wasted tax money on a frivolous government program, but that he did his job too well and that what the CPI represented was the government's malevolent foray into the dark arts of mass public manipulation.[105] Putting the personal attacks against Creel aside, the bulk of this accusation was correct—the CPI's "discovery" of the power of entertaining propaganda and information as a political weapon represented the passing of a figurative point of no return. Especially thanks to the advancement of film technologies, the disparate consciousness and imaginations of diverse populations could now be herded together and regimented along a single conceptual line. While the ranks of these individual minds could never be completely uniform and rigid, they could nevertheless be rendered sufficiently coherent and conformist to generate general approval (or contented neutrality) to the political aims and agendas of dominant assemblages of power in the world.

More important from the perspective of the United States was the profound change taking place in American society. Whereas barely 20 years prior to the outbreak of the Great War the population of the United States was content to tend its fields and mind its stores in the isolation of the vast North American continent, the prevailing sentiment as World War I came a close was that the United States was an exceptional nation that had to fight in Europe in order "to make the world safe for democracy." These sentiments waned as debates over the wisdom of the United States joining the League of Nations brought back the old isolationist refrain in American politics. Despite this, however, the seed of an imperial attitude, planted during the Spanish-American War, began to sprout during World War I. With the help of newly created audio technologies—including radio and motion pictures with a sound capability to match its already captivating visual power—this sprout would bloom into a fully grown empire.

The Sound of Depression and War: Radio, Audio Cinema, and World War II (1919–1945)

The immediate aftermath of World War I saw an enormous amount of resentment directed toward the personalities and institutions of public information and propaganda. Many outspoken groups expressed a certain queasiness with the revelation that a supposedly democratic state was learning how to pull the heartstrings of the masses so easily and quite possibly altering their behavior in the process. Congress especially was uncomfortable with the fact that a formal state propaganda agency (the CPI) existed during the war and took steps almost immediately after the cessation of hostilities to dissolve it into oblivion.[106] This skepticism and discomfort with state-based propaganda organizations continued to be a source of enormous tension for the next several decades.

Not everyone, however, saw the emerging apparatus of information management as a bad thing. As mentioned in the previous chapter, students of developing mass media capabilities like John Grierson saw the growth of these technologies as an opportunity to influence the public opinion in a positive way. For Grierson, this meant tutoring the masses of Great Britain through the methods of documentary filmmaking on the virtues of the empire and the imperial economy in a time of economic depression.[107] However, even Grierson's contribution to the processes of information and entertainment weaponization paled to that of the Austrian-born American Edward Bernays. As an indirect family relation of Sigmund Freud, Edward Bernays was keenly interested in how the insights of his uncle's theories of the human psyche could provide entry points into the collective conscious of the average person. After serving in Creel's CPI during World War I and then immersing himself in the early academic studies of wartime propaganda published by the likes of Walter Lippman, Bernays began laying the foundation for the science and technique of public relations.[108]

Like George Creel, Bernays saw the importance of using all the media platforms available in order to disseminate one's message. Thus, one of the most important media for Bernays was the up and coming platform of radio. While conceding the future of the fledgling medium was still unclear, Bernays nevertheless wrote in his seminal pamphlet *Propaganda* in 1928, "The radio is at present one of the most important tools of the propagandist."[109] Bernays's interest in radio reflected the debates seen in Great Britain as the BBC sought to use a global broadcasting capability to suture together a collapsing empire. However, for a man who would soon have an abundance of corporate clients, Bernays's interest in radio was more about how to boost sales than saving an empire—even if both ideas would eventually become intertwined as the still young century progressed. Radio, however, was not alone in its importance. The motion picture, already the one medium that had greatest potential for mass persuasion in the decade after World War I, went through a technological revolution with the addition of sound to its moving pictures. Because of this improvement, Bernays claimed it (the motion picture) "can standardize the ideas and habits of a nation" and that because it "avails itself only of ideas and facts which are in vogue," the motion picture is "the greatest unconscious carrier of propaganda in the world today."[110] The reason for this, Bernays argued, is not due to the fact the motion picture is a platform of persuasion through reason, which might be true of print platforms that "purvey news," but because "[the motion picture] seeks to purvey entertainment."[111]

This section will examine how these two crucial media dealt a final blow to the American propensity toward isolationism and cultivated entertaining and enticing messages of freedom and democracy in an era when depression and totalitarianism threatened to undermine liberal principles. Of particular interest was the use of these media as informational weapons that supplemented the coercive implements of war on the world's battlefields during World War II. Indeed, the period between 1933 and 1945 represented a kind of communications "arms race" between the major axis and allied powers who sought to maximize their ability to utilize ever-more powerful forms of communication to realize their respective war aims. One of the reasons why the United States and its allies emerged victorious over the forces of fascism rested on their ability to more effectively deploy the weapons of information within the context of world war and ultimately be more effective at winning hearts and minds of the global populations alongside the struggle of winning battles and territory. So important were these victories that World War II represents the moment when prominent leaders in the United States contemplated the possibility that waging a war of information and entertainment over a variety of media platforms could take precedent (or perhaps replace) the waging of a war of violence on a battlefield.[112]

As with all forms of power, however, rival groups and interests competed with each other in order to claim its legitimate use. In the United States during World War II, these tensions were most apparent in the struggle between private and state institutions. Propagandists like Edward Bernays served most often at the behest of large corporations during the 1920s when the ability of factories to manufacture material goods began to outpace the size of consumer demand and American industries looked for ways to stimulate the public's urge to buy more "stuff." The techniques of advertising, salesmanship, and product branding—essential parts of the present-day corporate enterprise—began their process of maturity during this period.[113] The development of radio was a crucial ingredient in these processes. However, when the economy crashed in 1929 and as the world headed toward war after Hitler's ascension to power in 1933, the American state attempted to reprise its role as the central purveyor of mass communication "weapons." American state propaganda agencies like the Office of War Information (OWI) and the Office of Strategic Services (OSS) quickly formed and performed similar functions during World War II as the CPI did in World War I. Such revivals of state information capacity, however, were not without controversy. Amid the debates of these turbulent decades over which institution was best suited to wield these potent weapons of information and entertainment, a larger transformation was taking place within the United States—that of a rising power deploying an embryonic soft power capability to expand, solidify, and legitimize its dominance.

Up until the 1920s, however, this nascent empire had no soundtrack. Radio quickly changed all this with its arrival as a form of mass media after World War I. As discussed in the previous chapter, Guglielmo Marconi's invention of a device that could transmit, capture, and broadcast audio signals was of high interest to great powers that saw the strategic potential of such a platform. In Great Britain, the government led the way in researching and developing the medium for public use both at home and in the far corners of its still substantial empire by creating the BBC and using it as a tool for creating greater imperial cohesion. In the United States, however, the incorporation of radio into the daily life of the nation took a different route. Whereas the broadcasting capability of Britain (as well as much of the rest of Europe) remained under the strict control of the state, in the United States, the government played a subordinate role to the private radio manufacturers and broadcasters who were largely the ones who produced and transmitted the content of radio programming.

Because American radio remained largely in the hands of private entities, the type of programming varied significantly from the government produced content of Great Britain. Whereas John Reith, the first director of the BBC, sought to use radio as a tool of mass education (which included educating the British people at home and in the colonies of the importance of the empire), in the United States, radio was from its earliest stages a medium in the control of the private sector—meaning it had to yield some means of profitability for those who owned and controlled the means of broadcasting and reception.[114] In the early days of radio, these were manufacturers like General Electric, American Telephone and Telegraph, and Westinghouse, and the key to their success as for-profit companies centered on the ability to create demand for both the hardware of individual radio receptors and the "software" of broadcasted programming by mass audiences throughout the country. Edward Berkowitz described the challenge this way: "Radio remained a product with a great deal of recognized commercial potential but without the killer application that would bring it into everyday use."[115] In other words, how should the radio manufacturers compel the American population to not only purchase radio receivers, but also to make listening to radio content a regular part of their day?

Overcoming this problem required two things. The first was the development of cheap radio receivers that would facilitate the creation of a mass audience and present lucrative opportunities for businesses intent on expanding their potential customer base. Throughout the 1920s, bulky radio sets slowly gave way to smaller and cheaper units thanks to the techniques of mass production and miniaturization. Eventually, 44 million small and versatile radio receivers (still somewhat bulky compared to the smart phones of today) saturated the consumer market by 1939.[116] However, cheap radios were not enough—the population at large needed a reason to go out and buy one of these radio receivers in the first place. For this, the radio manufacturers had also to be the producer of attractive content that could reach the millions of listeners in the audience as well as hold their attention for an extended period of time.

From this, radio producers created the commercial broadcasting network—an interconnected set of stations through which content produced on any part of the network could be broadcasted via the other parts to the entire country. Originally set up by the radio manufacturers themselves, these companies eventually abandoned their broadcasting operations to focus on other ventures and left the responsibilities of producing content to the commercial networks familiar today. The first was the National Broadcasting Corporation (NBC) in 1926 followed closely by the Columbia Broadcasting System (CBS) in 1927.[117] From the first moment these broadcasting networks came into existence, their sole focus, unlike with the BBC over in Britain, was on entertainment. In this sense, they brought to broadcasting the same ethos the tabloid newspapers did in the later nineteenth century with their focus on human-interest stories, comedy, and sports. To be sure, highbrow programming and educational content was available on American radio in the 1920s and 1930s—a single broadcast of a concert by the New York Philharmonic could gather a larger audience than the total cumulative in-person attendance of the symphony for the previous hundred years.[118] However, when the average radio listener turned on his receiver set in the 1920s and 1930s, he or she was far more likely to hear comedy and variety programs like *Amos and Andy* and the *Jack Benny Show*, smooth singing crooners like Bing Crosby, or sports spectacles like the Joe Louis/Max Schmeling boxing match of 1938—the latter of which was listened to by half of the entire American radio market of the time.[119]

The motivation for gathering these large audiences stemmed less from any noble pursuit of educating or enriching the lives of the masses than the need to generate revenues by capturing the ears of millions of people who would hear product advertisements alongside a network's programming. As foreseen by Edward Bernays, private radio networks were a bonanza of opportunity for advertisers and public relations professionals to tap into the imaginations of the public and stir the desires of the masses toward the products and perspectives of the clients of these agents of publicity. By paying the cost of producing a particular radio program or inserting a promotional message during a break in a station's primary programming, American radio was able to disseminate unlimited hours of entertaining content without recourse to additional taxes or other means of fee collection. The appeal of this model can be observed in the boost to advertising sales for radio between 1927, when radio stations billed $4.8 million, and 1944, when this amount soared to $392 million.[120]

For much of the interwar period, this model worked out fine for all parties. However, the combination of economic collapse and the gathering storm clouds of war meant that changes were on their way. In dealing with the consequences of the Great Depression, the Roosevelt administration initiated one of the largest expansions in American history of the scale and size of the federal government. To allay the skepticism of a public acculturated within a tradition of isolationism, individualism, and government restraint, Roosevelt sought to fully exploit the power of radio and its ability to burrow into the consciousness of the American people. Roosevelt's confidence in radio's power revealed itself in a conversation with Merlin Aylesworth, then president of NBC, when Roosevelt said, "Nothing since the creation of the newspaper has had so profound an effect on our civilization as radio."[121] As he began implementing his New Deal program, Roosevelt made periodic radio broadcasts where he gave detailed outlines and justifications for his reforms and answered any critiques made by his political rivals.[122] Dubbed "fireside chats," these broadcasts played a crucial role in legitimizing Roosevelt's reform agenda due to the fact they were among the most listened to radio communications in the United States with some of them garnering an audience of 30 million listeners. When Japan attacked the United States at Pearl Harbor in 1941, Roosevelt's "Day of Infamy" broadcast was heard by an astounding 62 million Americans.[123]

Roosevelt's ability to merge presidential politics and the medium of radio was a crucial step in incorporating this potent new media weapon into the American communications arsenal. Yet the memory of Creel's boisterous propaganda efforts was still fresh in the mind of many politicians in Washington, and even in the face of total war, great reluctance persisted over the wisdom of putting such powerful weapons like radio in the hands of the government. Amid a still vigorous debate in Congress and among the political elite in Washington, Roosevelt authorized in the summer of 1942 the creation of the OWI to manage all nonmilitary informational output by the American government for the duration of the war. From the moment of its inception, however, the tensions over how best to handle the growing power of these mass communication platforms plagued the agency's operations.[124]

The controversy connected with how much government control should be given over the nation's radio broadcasting capabilities should not be taken to mean that the role of radio in World War II was negligible or that powerful programming that was both patriotic and entertaining was absent during this period. In many ways, the totalitarian nature of the German and Japanese threat as well as the easy collusion of patriotism and the profit motive obviated the need for a large state-run propaganda agency. The private sector titans of American radio infrastructure were just as keen to see totalitarianism defeated as was the US government and were just as prepared to deploy the power of mass broadcasting to this cause.[125] As Gerd Horten summarizes, "it [radio] entertained large national audiences while selling the products of commercial sponsors. It provided national and international news coverage, and during World War II it made Americans as well informed as they ever had been."[126] Unique only to radio at this time was its ability to broadcast world events almost as if they were live. Pivotal moments like the 1938 Czechoslovakia Crisis were "news events extraordinaire... that allowed Americans to listen to history in the making."[127]

Indeed, "reality-based" news programming proved to be the most popular of all the various content formats outside of traditional comedy, music, and sports. Like the CPI, the OWI sought to provide private news outlets with facts and data upon which ostensibly neutral news reports could be written. When the OWI did try to steer the messaging and content in nonnews programs during World War II, the results were often mixed. Popular commercial radio programs like *The Green Hornet*, "integrated propaganda messages into their plot structures voluntarily, under the direction of the Office of War Information" while not so popular government programs like *We Hold These Truths* and *This Is War* offered regular doses of Allied goodness and Axis treachery.[128] In the case of the latter, the less than stellar ratings may have been due in part to commercial radio stations consigning such programs to times of reduced listenership late at night or early in the morning.[129]

When it came to using radio to appeal to overseas audiences, however, the private sector approach of the United States fell short when compared to that of the BBC in Great Britain. With its interest in keeping the collective consciousness of the far corners of the British Empire stitched together in the face of the threat posed by the Axis powers, international radio broadcasting proved to be an invaluable asset. In the United States, this capability was less appreciated among the most influential members of society—but not all. Recognizing that Nazi Germany had set up broadcasting facilities in Latin America, Nelson Rockefeller, who had numerous financial interests in the region, consulted with Franklin Roosevelt in setting some kind of public relations firm that would use the latest media technologies available to make appeals to Latin American countries and win their support for United States' war interests. Going through several name changes in its early days, the organization eventually acquired the title of Office of Inter-American Affairs (OIAA) and began a quiet propaganda campaign in Latin America designed to out-broadcast German radio programming. From the beginning, the producers at the OIAA sensed what made for the best kind of counter-Nazi programming—"tastes for the American way of life and its popular music."[130]

After Pearl Harbor, the OWI emulated many of the OIAA tactics as it established its own global radio network that eventually came to be called the Voice of America (VOA).[131] This service focused almost exclusively on news and broadcasted simple English language bulletins to large swaths of the globe that received its signal. Soon after the establishment of the VOA and after the United States had a foothold in Europe, a separate broadcasting outlet called the American Broadcasting Station, a European-specific service, dedicated a third of its airtime to German language programming. However, this service went beyond the simple news reporting of the VOA and attempted to incorporate more entertainment programming into its schedule. One example was a broadcast called "Music for the Wehrmacht," that interspersed popular American singers like Bing Crosby and Dinah Shore with German language hosts.[132] The success of these programs fueled more broadcasting operations, and by the end of the war, the OWI operated 30 shortwave transmitters and was capable of broadcasting 24 hours a day in 40 languages in every major theater of the war.[133] However slow and scattershot the American experience was with deploying radio capabilities during World War II, the experience eventually paid off in a significant way after the war ended and radio became a primary communications weapon against the Soviet Union in the Cold War—a topic that will be taken up in the next chapter.

During World War II, the United States was far more practiced and comfortable handling the medium of film. With World War I giving the United States the global monopoly on film production in the world, American films became one of the most effective platforms for exposing the world to American values, tastes, and aspirations. This dominant position, while weakened initially by the recovery of European cinema after World War I, actually grew more solid as technological improvements to the medium enabled the playing of an audio track that corresponded to the visual action of the motion picture. With the film medium already seen by such cinematic patriarchs as D. W. Griffin as a uniquely American platform, the sound innovations that were coming out of the United States in the 1920s (Warner Brothers premiered the first sound film in 1926 before the other studios quickly adapted the innovation to their own productions) ensured that this awe-inspiring medium remained an effective booster of American interests. Much of this had to do with the increasing homogenization of the filmmaking process—with cameras, projection equipment, and now, sound mixing and editing techniques being standardized in Hollywood. Increasingly, to be a filmmaker anywhere in the world meant at minimum gaining access to American equipment and internalizing the American filmmaking technique, and at maximum relocating to Hollywood and seeking the tutelage of established motion picture directors.[134]

The changes brought about by sound to motion pictures were not relegated to behind the camera. At first, the stars of the silent era were the stars of the sound era. Popular actors like Charlie Chaplin, the Marx Brothers, and other denizens of early Hollywood made a relatively smooth transition into the pictures where actors were expected to sing and talk in addition to dance and act. Eventually, however, performers like Katherine Hepburn, Clark Gable, Fred Astaire, and Ginger Rogers were fronting major motion pictures that, while being more expensive to produce, were selling unprecedented amounts of tickets at the box office.[135] This potency of film power was seen in the ability of motion pictures to survive the Great Depression. While it was true that the worst years of the depression from 1930 to 1933 saw three major studios (Paramount, Fox, and RKO) go into bankruptcy and overall film industry profits decline by 41 percent from all-time highs posted in 1929, by 1934 the industry was once again reaping profits and Hollywood was one of the few sectors of the American economy that was not stagnant during the later 1930s.[136]

In a strange way, the onset of the Great Depression gave even more power to this type of media experience since those enmeshed in poverty sought anything that might temporarily distract them from their desperate economic situation. Speaking in regard to film especially, Robert Fyne suggests, "Motion pictures...eschewed the harsh realities of an American economic system that virtually collapsed overnight (and) highlighted frivolity and choreography."[137] While the Great Depression featured many episodes of unrest and social turmoil that often required the state to use violent force to put down the dissent, revolutionary fervor may have been more pronounced if the nickelodeons and movie houses did not offer merry and entertaining productions of telegenic actors and actresses singing, dancing, dramatizing, pratfalling, and otherwise brightening the mood of bleak times. In perfecting a method of neutralizing the psychological and emotional effects of poverty, social inequality, and powerlessness, the producers of cinema unlocked a formidable means of protecting the status quo.

Once the United States declared war in 1941, motion pictures held fast to their roles as entertainers, but slowly blended pro-war and pro-American sentiments into their screenplays. Starting in 1938 with the film *Blockade* about the Spanish Civil War, American filmmakers incorporated topics that ranged from the threat of totalitarianism (*Confessions of a Nazi Spy* and *Manhunt*) to American heroism (*Sergeant York*) to celebrations of capitalism and the consumer lifestyle (*An American Romance*).[138] The vast majority of these films were unremarkable and often patronizing, yet the list also contains some of the greatest films in the entire American film oeuvre.

A handful stand out for special recognition. The first was Charlie Chaplin's *The Great Dictator*. Received well by most critics and embraced by audiences around the world, the film was the highest grossing of all of Chaplin's films. The movie did, however, manage to upset some audience members with its closing admonition: "Now let us fight to free the world—to do away with national barriers—to do away with greed, hate, and intolerance. Let us fight for a world...of reason—a world where science and progress will lead to the happiness of all." Some critics found these words a little too radical and communist for their tastes.[139] Second was Frank Capra's documentary series *Why We Fight*. As an attempt to explain to a broad American audience the various threats posed by the Axis powers, the films gave a sober and straightforward rationale why the United States was obligated to fight that also managed to be emotionally stirring. Indeed, the films were considered so engaging in their emotional power and moral disposition that they were shown to all military recruits during their training.[140] Outshining all of these was *Casablanca*. Regarded as perhaps the greatest film ever made, *Casablanca* deployed the best American filmmaking had to offer—potent star power from an international cast (some of whom were refugees from Nazi power overseas), high production values that included the latest sound technology, catchy songs like the now famous *As Time Goes By*, and the fact the film's eponymous city was in the headlines at the same time as the picture was released in 1942.[141]

Though the aforementioned films were made in the United Stated and were mostly intended for American audiences, their popularity and transformations into classics in the art of cinema were due to their international acclaim and popularity. Often however, this kind of acclaim was a fortunate accident and not necessarily the result of shrewd information management. During World War II, American propaganda efforts overseas, especially those involving film productions, lacked the central resource planning and message coordination that the CPI provided under the leadership of George Creel during World War I. Generally speaking, the American state refrained from any formal participation in propaganda filmmaking and took only an advisory role. Part of the reason for this was that with regard to foreign information management, the OWI had a rival in the OSS. Charged with dealing with the management of military information and psychological warfare, the OSS was less interested in spreading "big ideas" or mass entertainment than with utilizing informational and psychological warfare to supplement actions on the battlefield.[142] The OSS tended not to be interested in winning the hearts and minds of the general populations, though this would change in the future when it became the Central Intelligence Agency (CIA) and soft power became a prime component of its activities during the Cold War.

Another reason why the OWI was less successful at deploying entertaining information overseas during World War II centered on a debate that was going on simultaneously in Great Britain as seen with the friction between the BBC and Radio Luxembourg. Decision makers within the OWI were unsure whether the agency should concentrate solely on news releases and the output of raw data or create campaigns—sometimes through film productions—to elicit more passionate and emotional responses.[143] The conflict was never resolved satisfactorily, evidenced by the fact much of the OWI overseas staff "complained bitterly that the fuzzy lead they received [from their supervisors in Washington] made their own task difficult or even impossible to perform."[144] Eventually, however, the OWI did set up a Psychological Warfare Branch under the supervision of the military that established 40 foreign news bureaus as well as "propaganda shops" that showcased Allied print and pictorial material lauding the American and Allied efforts in the war. The activities of these shops rarely included cinematic operations.[145]

Toward the war's end, the OWI did flirt more heavily with the idea of establishing its own film studio to make propaganda pictures. However, still feeling resistance from movie studio executives and libertarian politicians leery of the idea of a state-based film propaganda capability, the OWI opted in the end to form a partnership with the major film production companies in Hollywood. While the bulk of the films made under this partnership had American audiences in mind, the OWI/Hollywood alliance did manage to produce a few films targeted primarily at foreign audiences. Few of these productions are widely remembered today, with perhaps the exception of *Wilson*, a celluloid homage to Woodrow Wilson that lauded his internationalism and portrayed his struggle for the establishment of the League of Nations as a heroic quest.[146] This unimpressive output and mediocre result demonstrated that while the United States understood and embraced the power of media technology as a necessary component of realizing its national interests, significant doubt and debate existed over the best means to procure and deploy this power. Such tensions continued to persist as World War II ended and the Cold War began.

Conclusion

The period between 1898 and 1945 saw the United States transform from a large but provincial nation to the most dominant state in the world with aspirations for planetary control. This transformation took place amid a series of tumultuous events that included three wars and a major collapse of the global economy. Amid all this turmoil, however, the opening decades of the twentieth century saw several momentous innovations in the art and science of communications. As it attempted to shake off its isolationist worldview, the United States led the world in adapting these new communications technologies toward political ends.

The most influential of these advances came with the invention of motion pictures, which played a significant role in transforming the traditional isolationist dispositions of the American people into a frenzied support of early American imperialism during the Spanish-American War. During World War I, the power of cinema as a weapon of entertainment expanded thanks to the development of a large filmmaking industry combined with the creation of the CPI, a government propaganda organization that recruited the power of cinema (among other media platforms) to the war aims of the United States. Finally, during the Great Depression and World War II, the invention of audio broadcasting and reception technologies enhanced the power of cinema and created a new platform of information and entertainment in the form of radio. As a result of these advances, the power of amusement at the theater, movie house, or nickelodeon became a more intense sensory experience while the daily home life of the average American became susceptible to a nonstop bombardment of broadcast entertainment.

This ability to reach into the intimate spaces of the nation was important for the larger prospect of American power. The coming years were to be very challenging for the nation as it confronted a threatening superpower with an "evil" communist ideology that had to be defeated regardless of the costs. Though a debate existed over the proper ownership balance between the public and private sector, it was nevertheless in the interest of all segments of American ruling interests that the larger public at most understand the nature of the Soviet threat and support the decisions of the prevailing complex of power, or at minimum be sufficiently amused and distracted by trivialities so as not to impede the status quo. As the Cold War began and the Soviet Union developed its own informational capacity, it became more important than ever to appeal beyond the domestic population—audiences in other countries outside the sovereign reach of the

United States also needed to be either won over or neutralized. The United States had discovered much in the previous years about the techniques and methods of deploying mass media and its power to win hearts and minds. Facing the Soviet threat, it now had to put these lessons to use in its bid for total world dominance. In doing so, it took the first steps in developing new technologies and new communications platforms that would make its arsenal of entertainment even more powerful and open up the possibility of exercising a form of imperial power not seen before in history.

3

Spreading Liberalism: Broadcasting, Consumerism, and the Maturity of the American Empire (1945–1968)

Introduction

Once the fires of war had finally burned out in 1945, a bleak and austere world full of hardship and depravation remained. For the United States, victory in the war meant making important decisions with regard to how it would deploy its surpluses of power to facilitate economic recovery and lay the foundations of a new international order. Some indication of the direction the United States wished to go was given before the end of the war at the Dumbarton Oaks Conference in 1944 where the ideals of liberal economics and institutional global governance were the primary topics of discussion. However, a consensus among the principal Western allies on the virtues of a managed international capitalism in no way translated to an agreement among the rest of the world, especially with a powerful Soviet Union offering what appeared to be a viable communist alternative and a collection of former colonies seeking independence and eager to discard anything that reeked of imperialism. In the crucial years after the end of World War II, the United States faced the daunting challenge of not only reducing the appeal of communism, but also winning global assent (or disinterest) to its own ambitious effort at global expansion.

To accomplish this, the United States created a new foundation of legal authority based on the provisions of the United Nations Charter and the Bretton Woods agreements that gave birth to the International Monetary Fund, World Bank, and General Agreement on Tariffs and Trade. Together, these institutions formed the nucleus of new assemblage of power that eschewed the discredited formal imperialism of the past for a new kind of international administration. Ostensibly, independent intergovernmental actors used attractive economic incentives (low-interest development loans and fixed monetary standards) and the rhetoric of human rights to maximize voluntary participation by sovereign states.[1] However, this chapter argues that the creation of this legal apparatus of international authority was but one element in a much more ambitious effort by the United States to construct a framework of informal empire. After 1945, this included the first steps in the creation of a global broadcasting infrastructure for the dissemination of information and entertainment. Using established forms of communications like international radio broadcasts and international exhibitions as well as more novel technologies like television, the United States hoped to create a stable liberal world order that could be managed without recourse to physical coercion.

The importance of minimizing formal military and political authority was a key component to the American strategy. General Eisenhower's aforementioned desire expressed near the end of the war reflected a larger awareness of the importance of avoiding the past mistakes of British colonialism in bringing about global acceptance of American dominance.[2] For this reason, it is worth pausing a few moments to reflect how the historical situations of Great Britain and the United States were different during the growth phase of their respective imperial developments and why communications technologies made it possible for American leaders to believe that a less abrasive form of rule was possible in 1945.

The early days of American hegemony shared much in common with the early days of British hegemony. Fear and uncertainty led to policies that were often incoherent and contradictory as new ideologies designed to create a new and better world confronted the political and economic wreckage of recent wars and depression. In the case of Great Britain this was the end of the Napoleonic Wars and the final defeat of the French Empire in 1815, and for the United States, of course, this was the defeat of Nazi Germany and Imperial Japan in 1945. Like Great Britain, the foundations of American hegemony rested upon a conception of liberalism that emphasized the free flow of capital, commodity and labor markets, protection of property rights, and republican political principles designed to legitimize the entire socioeconomic package. In this scheme, the state would play an important, but limited role in protecting markets by enforcing contracts and deploying military force to safeguard trade routes and when necessary, open up foreign territories for resource and demographic exploitation.[3] For Great Britain, however, the inability to access any kind of effective global communications apparatus until the 1920s meant that this ideology often had to be promulgated through colonial dictate and enforced with soldiers and gunboats. Even where a communications infrastructure did exist, such as with the worldwide British Broadcasting Corporation (BBC) radio broadcasting capability that began to come online after World War I, the legacy of racism and perception of colonial populations as being incapable of civilization (despite Kipling's poetic admonition to "take up the white man's burden") neutralized whatever potential existed to persuade the rest of the world of the virtues of liberalism.

Because of the contradictions between British imperialism and the universalism of liberalism, the United States offered a different package of liberal principles after World War II. These changes were encapsulated in the idea of embedded liberalism, which signaled "how market processes and entrepreneurial and corporate activities were surrounded by a web of social and political constraints and regulatory environment that sometimes restrained but in other instances led the way in economic and industrial strategy."[4] Whereas the early nineteenth-century British liberalism decried most nonessential interventions into the economy by the state and imagined a perfect free market by equal actors at the international level, the twentieth-century American liberalism after World War II gave the state an expanded role vis-à-vis private enterprise and industry in economic decision making. This meant the state would take responsibility for providing financial support to troubled industries and corporations, provide a social safety net for vulnerable social groups in society, and acknowledge economic inequality in mediating conflicts between highly developed states and lesser-developed ones that had previously been the subjects of imperial domination.[5] In essence, the social reforms that took a century to develop during the rise and fall of the British Empire were present at the very beginning of the American Empire. It was this state intervention that was mostly responsible for the construction of public airwaves and international broadcasting platforms that would allow both private and public broadcasters state-of-the-art media to transmit their messages, news, and spectacle.

Pro-liberal advocates in nineteenth-century Britain also had the luxury of focusing their initial efforts at constructing hegemony in British society on winning over the sentiments of industrial workers and middle-class shopkeepers before turning their attention to the wider world. The absence of a powerful rival in 1815 relieved the British bourgeoisie of a significant political burden in its battle to assume the leadership of British society. This benefit, however, eventually turned into a liability as Great Britain was unable, because of insufficient technological development, and unwilling, because of nationalist fervor, to redirect some of its propaganda output toward foreign audiences except in notable cases like the Great Exhibition. In the United States, however, a liberal domestic consensus had to be maintained while simultaneously persuading foreign audiences to side with the United States rather than with the Soviet Union and communism. Though an extended confrontation with the Soviet Union was not inevitable by the end of 1945, the tensions that existed at the allied conferences at Yalta and Potsdam suggested some sort of international rivalry would persist after the defeat of Germany and Japan. The United States thus faced the difficult task of maintaining the social status quo domestically while portraying the liberal internationalist assemblage of command backed by American power as progressive and universal to diverse and scattered audiences around the world. The inquisition of suspected domestic communists by such individuals such as Joseph McCarthy (discussed in the second section of this chapter) represented some of the difficulties the United States had in maintaining this balance.

Finally, the emergence of a nuclear standoff during this period between the United States and the Soviet Union gave even more prominence to the need for informal control and rule via intermediating institutions and enticing communications. Whereas Britain during its imperial rise could intervene militarily almost anywhere in the world without worrying about reprisals from other great powers until much later in the nineteenth century, the United States had to be very careful about intervention since a miscalculation could trigger a nuclear crisis. This did not mean, of course, that the United States did not intervene in foreign countries. However, the decision to intervene was a far weightier matter in the mid-twentieth century than in the mid-nineteenth century. Within this unique environment, the ability to persuade and seduce via clever deployments of information and entertainment gained a heightened importance that was neither present nor appreciated in the early days of British imperial development.

The three periods discussed in this chapter mark the development of the informal imperialism of the United States between 1945 and 1965 where innovations with mass communications platforms conveyed compelling variations on themes of American administered liberal institutionalism. The first period, encompassing a brief period of postwar euphoria between 1945 and 1948, saw the ideas of human rights and institutionalism form the first variation on the larger ideological theme of a postwar liberalism. Relying heavily on state-based bureaucracies and agencies, the United States unleashed a barrage of radio, film, and other forms of news and entertainment to persuade nations devastated by decades of war and depression that basic human rights could be protected and advanced through international organizations like the United Nations and the Bretton Woods institutions. The second period occurring between the years 1949 and 1959, feature the era of McCarthyism. Utilizing the newly arrived power of television, Joseph McCarthy put forth a harsh rhetoric that was more skeptical of liberal institutionalism and that often associated it with communism. Because of the power of television, this burst of populist fervor, though engaging a large audience at home, caused significant damage to the ability of American overseas persuasive and entertainment outlets to neutralize actual communist dissent in Europe and other volatile zones of superpower confrontation. Finally, in the years between 1959 and 1965, a more positive, pleasing, and most importantly, entertaining idea of liberalism in the form of consumerism arrived on the scene via a series of international expositions and world's fairs. The most notable of these was the 1964 World's Fair, which served as an informal celebration of the dominant position of the United States in the world and inspired the type of theme park entertainment seen in the present day in places like Disneyland and Epcot Center.

Airwaves amid Airlifts: International Radio Broadcasting (1945–1949)

Like Great Britain during its hegemonic rise at the start of the nineteenth century, the United States offered the world a liberal vision upon which peace and prosperity could be built. In promoting the creation of the United Nations, the Bretton Woods development institutions, and the Universal Declaration of Human Rights, the United States sought to rid the world of the scourge of war and poverty in the same way Great Britain sought to use its power to end slavery and starvation during its rise to prominence. In pursuit of its goals, Great Britain hoped to consolidate the class antagonisms that existed within its society at the time and forge a consensus in support of imperial expansion. The liberal project the United States pursued posed a more complicated challenge. Rather than merely consolidate class differences at the national level, the United States also had the task of incorporating whole nations into the grand international scheme it promoted. In accomplishing this task, however, it could not routinely rely on coercive force as Britain did in the previous century. With this in mind, the United States offered genuinely attractive humanitarian ideals embodied in the UN Charter and the Universal Declaration of Human Rights and hoped this soft power approach would spare it many of the seedier tasks of imperial management.

Unfortunately for the United States, there were signs early in the aftermath of World War II—a war brought about in part due to the excesses and extremes of capitalism—that many nations were not prepared to give liberalism a second chance. Strong communist parties existed in France and Italy while radical insurgents were already organizing armed resistance to liberal governments in Greece and Turkey. Anticolonial groups in Asia and Africa pursued independence on a model of self-determination heavily infused with the writings of Marx and Lenin. Of course, the presence of the Soviet Union as the other great superpower to emerge out of the fires of war meant that any political party or resistance group that opposed Western capitalism had a stalwart supporter in the Soviet state. Thus, the liberal ideology promoted by the United States had substantial historical baggage and was viewed with both skepticism and hostility throughout the world. Given this challenge, simply proclaiming the virtues of liberalism would not be enough—mechanisms of persuasion and methods of neutralizing dissent would be necessary if the liberal internationalist vision was to succeed.

This first sign that the role of media rose in importance among key decision makers in the American government can be seen in how media and government began to merge after 1946. Whereas during the war, the American state had gone out of its way to minimize governmental control or oversight in the production and dissemination of war-related content, several key developments in the early Cold War revealed the need for state-based information capacities to promote the idea of liberal institutionalism.

Almost all of them were connected in some way to the emerging antagonism taking shape between the United States and the Soviet Union. The
first was the publication of George Kennan's now famous "Long Telegram"
in February of 1946 in which he anticipated the coming intractable standoff between the Soviet Union and the United States due to the conflicting
ideologies of the two nascent superpowers. Kennan identified Soviet propaganda as "basically negative and destructive," and suggested, "It should
therefore be relatively easy to combat it by any intelligent and really constructive program."[6] A few lines later Kennan criticizes the lack of attention
information activities have garnered by American political elites: "We must
formulate and put forward for other nations a much more positive and constructive picture of the sort of world we would like to see than we have put
forward in the past."[7] Kennan then anticipates some of the objections of
those who would argue that liberal freedoms provide their innate justification, and warns that reluctance by the United States to legitimize itself will
only empower its adversary:

> It is not enough to urge the people of the world to develop political processes
> similar to our own. Many foreign peoples, in Europe at least, are tired and
> frightened by experiences of the past, and are less interested in abstract free-
> dom than in security. They are seeking guidance rather than responsibilities.
> We should be better able than the Russians to give them this. And unless we
> do, the Russians certainly will.[8]

Kennan's warning sent a chill up the spines of enough congressional lawmakers to persuade them that more proactive measures were necessary to
confront Soviet expansionism and that the state might have a role to play
in the development of an information and propaganda program. Advocates
in Congress of an aggressive communications apparatus took advantage of
this change in attitude to begin pushing for funding a multimillion-dollar
foreign information and cultural diplomacy effort.[9]

A second boost came from newly appointed Secretary of State George
Marshall. In June of 1947, Marshall had given his now famous speech at
Harvard University outlining the principles of the European Recovery Plan
that was later dubbed the Marshall Plan. In the speech, Marshall made an
eloquent argument that sought to justify massive economic assistance to
Europe based on the core liberal values of stability, abundance, and liberty:
"Our policy is directed not against any country or doctrine but against
hunger, poverty, desperation, and chaos. Its purpose should be the revival
of a working economy in the world so as to permit the emergence of political and social conditions in which free institutions can exist."[10] These ideas
fueled not only the Marshall Plan, but also the decision to undertake the
Berlin Airlift a few months later. Marshall's next move, however, suggested
aid by itself was not enough to win the hearts and minds of Europeans. On
June 10, 1947, three days after the speech at Harvard, Marshall was back
in Washington, DC, to testify before the Senate Appropriates Committee.

Of principal concern to him was the restoration of some $31 million to the budget of the Office of International Information and Culture that had been tentatively cut by the committee. Marshall insisted that the success of reconstruction efforts in Europe demanded an ability to communicate with the peoples who lived in the difficult conditions there and to share with Europeans the humanitarian aims and objectives of redevelopment aid.[11]

Yet a full understanding of what was at stake in the emerging struggle with the Soviet Union and the importance of media weapons in this struggle came when a 22-member congressional delegation visited Prague in the hopes of gaining a firsthand account of the political tensions reverberating in Central Europe. Upon discovering that many anticommunist leaders and activists had experienced repression at the hands of Soviet-friendly officials, the delegation made a statement reminiscent of George Creel 30 years earlier: "[There is] a vast battlefield of ideologies in which words have to a large extent replaced armaments as the active elements of attack and defense."[12] Sentiments such as these captured perfectly the emerging shape of how power was transforming from physical violence to mental and psychological influence, and unsurprisingly, those lawmakers who participated in the tour conceded to their colleagues that the United States was badly outgunned in this new form of warfare. From their testimony, the need for a state propaganda agency to persuade foreign audiences of the honest intentions and mutual interests of American leadership became widely accepted. On January 16, 1947, Congress passed the Smith-Mundt Act, thus formally establishing an American foreign communications and propaganda apparatus.

The passage of the Smith-Mundt Act committed the United States to using state resources to win the favor and approval of foreign audiences by communicating the values and ideals of the United States and the aims and objectives of its foreign policy. In establishing this infrastructure, the United States attempted to legitimize its new status as the world's most dominant superpower and its intention to retain this position indefinitely. Monies from the Smith-Mundt Act funded a wide array of informational and cultural activities including the publication of newspapers and magazines, production and distribution of motion pictures, foreign exchange programs, and overseas libraries. These activities went a long way in persuading many national leaders and populations of the importance of liberal values and the need for a strong American state to protect them.

However, the debate over the passage of the Smith-Mundt Act revealed a core antagonism in the approach to legitimizing American values abroad that undermined the effectiveness of its newly minted communications activities. The main fissure developed in the distinction between content understood as news and information and content understood as cultural and educational exchange. News operations included activities such as the publication of newspapers full of headlines from the United States and distribution of glossy photographic magazines with pictures of the material trappings of American society. This style of content was directed toward mostly mass audiences with the hope they would develop a favorable opinion of the United States and direct the policy of their particular nation toward a more friendly posture. Cultural operations featured exchange programs with students, scholars and artists, touring symphonies and art shows, and receptions and parties held between visiting American dignitaries and their local counterparts. These cultural activities were directed toward the elite decision makers and social trendsetters of a nation in the hope of cultivating friendly relations among elites who occupied the local halls of power.[13]

Combined, both approaches gave the United States a broad front of soft power to win the opinion of the world. However, both these approaches were time consuming—it might take years to set up worldwide distribution networks for American publicity publications or cultivate deep relationships between American elites and their overseas counterparts. As the alarm over the rising red tide of Soviet power increased, some new dynamic was needed to quickly convince large swathes of the global population to love the United States—or failing this, at least see it as the lesser of two evils. The American ambassador to the Soviet Union, Walter Smith, understood this best when he insisted American programming include "humor, bright music, folk songs and any form of entertainment which offers an escape from the grim reality of daily existence."[14]

More entertainment, however, was only part of the equation. The medium that conveyed this brighter and more compelling narrative about the United States also had to be more dynamic. While television broadcasting was making inroads into American domestic society in the days after World War II, it was not yet a platform that could speak to the global masses who largely did have access to television sets. By far, the "hottest" global medium of the mid-twentieth century remained the radio. Great Britain demonstrated how to capture the minds and imaginations of millions of people with radio broadcasting during World War II. The BBC, with its devotion to truth and objectivity made it the preferred choice among most Europeans for news about the war. However, the straight and dispassionate tone of the BBC rarely stoked the passions or fostered an emotional response of the audience members. While it was on the air, Radio Luxembourg provided a livelier package of news, popular music, and human-interest content that made it popular among listeners in Western Europe.[15] Thus, the United States, taking its cue from the British experience, sought to cultivate a broadcasting infrastructure that would woo the audiences of the world with a combination of objective news and cultural programs wrapped in American-style entertainment.

The most famous of the great radio assets of the United States was the Voice of America (VOA). Created by the Office of War Information (OWI) during the war, the VOA had the responsibility of broadcasting the news of the day to foreign audiences as well as explaining the aims and objectives of American foreign policy.[16] After the war, the VOA looked to be headed toward the chopping block as a new influx of budget-slashing Republicans entered Congress after the elections of 1946.[17] The service was saved, however, when William Benton, a veteran of the New York advertising agencies and senator from Connecticut, along with key Republican members of Congress like Karl Mundt and George Bender, persuaded members of their own party that foreign broadcasting was a key part of neutralizing the spread of communism. To bolster the defense of the VOA as the budget deliberations continued, the State Department announced it would utilize new technologies to begin broadcasting operations in Russian that would be beamed directly into the Soviet Union. The programming consisted of news reports and discussions of current events, explanations of the American political system, and perhaps most importantly, samplings of American music in between the spoken-word content. According to Walter Smith, the audiences that he observed did not care too much for the lessons on political theory, but apparently they all smiled in unison when Cole Porter's "Night and Day" radiated over the airwaves. One listener commented, "This is what we have been waiting 45 minutes for."[18] After mostly positive reports came in from the Soviet Union on the public reception of the VOA, programmers tweaked the original scheduling to include more "jazzy song and news items."[19] These insights revealed the important role entertainment would play in the power struggle with the Soviet Union.

Smith's observations were borne out by the limited audience data collected from Eastern European and Soviet audiences during the Cold War. Surveys taken by the Soviet government in the mid-1970s revealed that the primary reasons for listening to Western radio programs were music and entertainment.[20] Throughout the Eastern Bloc, a small but notable cadre of radio celebrities grew thanks to American radio broadcasts. The most popular of these was DC-area deejay Willis Conover, the host of an immensely popular VOA program called *Music USA*. According to Wilson Dizard, a noted historian of American public diplomacy,

> The introduction of [the] two-hour nightly jazz show, *Music USA*, played a special role in expanding listenership. Originally targeted to audiences in Soviet-controlled areas, the show was soon expanded to reach a worldwide audience. Washington disc jockey Willis Conover, the host of Music USA, was a knowledgeable jazz enthusiast with a personal record collection of over sixty thousand selections. His program regularly featured interviews with popular artists form Duke Ellington to Frank Sinatra. (He drew the line at Elvis Presley.)[21]

Entertaining programs like *Music USA* over time built large audiences that on a good day could reach over half the population of the Soviet Union or any of the countries of Eastern Europe. Survey data taken later in the Cold War testified to how powerful these programs were and how many millions of people experienced them. Though the Soviet Union jammed many of the transmissions of Western radio broadcasters during the early days of the Cold War, by the 1970s this interference had largely ended, and surveys revealed that half the urban population in the Soviet Union listened regularly to Western radio programming.[22] Audience numbers outside of the Soviet Union could be even bigger. Broadcasts of Radio Free Europe—a service that directed programming solely to Eastern Europe—had potential audience sizes in Poland as high as 70 percent of the population, above 50 percent of the population of Hungary, as high as 60 percent in Czechoslovakia, and over 60 percent in Romania throughout the 1960s and 1970s. Music and show businesses were not the only reasons for listening. News and informational programs also proved to be sources of interest and curiosity as well as important sources of information that were more trustworthy than the state media monopolies. After "music and entertainment," the most common reason for listening to Western radio programs was "searching for information that differs from official point of view."[23] The simple search for independent information not manipulated or fabricated by the government appeared to be its own form of entertainment.

While the VOA and Radio Free Europe directed most of its attention toward Europe, other broadcasting outlets targeted different regions of the world and often used a more cultural approach to their operations. In Latin America, the General Advisory Council (GAC) and Office of Inter-American Affairs (OIAA) took the lead in legitimizing American interests in the area. In the former, the GAC sought to overcome the worldwide perception that the United States suffered from cultural inferiority compared with European and Latin American states. Under the leadership of Ben Cherington, the GAC focused much of its work on exchange programs for students, artists, and musicians—many of whom were recording stars locals had heard singing on local stations.[24] In the latter, the OIAA worked with local governments and provincial elites to cultivate an environment that was friendly to foreign investment (especially to the OIAA's founder, Nelson Rockefeller). Part of this process included providing educational resources and training in the methods of liberal economics and entrepreneurship as well as forging close cultural bonds between North and South Americans. The OIAA also had a substantial informational capacity that included distribution networks for printed material and radio broadcasts of a rich array of radio programming in Spanish.[25]

As countries occupied by the Allies, Germany and Japan had their own unique cultural and informational programs that brought handpicked members of the defeated nations to the United States for exposure to the values and methods of liberal democracy. The hope was that the magnetism of American soft power—especially its abundant entertainment resources, seeped into the minds of the visiting dignitaries and echoed in their heads as they made important decisions about the future of the their societies. In other cases, local decision makers not associated with the previous regimes were provided with local on-site tutelage by American military and political occupiers.[26] The United States also played a pivotal role in establishing the United Nations Economic, Social and Cultural Organization (UNESCO), an arm of the United Nations devoted specifically to foster closer cultural ties between nations. To top it all off, the United States in 1946 established the Fulbright Scholarship Program, which would select and fund scholars and future leaders from around the world for extended stays in the United States to study, research, and teach. After their stays in the United States, the hope was the selected individuals would return to their home states imbued with liberal values and enter the local ruling structure prepared to implement these values.[27] At the heart of all these programs was the belief that American culture was more entertaining and enticing than that of the Soviet Union and that the average foreigner need only sample a small bit of it before he or she became an advocate of American power.

Unfortunately, these successes in exercising American soft power were often undermined by the still persistent domestic squabbling over the role of government in state media operations. Shortly after the VOA received substantial funding after the passage of the Smith-Mundt Act, the operation was back in the critical spotlight when scripts of a VOA series called "Know North America" that contained certain unflattering depictions of particular regions of the United States were discovered.[28] Members of Congress brought the directors of the VOA to their committees, grilled them on the inappropriateness of such content, and threatened to remove the precious funding they had only recently won. Calmer heads prevailed when newly appointed Office of International Information chief George Allen and VOA chief Charles Thayer pointed out the disputed program was a National Broadcasting Corporation (NBC) production (Smith-Mundt demanded that a sizable percentage of VOA content come from private sources) and promised to put the State Department in direct control of future programming content.[29]

These internal divides came at a critical time for the development of a fledgling American Empire built on a foundation of liberal institutionalism. Thanks in part to the promotional activities made possible by the Smith-Mundt Act, the United States enjoyed substantial amounts of success in promoting many of the ideas behind liberalism as evidenced by the wide participation of most of the world's states in the United Nations as well as a significant number of European states receiving redevelopment money from the Bretton Woods agencies and the Marshall Plan. Though the heavy presence of US troops remained in Europe and Japan, politicians and many of the people they represented cooperated with American-led redevelopment initiatives due in no small part to the appealing content they were hearing on the VOA or reading in glossy magazines put out by American information agencies.

However, the fear of communism among powerful segments of American political society triggered a dramatic reevaluation of the wisdom of state- and institution-managed liberalism as the 1940s drew to a close. At the heart of this reevaluation was the rise of Joseph McCarthy and the belief that any institution that contemplated high levels of state intervention bore the taint of communism and needed to be relentlessly resisted. Out of this movement emerged a new spin on the imperial messages of the immediate postwar period that placed an anticommunist ideology at its center and sought to purge all domestic institutions of any hint of collectivist sympathies. Naturally, these impulses would change the way the United States represented itself to the rest of the world and pose a threat to the informal cultural and informational connections the United States had already forged. Moreover, the tones and themes of anticommunism left little room for the frivolity and pleasure of the forms of entertainment that were proving to be one of the most popular elements of the American informational apparatus. Beyond all this, however, was the introduction of the most powerful weapon of information and entertainment yet developed and deployed in the American communications arsenal: television.

The Rise and Fall of Joseph McCarthy: Anticommunism and Television (1949–1959)

By 1949, it was clear to many key decision makers in the government, including Wisconsin Senator Joseph McCarthy, that the rhetoric of liberalism lacked the aggressive edge necessary to confront the ideological threat of communism. Between 1949 and 1959, the drive to add this edge became an important part of the development of an informal American imperial apparatus, though not a part that necessarily led to its growth. Indeed, the anticommunism of the early 1950s, while certainly attracting great interest both inside and outside the United States, showed how media weapons could do as much damage to the possessor of these capabilities as the intended targets. While this lesson was apparent to the close observer of motion pictures and radio during the previous decades, it did not fully reveal itself until the arrival of television, a platform that had perhaps the most profound impact on American soft power during the twentieth century.

Thus, this section will argue that the success of the intrusion of acidic anticommunist rhetoric into the heavily managed narrative of international institutionalism was made possible in large part due to the proliferation of television into American society. This new technology increased the potency of broadcasting by combining live real-time moving pictures and audio beamed directly in an individual's home giving political messages access to an individual's most intimate settings. McCarthy's appearances on television had the effect of not merely raising the specter of communist infiltration in the United States, but also providing a macabre form of entertainment that distorted a more accurate representation of the Cold War struggle. McCarthy's actions as they were presented on television made the already difficult task of legitimizing liberal values more difficult. Despite this, however, the McCarthy episode and its aftermath also demonstrated the fickle nature of the medium, as critics of McCarthy, such as noted radio and television reporter Edward R. Murrow, used television to combat the excesses of McCarthy and demonstrated that television, like most media weapons, could be used by anyone for any cause.

The starting point of McCarthyism was February 9, 1950. On that day, Joseph McCarthy, the junior US Senator from the state of Wisconsin, gave a speech to the Ohio County Women's Republican Club in Wheeling, West Virginia. Most of the speech, according to the local newspaper that reported the event, was an unremarkable reiteration of anticommunist utterances from other prominent Republicans on the national political scene. At one dramatic point in the speech, however, the senator held up a piece of paper and claimed, "I have in my hand a list of 205 that were known to the Secretary of State as being members of the Communist Party and who nevertheless are still working and shaping the policy of the State Department."[30] With this utterance, one of the most famous political dramas of the twentieth-century American politics began.

There were no television cameras to record McCarthy's speech in West Virginia, but this would prove to be one of the very rare occasions when the senator and the increasingly ubiquitous technology of television failed to share the same room. The city of Washington, DC, was becoming increasingly cluttered with the large cameras, bulky transmission cables, and intense floodlights associated with a television broadcasting apparatus. The propaganda potential of television was also readily apparent in the medium's early days, with the Radio Corporation of America's (RCA) president declaring at the world's fair in New York in 1939 that television is "an art which shines like a torch in the troubled world, a creative force which we must learn to utilize for the benefit of all mankind."[31] This magnanimous vision soon gave way to a troubled reality, as the televised spectacle of suspected communist saboteurs being excoriated before the House Un-American Activities Committee (HUAC) contributed to the imprisonment of 150 suspected communist sympathizers, a Hollywood blacklist that swelled to over 300 names, and an era of conformity in American society where dissent and critical thinking were stifled.[32]

Television's appeal as a communications medium lay not merely with its unification of words and moving pictures—film had accomplished this decades ago—but with the ability to permit a mass audience to observe real performances and events as they happened. This immediacy created an entirely different sensation for both the "performer" and the audience that was absent in the film medium. As John Crosby suggested in 1953, "film possesses no sustained acting or mood, little of the tremendous feeling of urgency and immediacy of live TV."[33] Thomas Doherty expands on this observation by insisting that "live television happens in the same temporal frame: for beheld and beholder, the same existential moment, the same imaginative space."[34] The result of this shared experience of vitalism that television enables is a hypnotic effect that seizes the consciousness of the viewer as an event or drama taking place far away and having otherwise little consequence is now the sole focus of attention for millions of people. The hypnotic effect was of obvious benefit for purposes of entertainment, with the emergence in the 1950s of live serial dramas and variety shows that became a staple of television programming worldwide. But the effect also, perhaps in a way not fully anticipated at the time, impacted the perception of political events and the daily news cycle. As Doherty observes again, "when telecast live, news events and political hearings exerted the same hypnotic influence as the anthology series—and, occasionally, the same improvisational delights of the variety shows...Washington D.C....originated some of the most compelling programming on early television."[35]

The hypnotic effect of television, however, relied on the ability of the masses to obtain the equipment necessary to receive, process, and view the messages encoded in the broadcasting signals. Though television technology existed for several decades prior to 1949, the high cost of early "television sets" combined with the low Depression-era incomes and wartime restrictions on manufacturing limited the diffusion of this equipment. By the end of the war, however, this began to change rapidly. In 1950, about 9 percent of households had a television set with a total of 4 million units. By 1959, that number had grown to 86 percent of all households with a total of 44 million sets. To provide content for all these new units, broadcasting stations increased from 69 to 609 in the same period.[36] Television sets soon made the transition from eclectic luxury item enjoyed by a privileged few to essential consumer item that every American family had to have lest they be left out of mainstream culture.[37]

Related to the growth of this new mass medium was the question of who would control its content and distribution. As seen in the previous section, the state played a central role in the dissemination of information to foreign audiences, and in many other nations around the world, the state was already taking a dominant role in controlling television transmission rights and privileges. In Great Britain, the BBC assumed a similar authoritative role with television broadcasting as it had with radio broadcasting that sparked the familiar debates between advocates of state-run television creating programs that would give the people what they ought to have versus privately procured content that gave the people what they wanted.[38] Back in the United States, however, television was not yet seen as a tool for promoting American interests overseas but rather a forum through which entrepreneurs could make money. Thus, unlike with international broadcasting and unlike other nations in Europe, the American state made no movements toward collective ownership of televisual airwaves and instead assumed a loose supervisory role over private media companies that were rapidly adding television broadcast capabilities to their already existing radio operations. By 1955, the two titans of radio, NBC and Columbia Broadcasting System (CBS), along with the newer upstart American Broadcasting Company (ABC), had effectively divided the nation's airwaves among each other under the auspices of the Federal Communications Commission. This assemblage of media power continued to cooperate in this way to preserve the oligopolistic status quo for several decades to come.[39]

Meanwhile, the anticommunism movement in the United States already enjoyed a robust life long before Joseph McCarthy entered the scene. Formed in 1938, the Congressional HUAC served as the primary instrument for the movement by investigating citizens suspected of associating themselves in any way with collectivist or socialist sympathies. By the time McCarthy waved his list of names in West Virginia, HUAC had already held hearings that led to the conviction of Alger Hiss for perjury, and blacklisted the names of a handful of Hollywood screenwriters and directors, known then as the Hollywood Ten, for their suspected ideological and political allegiances with the American Communist Party. The activities of HUAC were augmented by the Federal Bureau of Investigation (FBI) and its fire-eating director J. Edgar Hoover, who "felt almost personally threatened by radical ideologies and individuals."[40] Outside of government was a wide network of industrialists, small-business entrepreneurs, religious leaders, and grassroots organizations that waged their own local battles against suspected communist groups and individuals while providing a foundation of support for similar efforts at the national level.[41]

Amid this social milieu arrived Joseph McCarthy. Elected in 1946, he took his seat in the Senate as one of its youngest and most vibrant members. Despite this vigor, however, his early days in the Senate were unremarkable save for his curious championing of the cause of 73 German SS troopers convicted of massacring American soldiers in Belgium in 1945. Hoping to win favor with German-American constituents in Wisconsin, McCarthy engaged in a barrage of accusation, intimidation, and fiery language in denouncing the final report of the investigating committee that so disgusted its chairman, Senator Ray Baldwin, he resigned his seat and quit politics.[42] This incident allowed McCarthy to hone his rhetorical skills as a political interlocutor, but he still lacked a single issue that that could galvanize his reelection campaign and bring him the notoriety he craved. Then one night, as he dined with Father Edmund Walsh, head of the Georgetown University School of Foreign Service, McCarthy listened as Walsh complained of suspected communists in the foreign communications sections of the State Department.[43] Walsh had not proof of these claims, but not long afterward, McCarthy was in West Virginia with his intense passion, his fierce rhetoric, and his list of 205 members of the communist party working in the State Department.

With a message, all that was lacking was a medium. McCarthy had already proven himself to be an astute man in his dealings with print reporters, giving them a scoop or a quote when there was little else to report.[44] But it was the actions of a fellow senator, Estes Kefauver from Tennessee, that revealed the power of television to McCarthy. Kefauver was the chair of the Senate Committee to Investigate Crime and Interstate Commerce, and in January of 1951, he and his committee embarked on a three-month tour of the United States where they held hearings over fears of a nascent organized crime wave gripping the nation at the dawn of the decade. Kefauver's committee made stops in several cities, where local television stations often carried a portion of the day's scheduled hearing live. The broadcast of the hearings proved especially popular, as suggested by this magazine report from the Detroit panel: "Every other activity paused as televiewers riveted themselves before an estimated ninety percent of the city's screens to watch hoodlums squirm under the relentless questioning of the committee."[45] Though the list of subpoenaed witnesses included the famous gangster Frank Costello and crime boss concubine Virginia Hill Hauser, the real celebrity of the hearings was Kefauver himself. Despite his tall awkward frame and propensity to speak annoyingly slow, Kefauver gained a national following through newspaper stories and appearances on television interview shows. Indeed, at one point during the crime hearings, Kefauver appeared on the quiz show *What's My Line* as the "mystery guest." Though reportedly angry and envious of all the attention Kefauver was getting, McCarthy nevertheless knew that organized crime was not his issue, and waited for the right opportunity to reveal a dangerous new threat to the television cameras of the nation.[46]

In early April of 1950, McCarthy made his first move. Having accused a high-ranking State Department employee, Professor Owen Lattimore, of being a communist *and* an agent of the Soviet Union, McCarthy managed to persuade the Senate Foreign Relations Committee chair, Millard Tydings, to hold a hearing. Professor Lattimore appeared before the committee, but McCarthy never got a chance to publicly pillory him. Since the Democrats were the majority party in the Senate and controlled the committee proceedings, they prevented McCarthy from questioning Lattimore. Instead, it was McCarthy himself who had to sit silently as the esteemed professor declared, "It is only from a diversity of views freely expressed and strongly advocated that sound policy is distilled...He who contributes to the destruction of that process is either a fool or an enemy of his country...Let Senator McCarthy take note of that."[47] McCarthy would be unable to create televised spectacle for political gain until he could control the committees himself.

In 1952, the American people handed him this tantalizing power. With the election of a wave of new Republicans to Congress, McCarthy was now in the majority caucus and expected to be granted chairmanship of several key Senate committees, including the Permanent Subcommittee on Investigations (which eventually became known as the "McCarthy Committee") from which the senator could savage most of his targets. McCarthy wasted no time going after that portion of the government he believed was the most infected with communist subversives: the State Department's foreign communication operations. Of particular distaste was the VOA, the primary overseas communication organ and, as previously shown, a focal point of the effort to persuade foreign populations of the mutual benefits of American-led liberal hegemony. Taking his cue from earlier hearings from then Senator Karl Stefan over the funding of the VOA, McCarthy used the existence of lewd and explicit content in overseas libraries and radio programs to portray the entirety of the foreign communications apparatus as bursting at the seams with communists. In February 1953, McCarthy began a series of hearings that saw a plethora of VOA employees and managers brought before the committee for aggressive questioning before a national television audience. The power of television combined with McCarthy's new position of power turned him into one of the earliest examples of a Washington media celebrity.

McCarthy also benefited from the fact that anticommunist activities and television enjoyed a previously existing symbiotic relationship. The hearing that saw HUAC berate the Hollywood Ten in 1947 had been recorded on newsreel and shown on television and in movie houses. While the scenes of incivility that were the hallmark of this event drew numerous condemnations, they also proved to be especially popular among viewers.[48] The following year, HUAC hearings on Alger Hiss were only the second time in American history that congressional testimony had been carried live on television.[49] Perhaps seeing the Frankenstein monster they were creating, HUAC banned most media recording equipment from future hearings in 1949, but by this point, the monster was already alive and about to wreak havoc on the American media landscape. As HUAC gathered in 1951 to hold hearings on communist infiltration into the motion picture industry, a local television station manager named Dick Moore persuaded the committee to allow live audio recordings while his station broadcast still pictures of the committee members and witnesses. Outside the hearing room, Moore had his reporters and cameramen ambush committee members and pepper them with questions about why media coverage of the hearing was forbidden. Meanwhile, the station and the federal building where the hearings were being held received an avalanche of phone calls demanding the hearings be carried live. In the days before audience ratings could be accurately measured, this flood of phone calls amounted to a mass citywide outcry. From that day forward, all or part of that month's HUAC committee hearings were carried live.[50]

McCarthy's fame, then, comes from being neither a member of the anticommunist vanguard nor a media visionary. His novelty and notoriety came from his subconscious ability to exploit the hypnotic influence of live television in such a way as to make the extreme anticommunist agenda and ugly process of rooting out suspected red subversives compelling to the mass public. Such a phenomenon was an important step in the weaponizing of information and entertainment, as McCarthy's actions were less about providing a coherent argument on the liabilities of the communist worldview and more about creating a spectacle that distracted from the changes in the prevailing political consensus anticommunism sought to make. As the public watched, enraptured by the sight of government bureaucrats, labor leaders, intellectuals, and artists defending themselves from McCarthy's intimidation, real changes were taking place in civil society that would have a lasting impact on the American political landscape. As early as 1952, Supreme Court Justice William O. Douglas lamented in a *New York Times Magazine* essay that "the black silence of fear" was settling over the nation creating a mass conformity more dangerous than "inflation, national debt, or atomic warfare."[51] More importantly perhaps, the spectacle of McCarthy's public pillorying directly contradicted the efforts of the United States to maintain its hegemony based on liberal principles that were supposed to value freedom of consciousness and government restraint. Perhaps the greatest irony of McCarthy's first major set of televised hearings on alleged communist infiltration in the VOA was that they featured "a politician using television to propagandize against the propaganda arm of the government for insufficient zeal in propagandizing the government."[52]

It is common for spectacle to begin as banality, and the early VOA hearings were a clear example of this. McCarthy needed some kernel of legitimate impropriety around which he could paint a vivid picture of communist infiltration. In the case of the VOA, it was mismanagement of the efforts to counteract Soviet jamming of VOA broadcasts with the construction of newer and more powerful transmission towers. Unfortunately, these towers were placed in positions where magnetic interference disrupted the signal, resulting in skyrocketing expenses as radio engineers attempted to correct the problem. It was this excessive cost and incompetence on which McCarthy pounced, using them as the entry point through which a sordid world of subversion and perfidiousness could be revealed.[53] Relying heavily on dubious information funneled to him from an anticommunist group within the VOA called "The Loyal Underground," McCarthy brought key members of the VOA to testify on live television before his committee. The spectacle proved to make for popular viewing as both NBC and ABC carried the morning sessions live and all three major networks recorded the bulk of the hearings for editing and broadcast in evening news programs.[54]

As described by David F. Krugler, McCarthy "targeted the lifestyles and religious beliefs of individual VOA employees in order to substantiate charges of communist influence."[55] Thus, witnesses were asked not if they were a communist per se, but if they were a member of an urban housing cooperative or an atheist. In an example of the first, Troup Matthews, chief of VOA's French desk, was accused by McCarthy of trying to recruit colleagues into a "Marxist free-love collective." In an example of the second, director of VOA's religious programming, Roger Lyons, was accused of being an atheist based on a coworker's testimony that he did not know what Lyons's religious beliefs were.[56] The nadir of the hearings came with the four-day grilling of VOA chief Reed Harris. McCarthy dug deep into his past to paint the civil servant as a radical subversive, spending hours questioning his support of a Marxist professor fired from Columbia University and the seditious ideas he expressed in a book he wrote, titled *King Football*, in which he made the treasonous claim that universities spend too much money on athletics.[57]

In all these cases, McCarthy had a keen sense of how to manipulate broadcasting procedures to heighten the drama and maximize the appearance of guilt by the witness. The television critic Marya Mannes commented that with "the telephoto lens, bringing each human element close to the eye, [it] makes it an experience probably more intense and disturbing [when viewed on television] than actual presence in the committee room."[58]

When the witnesses looked to be too feisty or credible, McCarthy often prevented these individuals from being able to make statements to defend themselves (often insisting all questions be answered "yes" or "no") or made sure any rebuttals would take place during those times when the hearings were not carried live.[59] Outside the committee room, McCarthy was always willing to go on television to do interview programs like *Meet the Press* or *American Forum of the Air*. While such shows required him to be questioned by incredulous reporters, McCarthy nevertheless used these platforms to continue his cavalcade of accusation and innuendo as if he was back in his committee chamber. Though often challenged vociferously by the journalists on these shows, McCarthy was never interested in winning a debate or persuading the assembled newsmen that his cause was just. His primary concern was to augment the spectacle taking place in his committees by engaging in rhetorical combat with nationally known members of the media. McCarthy's responses to the reporters' questions visibly irritated many of the august members of the national press—indeed, McCarthy often intentionally mispronounced their names when answering their questions to get rise out of his interlocutors. In the end, however, he was always invited back for another appearance.[60]

On the fourth day of his interrogation, Reed Harris finally lost the ability to maintain his cool demeanor and rebuked McCarthy by declaring his resentment for "the tone of this inquiry" since its "my neck, my public neck, that you are, I think, very skillfully trying to rebuke."[61] Recording this exchange was a cameraman who worked for the news reporter Edward R. Murrow, a man widely lauded for his radio reports from London during World War II and now hosting a weekly news magazine show called *See It Now*. Murrow and his colleagues had been working to use their prominent placement on television to restore some of the lost credibility on McCarthy's victims and wage a televised counteroffensive against McCarthy's on-air attacks.[62] Shortly after Harris's testimony, Murrow put together an episode that ostensibly was to mark the occasion of the recent death of Joseph Stalin, but Murrow and his staff had coyly added the aforementioned "my public neck" rebuke by Harris to the end of the episode. Joseph Wershba, one of Murrow's producers on *See It Now*, remarked about the episode, "The juxtapositioning of Stalin and McCarthy was not lost on viewers...it was a case of one dictator dead, another potential dictator on the way up."[63]

After the VOA hearings, McCarthy's reign of accusation expanded. Seeming to have effectively silenced the nation's subaltern groups, McCarthy set his sights on the dominant figures and institutions of the Cold War consensus, including members of the military, the Republican Party, and former war heroes. McCarthy had already accused former general and Secretary of State General George Marshall of being part of "a conspiracy on a scale so immense as to dwarf any previous such venture in the history of man" on the Senate floor in 1951, but now McCarthy was going after current officers of the military, including Lt. Milo Radulovich of the

Air Force Reserve.[64] Murrow devoted several episodes of *See It Now* to honoring George Marshall and restoring the honor of Lt. Radulovich, the latter of which enjoyed a full exoneration by Air Force Secretary Harold E. Talbott at the beginning of one episode.[65] Then, McCarthy played fully into Murrow's hands by screaming at Army General Zwicker that he was "not fit to wear the uniform" for going to see an army dentist accused of being a communist.[66]

Now live television worked against McCarthy as his swagger and demeanor were no longer able to obscure the gravity of his politics. The sight of McCarthy excoriating a decorated general was self-destructive in its own right. Murrow, however, was going to put the hypnotic influence of the medium to even greater effect with his special *See It Now* report titled "A Report on Joseph McCarthy." In this episode, Murrow combined the appeal of live television with another of the medium's great propagandistic virtues that was beyond McCarthy's ability to control: editing. Murrow's special McCarthy episode began with Murrow suggesting the following content is little more than a rendering of McCarthy's actions in the senator's own words. From there, Murrow provided the voice-over for a montage of key moments in McCarthy's recent parade of impugning and accusation, with particular attention paid to his berating of helpless witnesses and his disdain for anyone who criticized him, including the intentional mispronunciation of their names.[67] The editing job depicted McCarthy as ugly and vile—a man who shamelessly exploited his power as much for his own twisted gratification than for any fidelity to the cause of anticommunism. Murrow was not done, however. When the montage ended, he gave a final live soliloquy that Thomas Doherty describes as "the most dramatic, eloquent, and influential oration ever delivered by a television journalist."[68] Included in this oration are lines that epitomize what Murrow believed was at stake in his effort to discredit McCarthy and ensure that the projection of American power overseas was not undermined by the opportunistic ravings of a megalomaniac: "We proclaim ourselves—as indeed we are—the defenders of freedom where it continues to exist in the world. But we cannot defend freedom abroad by deserting it at home."[69]

Murrow's report was not only a piece of entertaining political television, but also showed how the medium's hypnotic effect could be enhanced by combining live television with prepared pieces edited for maximum effect. The report, however, was deliberately designed to argue a specific point, and in this way, was little different from a newspaper editorial. Live unedited television, the medium that McCarthy had managed so well, had yet to fully betray him—until June 9, 1954, when Joseph McCarthy found himself a beleaguered witness at a Senate committee hearing rather than an interlocutor. Called to investigate the efforts by McCarthy's chief counsel, Roy M. Cohn, to get one of McCarthy's staff members out of military service after being drafted, the Army-McCarthy hearings quickly became a referendum of sorts on the last two years of McCarthy's red baiting. When the hearings began, the room was a veritable television studio, with countless cameras in every nook and cranny of the already crowded committee room and makeshift platforms providing elevated spaces for those television cameras that could not secure a place on the floor. In a telling moment that signified the new place of television in the American cultural and media landscape, committee chairman Karl Mundt demanded that newspaper photographers remain in a kneeling position as they made their snapshots lest they block the view of the television cameras that were covering the event live. When these cameras were not focused on testifying witnesses, they would pan onto an assortment of celebrities and other VIPs that secured prime seats in the front rows of the committee room.[70]

No spectacle, however, was complete without advertising and product promotion. Television networks began to complain early in the hearings that the costs of broadcasting the event were proving to be prohibitive and that arrangements had to be made to allow some sort of advertising to take place for broadcasters.[71] These concerns reflected an interesting trend that emerged slowly alongside McCarthyism: the rise of a televised consumer culture in the United States that drove rapid economic growth and required large amounts of airtime to promote the panoply of new consumer products. Even Edward R. Murrow needed corporate sponsorship for his shows in order for them to be aired, and reeled when such sponsorship was lost in the aftermath of his McCarthy reports in 1953. Aware of this, the committee chairman, Senator Karl Mundt, the same man who had given his name to the *Smith-Mundt Act* that had established government propaganda overseas, agreed to allow broadcasters to insert advertising into their coverage of the hearings during naturally occurring pauses, such as when witnesses were dismissed and new ones were seated. This resulted in odd juxtapositions between the drama of the hearings and the plugs of advertisers—in Los Angeles, for example, the hearings were sponsored by Shinola! shoe polish.[72]

Two months after the start of the Army-McCarthy hearings, the main event arrived. McCarthy and Cohn were both witnesses as the committee attempted to uncover some of the investigative tactics of McCarthy's staff. As the questioning progressed, Senator Joseph N. Welch, who had just completed an aggressive interrogation of Roy Cohn, found himself under verbal attack by McCarthy, who accused Welch of associating with a local attorney accused of being a communist. Welch shrugged off the accusation as being unimportant to the questions he was trying to get answered, and as McCarty continued to belabor the point, Welch finally exclaimed, "Have you no sense of decency, sir, at long last? Have you no sense of decency?"[73] Welch followed this up by angrily asking for the next witness before McCarthy could respond with another accusation or insult. As the television cameras continued to broadcast the exchange live, applause erupted from the audience assembled in the committee room. Perplexed at what he was seeing, McCarthy could do little more than utter, "What happened?" Thomas Doherty answered this question most ably when he said, "What happened was that television, whose coverage of McCarthy's news conferences, direct addresses, and senate hearings had lent him legitimacy and stature, had now become the stage for his downfall."[74]

Murrow's comments at the end of his special episode on McCarthy epitomized the contradiction of the American effort to justify its hegemonic power in the early Cold War through appeals to liberalism. The effort to enforce ideological homogeneity through the totality of American society alienated not only domestic groups who had otherwise submitted to the liberal Cold War consensus after World War II, but also political groups and governments overseas, including those committed to American leadership in the geostrategic struggle against communism and the Soviet Union. During one of McCarthy's appearances on *Meet the Press* in which he accused Great Britain of betraying its alliance with the United States for trading with China, Reuters journalist and British national Paul Scott Rankine scolded McCarthy for the damage he was causing to the flattering image of the United States. "Once," Rankine began, "the United States was recognized as a sanctuary for independent thinkers and rugged individuals, [but now, McCarthy] was erecting a climate of fear under which people were afraid of confessing political misjudgment or else suffer the loss of their jobs, intimidation, and social distrust."[75] After attending sessions of the Army-McCarthy hearings, the conservative French intellectual Raymond Aron stated that he could no longer be an advocate for the United States in a country that was already skeptical of American hegemony and the liberal consensus.[76] Throughout Western Europe, leaders expressed and public opinion polls indicated the notion that McCarthy's purges were not reflective of the democratic values the United States was allegedly advocating.[77] Moreover, in other nations outside of the direct orbit of American power and influence, McCarthy's actions gave the impression that democracy was, in reality, a rather feeble and fragile institution that could not resist the self-evident logic of communism.[78] In trying to make the case that the United States was the protector of the free world, McCarthy's televised antics were demonstrating to a global audience that the opposite was true.

Indeed, as McCarthy was going around the country accusing dissenters of being communists, the United States was going around the world toppling regimes it too suspected of being communist. In 1953, American and British intelligence operatives orchestrated a coup d'état in Iran that removed Mohammad Mossadegh from the presidency. Mossadegh had recently announced his plan to nationalize the oil fields of Iran, creating a crisis for Western-based petroleum companies and threatening a main tenant of the liberal economic order that demanded key resources be controlled by private firms. Sensing the danger, Secretary of State John Foster Dulles, a man who "had two lifelong obsessions: fighting Communism and protecting the rights of multinational corporations," gave the order for the planning and execution of the coup.[79] A year later, the United States orchestrated another clandestine overthrow in Guatemala. Like Mossadegh, Guatemalan president Jacobo Arbenz Guzmán had promised to nationalize large tracts of property, including those owned by the American firm United Fruit, and redistribute them among poor peasants in the countryside. Once again, John Foster Dulles instructed the Central Intelligence Agency (CIA) to topple Arbenz's regime and replace it with one more amiable to American leadership in Latin America.[80] In the run up to the coup, a highly complicated public relations campaign took advantage of the communist paranoia that McCarthy was spreading through American society in order to justify the operation.[81] Neither Mossadegh nor Arbenz were communists or openly expressed any fidelity to the Soviet Union, but their efforts to enact social reform were sufficient evidence in the age of McCarthy to begin violent overthrows of these democratically elected governments.

Clearly, the hypnotic effect of television had an impact greater than anyone suspected. Television empowered McCarthy far more than was possible for a surly and abrasive man having to get by on his own wit and charm—if anything, it was this cantankerous nature that added to the spectacle of McCarthy's rise to prominence. Thus, McCarthy's exploits showed that the early days of television were not solely a time of heroic journalism and wholesome entertainment as present-day myths suggest, but that the stench of "infotainment" and the scourge of celebrity were present even during the medium's infancy. One can see in the McCarthy experience protean versions of phenomena more familiar to the early twenty-first-century television viewer, including unscripted "reality" dramas, a celebrity political "commentariat" on cable news channels, and publicity stunts seeking to boost radio and television ratings.

Fear of communist infiltration waned (though by no means disappeared) in American society in the years after McCarthy's fall from grace (and his untimely death a few years later). Though anticommunism was still a priority at J. Edgar Hoover's FBI, it was clear that fear and paranoia were of limited value in creating a sustained and enticing entertainment that could win the hearts and minds of overseas audiences. Meanwhile, Senator Welch's demands for a sense of decency from McCarthy came at a time when the American economy provided its own persuasive narrative for the liberal way of life as the gross domestic product spiked from $1.6 trillion to $2.4 trillion by 1960.[82] More importantly, the election of Dwight Eisenhower in 1952 and his support of the tripartite liberal model meant that anticommunism, while always good for a rhetorical flourish now and then, remained on the periphery. Other nations aligned with the United States were also enjoying strong regeneration of their economies and societies. Western Europe saw their economies regrow to the point at which they were at before the outbreak of World War II as did Japan with the added bonus that most of the American occupation troops had gone home. Indeed, the liberal consensus of the postwar economic order clearly enjoyed successes that were their own best justifications for American hegemonic leadership and the rejection of the communist temptation. The challenge that emerged for the United States now was to use its advantage in media power to publicize the improvements made in the global economy and parley these successes into a worldwide expansion that could reclaim the tracts of global territory lost to communism. Unsubstantiated accusations against American citizens and clandestine overthrows of democratic governments were a severe liability to the grand designs of liberal expansion.

In accomplishing this goal, television would soon play a crucial role. The rise and fall of Joseph McCarthy demonstrated the power of television to captivate a mass audience. As the technology advanced even further with the promise of color pictures and crisper sound, the power of television became more profound as it became one example of a wave of consumer gadgetry representing a utopia of material abundance and consumer comfort. Increasing suburbanization of American society, with its offers of home ownership, rooms full of furniture, shiny new cars, and copious leisure time, could repair some of the damage McCarthyism had done and present a far more attractive vision of what capitalism and republican government could offer. Television became a powerful platform in depicting this pleasant lifestyle to domestic American audiences and allied countries that were in the middle of spirited economic recoveries.

However, television was not the only media through which to communicate the pleasures of consumerism. With a mild thaw taking place in the Cold War relationship between the United States and the Soviet Union and the return of high-profile cultural exchanges between the two superpowers, a new opportunity for that classic tool of foreign entertainment—the international exhibition—reemerged in the mid-twentieth century. As with Great Britain with its Crystal Palace in 1851, the United States made plans for a grand exhibition of its own in New York in 1964 to welcome the world to the American shores and showcase the consumerist lifestyle that was available to all so long as they accepted American leadership and values. In making plans for this world's fair, one of the most powerful weapons of entertainment took form.

Exhibiting Consumerism: World's Fairs at the Height of the Cold War (1960–1965)

Having endured two world wars, a great depression, a rearmament process to confront the perception of expanding Soviet power, and most recently, a war in Korea that resulted in the deaths of over fifty thousand American soldiers, the American population rightly felt entitled to some kind of reward for the world order they helped to construct and defend. By the time Eisenhower became president in 1952, the nature of this reward began to reveal itself in the form of suburbanization through mass home ownership, a spike in the purchase of motor vehicles, and a new focus on leisure time and recreation. Together, these social trends reflected the shift toward a consumerist orientation to the socioeconomic priorities of the American economy. By producing massive amounts of consumer goods, including cars, kitchen appliances, televisions and radios, and other household gadgets, full employment could be guaranteed and social strife mitigated. Moreover, the sights of ordinary Americans indulging in a life of consumerist luxury would provide a propaganda coup in the soft power struggle with the Soviet Union.

As the paranoia of McCarthyism subsided amid Eisenhower's embrace of tripartism, consumerism emerged as an ideal narrative to carry the banner of the free world into a new decade.[83] Thus, this section argues that the effort to promote and glamorize the abundance of consumer goods created a new and innovative way of stirring the masses through entertainment and spectacle during this crucial phase of the American Empire in the middle part of the twentieth century. While the material struggle for the protection and expansion of the free world wore on with the aforementioned secret interventions in Latin America and the more conventional war in Korea, the nonmaterial empire of images and lifestyle rose to greater importance as the American Empire matured. At the center of evoking the imagery of this consumerist utopia were grand visionaries like Walt Disney who sought to find innovative new ways of showcasing the fantasies of luxury and contentment to the masses in the United States and beyond. This drive to more vividly represent the pleasures of material abundance led first to Disney's primary innovation in the form of the theme park, and then to the effort to rechannel the celebratory mood of imperial triumph experienced by Great Britain at the Great Exhibition of 1851 by designing and constructing the substantial portions of the world's fair in New York in 1964.

Indeed, Disney's arrival on the scene came at a perfect time for the United States in its effort to win the hearts and minds of the world. While the power of consumerism was ready to be unleashed as early as 1952 as the Korean War came to an end, the dark presence of anticommunist paranoia eclipsed the luster of myriad consumer products displayed on television. Ironically, in the early days of anticommunism after World War II, Disney had been an active participant in the blacklisting of artists and writers from Hollywood who were suspected of being communists and went so far as to give names of former employees who had organized a strike against his studio back in 1938. In an appearance before the HUAC in October 1947, Disney gave the committee names of former employees he suspected of organizing that strike and implored to the committee the importance of "smoking out" communists from trade unions in the United States.[84]

Disney, however, was not an acolyte of Joseph McCarthy. He supported the presidency of Franklin Roosevelt at the height of the Great Depression and still saw a place in American society for trade unions. In this sense, he was a staunch believer in the postwar consensus that held fast through the controversies of VOA and the period of McCarthyism. As the Cold War tensions were beginning to ramp up in 1948, Disney commented, "If people would think more about fairies they would soon forget the atom bomb."[85] This sentiment hauntingly echoed across a century and an ocean, when in

1851 the poet and novelist William Thackeray, upon visiting the Crystal Palace in London, wrote the ode,

> A Palace as for a fairy prince
> A rare pavilion, such as man
> Saw never since mankind began,
> And built and glazed.[86]

To get the mass American public to think about similar fairies, Disney commanded a vast media empire that ranged from animated feature films like *Snow White* to television programs like *The Wonderful World of Disney* to air on the ABC television network. However, the medium that intrigued Disney the most was the theme park. Like Thackeray, Disney believed it was inside a space closed off from the outside world where an alternative reality could neutralize fears, make dreams come true, remove the conflict of the past, and allow one to peer at a utopian future constructed from the blueprint provided by American liberal principles.

In 1955, Disneyland, the first prototype of international theme park entertainment, opened in Anaheim, California. Opening day activities were broadcast live on television with several famous celebrities acting as on-air tour guides, including film and television star Ronald Reagan. Disneyland transcended any previous notions of what an amusement park was or was not supposed to be. In an interview with a California newspaper, Disney described Disneyland as "something of a fair, an exhibition, a playground, a community center, a museum of living facts, and a showplace of beauty and magic."[87] The park featured all the familiar attractions of a typical amusement park, such as midway rides, food stands, and souvenir kiosks, but dressed them up in a way that matched the theme of whichever sector of the park a visitor strolled. These themes, with names like Adventureland, Fantasyland, and Tomorrowland, evoked not only the aesthetic and characterization of Disney movies and television shows, but also the core values Walt Disney thought epitomized the American experience. Early Disneyland promotional material describes succinctly what Walt Disney wanted his magic kingdom to be:

> Disneyland will be based upon and dedicated to the ideals, the dreams, and the hard facts that have created America. And it will be uniquely equipped to dramatize these dreams and facts and send them forth as a source of courage and inspiration to all the world...It will be filled with the accomplishments, the joys, the hopes, of the world we live in. And it will remind us and show us how to make those wonders part of our lives.[88]

Disneyland was a direct legacy of the Great Exhibition of London in 1851 and the numerous international exhibitions that took place regularly in its stead. As the years passed, however, the size and scale of these showcases increased dramatically as nations around the world saw them as ideal situations to publicize themselves to a large multinational audience. All the bustling capitals of industrializing Europe and North America played frequent host to some sort of international exhibition, expo, or as they soon came to be known by the end of the nineteenth century, world's fair. As previously discussed, the London Great Exhibition was an event that offered the rich and poor from around the world a fantastic vision of a world transformed by the innovations of science and engineering developed by the power of the British Empire. Despite the utopian themes, however, the exhibition had a strong current of ribald nationalism that foretold of a future when such twitches of jingoism could heighten tensions between the imperial center and its colonies or with an upstart imperial rival.

Amid an intense rivalry with a dangerous foe, a world's fair held in New York City could be a perfect opportunity to highlight the wonders of the modern age, attract a large mass audience that transcended class, race, or nationality and depict a utopian future that promised comfort, ease, and leisure. At the same time, it was also an opportunity to solidify the tripartite equilibrium of the mid-twentieth-century economic boom that depended on a large amount of consumer spending to maintain the growth of the world economy.[89] These carnivals of consumer culture at international exhibitions also acted as "silent ambassador(s) for democratic ideals" and neutralized some of the communist propaganda about the evils of capitalism and American culture.[90] There was, however, one key difference in the American effort to showcase its material abundance and seduce the rest of the world with the prospect of creating consumerist utopias. Whereas Great Britain constructed the Crystal Palace as a way of legitimizing its status as the world's greatest imperial power, the United States would use the world's fair as another volley in the ideological war with the Soviet Union. The world's fair would not be a moment of triumph as it was in Great Britain, but the most potent platform in a larger emerging arsenal of entertainment that would either persuade the world that the United States ought to be triumphant in the Cold War, or amuse it into carefree submission.

With the pictures and imagery of the Korean War and other clashes of coercive power still taking center stage in the 1950s, few had the ability to recognize when a similar battle took place in the realm of soft power. However, in 1959, this began to change when a remarkable conversation took place between the leading politicians of the two superpower states of the Cold War that revealed the extent to which international exhibitions and world's fairs had become an entertainment battleground in the Cold War. The American National Exhibit, a traveling showcase that displayed a wide range of American consumer and industrial products, had just arrived in Moscow. The event included a scheduled tour of the exhibition by Vice President Richard Nixon and Soviet Premier Nikita Khrushchev. Nixon led Khrushchev around the exhibits, going out of his way to laud the advanced technology evident in many of the kitchen gadgets on display.[91] At one point, as the two men discussed the strengths and weaknesses of their respective societies, Nixon observed, "There are some instances where you may be ahead of us, for example, in the development of the thrust of your rockets for the investigation of outer space; there may be some instances in which we are ahead of you—in color television, for instance."[92]

Subsequent to this conversation, Nixon was severely criticized, most notably by John F. Kennedy, for trying to equate the banal technology of color television with the strategically more relevant technology of ballistic rockets. However, this criticism was misinformed. Whether he knew it or not, Nixon was celebrating the primary mechanism through which American Empire expanded throughout the later twentieth century. While the respective militaries (including their ballistic missile capabilities) of the United States and the Soviet Union remained in a nuclear stalemate, the American innovations in communications technologies, including color television, created a dynamic force of persuasion and entertainment that, while not apparent at the time, allowed the United States to emerge from the Cold War victorious. This "Kitchen Debate" between Nixon and Khrushchev was one of the earliest clues of this changing dynamic.

Other clues were also starting to reveal themselves as international exhibitions became hallmark events on the calendar of international politics. In 1955, at the Indian Industries Fair, the United States and the Soviet Union squared off in their efforts to woo the nonaligned host nation toward a partnership for an Indian nuclear power program.[93] In 1958, the rivalry intensified in Brussels at the Universal and International Exhibition, where the United States focused much of its display materials on cultural exhibits, including fashion shows and streetscapes that did not exactly capture the "Atomium" theme of the expo. Meanwhile, the Soviet Union had constructed a massive pavilion that went out of its way to show the technological progress of the soviet states, including advanced applications of nuclear energy technology, aeronautical engineering, and consumer goods. In a sentiment that anticipated the "Kitchen Debate" a year later, the consensus of the expo's organizers was that the American pavilion, while succeeding in humanizing the American people with its focus on culture and society, did little to show off the technological progress of the world's most powerful state.[94]

In 1962, the Cuban Missile Crisis demonstrated how unchecked military struggle was not feasible in the nuclear age without risking worldwide destruction. As a result, soft power in all its forms became extremely important to continue to ensure the Cold War struggle maintained its cool temperature. Rather than relying completely on saber-rattling, the United States and the Soviet Union moved toward a battle of industry, lifestyle, and consumerism. Such importance was not lost on President Eisenhower, who was "personally embarrassed" by what he considered was a poor show by the United States in Brussels with the overabundance of popular culture on display at its pavilion. Eisenhower was eager to "fire a peaceful missile" that would show off American "technological superiority and...celebrate international-style corporate capitalism."[95]

Eisenhower's desire for international redemption in the battle of super-power exhibitions converged with the plans already under way by local officials in New York City who dreamed of a massive world exhibition on the same site as the 1939 World's Fair in Flushing Meadows. The main advocate of this newer and bigger world's fair was longtime city planner Robert Moses. With a lifetime in New York politics having tarnished his reputation, Moses was eager to make the proposed fair "the greatest event in history" in the hopes that it would give him an honorable legacy. However, a unifying vision was needed to bring together the disparate components of such a massive endeavor. Moses had taken steps to create this coherence with the fair's tentative theme: "Peace through Understanding." Moses, however, was a bureaucrat and lacked the creativity to imagine what the greatest event in history would actually look like in practice. To give his ambition a concrete form, Moses turned to the man who had already created one magic kingdom on the other side of the country.[96]

As the planning for the fair began, Disney saw plenty of opportunities to weave the properties and power of Disneyland into the exhibition's essence. As early as 1960, Disney observed, "All the big corporations in the country are going to be spending a helluva [sic] lot of money building exhibits there... Now, they're all going to want something that will stand out from the others, and that's the kind of service we can offer them."[97] Disney hoped some of the technological innovations on display at Disneyland could provide the propagandistic punch many exhibitors at the fair wanted in order to make their pavilions and attractions capture the imaginations of the visitors. Two key innovations were at the heart of this effort. The first was a new way of conceptualizing movie theaters so as to immerse the audience into a panoramic experience of sight and sound, thereby assaulting their senses and making them more receptive to the message of the film being presented. The second was animatronics technology, or the use of robotics to create a lifelike simulation of an actual person, animal, or historical figure from the past. As the pavilions for the world's fair began to be constructed, Disney consulted with most of the owners of the major displays at the fair, and in the case of the exhibits for General Electric, Ford, Pepsi-Cola, and the state of Illinois, actually designed and built their exhibits.[98]

Several examples of the new technologies Disney brought to bear were found in the pavilion for General Electric. As described by Steven Watts, the pavilion relied on a new and innovative design in which "a revolving theater on which a segmented stage remained stationary as the audience moved around in their seats. This enormous revolving 'doughnut,' as it came to be known, rested on railroad wheels and allowed customers to view a series of six shows."[99] The shows themselves featured animatronic "actors" depicting a household scene from four different historical eras ranging from the early 1800s to the then present-day 1960s. In this way, audiences could marvel at how far American life had come since the early days of the nation and how household products by General Electric had made life better and more prosperous. The final show depicted a scene from "Medallion City," which starred still more animatronic characters using current and future household goods. Given the circular nature of the attraction, the pavilion received the label "Carousel of Progress."[100] At the Ford pavilion, a similar mixture of history and progress entertained and awed guests with panoramic stages and animatronic figures, including life-like robotic dinosaurs.[101]

The crowning achievement for Walt Disney at the fair was the Pepsi-Cola pavilion, which featured the exhibit "It's a Small World." Perhaps more than any other attraction, "It's a Small World" epitomized the liberal internationalist spirit of the fair, especially when one saw that the exhibit had support not only from Pepsi and Disney, but also from the United Nations Emergency Children's Fund.[102] Visitors boarded a small boat inside a giant exhibition hall that moved through a series of rooms, each representing a region of the world. Inside these rooms, an army of animatronic dolls dressed in local garb robotically danced, played, and sang the exhibition's theme song in their native language. Few lines at the numerous pavilions at the fair were as long as the one to await a chance to experience "It's A Small World."

Like in London in 1851, the 1964 World's Fair ran a fine line between celebrating universal harmony and brotherhood and glorifying the exploits of the host nation. Indeed, much of the early anticipation of the fair centered on the expected exhibitionist clash between the two superpowers, especially when Soviet planners rented the largest space available at Flushing Meadows. However, the spirit of cultural exchange and friendly competition soon gave way to Cold War realities, as tensions between the fair's host and its biggest tenant became burdened with political calculation. Preliminary Soviet plans for the tallest pavilion on the grounds forced American planners to redraw their own blueprints and add height to their already sizeable buildings. The Soviets responded in kind, this time making their specific plans a secret so as not to be outdone again by the American planners. Fair officials insisted their plans needed to be made public, triggering exasperation on the part of the Soviet contingent, and the decision shortly thereafter to withdraw completely from the fair in October of 1962.[103] Before ground was even broken for the construction of the first pavilion in New York, petty nationalism had ruined what was to be one of the fair's biggest draws.

Once the fair began, one need not look far to see efforts to champion American values, progress, and utopian future—and like at the corporate pavilions, the contribution of Walt Disney was readily at hand. At the Federal and State Area, where spaces were reserved only for displays from the United States, one could not walk anywhere without seeing Disney-inspired streetscapes. One of the main attractions of the original Disneyland in California was Main Street USA, an idealized reconstruction of the central strip of a prosperous Midwestern town designed to stir nostalgia and refuge among American visitors. Main Street USA was in many ways Disney's most sinister creation in the park since it gave the impression that American life was (and could be) simple and carefree (one of the areas in Main Street USA is called "Carefree Corner"). Yet the "truth" of Main Street USA, as pointed out countless times by cultural and political observers, was that the Main Street USA was little more than a "fictional image from the past" that made visitors yearn for something they themselves had never actually experienced nor had ever existed.[104] At the world's fair, many of the exhibitions from state chambers of commerce were variations of Main Street USA writ large. The New Mexico exhibit re-created a Southwestern Native American pueblo of adobelike buildings, the Oregon exhibit resembled a working timber camp, and the Louisiana exhibit featured a replica of Bourbon Street from New Orleans with "jazz bars and go-go dancers." The sum total of this replicated America created what Lawrence Samuel called "a dizzying mishmash of American iconography."[105]

By far, however, the most popular feature of the state exhibits was the animatronic Abraham Lincoln at the Illinois pavilion. The true-to-sized robot of the sixteenth president was the most lifelike animatronic figure of any at the fair in that it did not merely move its limbs back and forth but actually stood up from a seated position and made movements at its neck, eyes, and mouth. The Lincoln robot made these movements as part of show in which "he" delivered excerpts from famous speeches and lectured the audience on the "meaning of American liberty."[106] Those who saw the show report audiences "reacted with wild cheering, applause, and even tears at its conclusion."[107] Oddly enough, the spectacle of a robotic Lincoln at the Illinois pavilion stole some of the exhibitionist thunder away from the US government displays at the large rectangular Federal Pavilion, which besides screening promotional films about American history and the rise of the nation to greatness, included a Hall of Presidents that included statues of great American leaders and their assorted memorabilia. Though the exhibit proved popular, none of the statues in the Hall of Presidents moved or talked.[108]

Disney's magic touch could not be extended everywhere, and in those places where new media technologies and escapist consumer fantasies could not provide a pleasant shelter from reality, the tensions of the world in the mid-twentieth century crept into the fairgrounds. An example of this was present at the Futurama exhibit sponsored by General Motors. According to the Futurama brochure, the future bore an odd resemblance to the imperial age of the nineteenth and early twentieth centuries: "Everywhere you go, you will see man conquering new worlds, to a large degree because he will have available to him new and better methods of transporting machines, material, and people."[109] The number of automobiles would increase, but so would the size and speed limits of freeways. New sources of energy would be tapped at the bottom of the oceans and in the wastes of Antarctica. Life for a large cross section of workers, from farmers to laborers to nurses, would have their lives rendered free and leisurely with the advancement of robotics and automation that would usher in the oft-repeated phrase "the push-button age."[110] The language of conquest and expansion were not merely attempts to see into the future, but arguments that capitalism and American leadership were necessary for such a wondrous vision to actually come to reality.

Indeed, several aspects of the fair revealed the key tensions present in the discourse of consumerism and questioned whether a future of material abundance was truly utopian or wondrous. For example, traffic congestion and parking difficulties outside the exhibition grounds made accessing the fair a tedious process and in no way conformed to the rapid movement of people conveyed in the General Motors exhibition.[111] Moreover, the rapid suburbanization of the country that mass production of automobiles and consumer goods enabled was already beginning to create an alienated population. The beginnings of a counterculture were apparent throughout the country at the time, as Timothy Leary wrote his famous line, "Turn on, tune in, drop out," as the fair was coming to a close in 1965.[112] Promises of going to greater extremes to tap into energy reserves betrayed the truth about the finite nature of fossil fuels and the damage energy production and consumption had on the environment—Rachel Carson's *Silent Spring* was published the same year the Futurama opened in 1964.[113] Most troubling of all that year, the invulnerability of American coercive power was beginning its long slide into crisis as the Gulf of Tonkin Resolution passed the Senate two votes short of unanimity. For all the wonder and spectacle of this greatest event in the history of the world, the gates of Flushing Meadows could barely keep the straining social and political tensions of the real world out.

Perhaps it is of little surprise that by the end of the fair the whole venture had lost a considerable amount of money. Though Robert Moses had promised a total profit from the fair at around $27 million, the fair cost the city of New York $24 million and defaulted on 60 percent of another $30 million in privately financed bonds. Nevertheless, the fair's organizers pocketed substantial amounts of money, with the fair's primary organizer, Robert Moses, receiving over $1 million for his 7 years as president of the project plus a $200,000 bonus at the close of the event.[114] Adding insult to injury was the severe criticisms of the overall aesthetic of the fair's various buildings and the tackiness of the consumerist displays that attempted to combine images of banality with profundity. One writer who visited the fair commented,

> And I remember...a building called the Hall of Free Enterprise, with a screen façade of a freestanding Greek Doric colonnade on whose architrave was inscribed, "The Greatest Good for the Greatest Number," a design that was either the last surviving insult to the ardent spirit of the Machine-Age architecture...or the first straw in the campier winds of Post-Modernism. The giggling never seemed to stop.[115]

Rather than testifying to the utopian future of social harmony, consumer values, and a world made safe through American power, the fair wound up testifying to the dystopian future of social strife, clashing values systems, and the problematic deployments of American power overseas.

This appearance of corruption and bad taste damaged the legacy of the fair and the city government in New York, contributing to the demise of the very concept of a grand international exhibition. From 1965 to the present day, world's fairs, though still in existence, are far smaller and less momentous occasions. Indeed, Moses and his colleagues sought to make the 1964 New York World's Fair "the fair to end all other fairs"—and in a strange way Moses had accomplished this goal.[116]

Even Walt Disney, who hoped to open a second theme park on the fairgrounds in Flushing Meadows, found his designs rebuked by Robert Moses. Disney himself was dead a year later and his brother Roy led the effort to establish a bigger and better space to continue enchanting and entertaining the masses of the world. However, the lessons Disney learned at the world's fair in 1964 were not lost. In 1971, Walt Disney World opened outside Orlando, Florida, with the same themed sectors of the park found in California as well as EPCOT (Experimental and Prototype Community of Tomorrow) Center. Featuring corporate-sponsored pavilions about future ways of life, EPCOT was the application of the world's fair consumerist utopia into the practical day-to-day world. EPCOT and Disneyland were also the place where Disney's most cherished creations—the animatronic Abraham Lincoln, "It's a Small World," and The Carousel of Progress—wound up after the fair ended.[117] In subsequent years, the massive entertainment complex that represents the core of the Disney brand grew to become one of the most beloved corporate entities in the world. The millions that flock to the Disney-owned theme parks around the world testify to the power of amusement and entertainment and the rich rewards that await the state or empire that can learn how to harness this power.

Conclusion

Like its British forbearer, the United States used entertainment and spectacle to consolidate disparate social classes behind a vision of American power as the protector of a liberal blueprint for world order. In the first half of the twentieth century, radio and motion pictures overcame the isolationist impulses of the American public and launched the United States into the arena of international politics. Between the years 1945 to 1965—a crucial phase in the development of a fully fledged empire—the United States faced the additional challenge of consolidating disparate nations to a Western alliance against the appeal of Soviet power organized along an alternative communist model. Thanks to innovations in the communications technology of the mid-twentieth century, the United States succeeded in preserving its domestic tranquility while simultaneously drawing key nations of Asia and Europe into its ideological orbit without frequent overt use of coercive force.

The increasing use of information technologies to quell insurgent impulses, however, did not occur without major hiccups that threatened to undermine the appealing messages of liberal freedom and consumer abundance. As part of its plan to rebuild the global economy through the ideals of a managed capitalist global infrastructure that included the United Nations, the Bretton Woods development institutions, and the Universal Declaration of Human Rights, the United States constructed a parallel complex of news and entertainment that provided worldwide radio news via the VOA as well as made cultural overtures to elites in key foreign capitals. These efforts at using the power of spectacle were not only successful in helping to consolidate the West in the precarious days after the end of the war, but they also revealed some of the major ideological fault lines within American society and the larger world that threatened to undermine future innovations in the use of information and entertainment as a less costly tool of global power.

These tensions fully revealed themselves in the 1950s. The campaign by Senator Joseph McCarthy to purge all suspected communists from the government of the United States provided a counterpoint to the rhetoric of liberal freedom and illustrated how not all members of American society were on board with the postwar consensus that was taking shape. Aided in large part by the advent of television and its "hypnotic effect" over mass audiences, McCarthy offered an alternative vision of the priorities of American power reflected in several key interventions of the early 1950s, including the overthrow of the governments of Guatemala and Iran. However, McCarthy's antics caused an image crisis among many states allied with the United States who had bought into the idea of an American-led international order. To undo the damage caused by McCarthy a different and more pleasing kind of spectacle would be necessary.

This newer and more positive form of entertainment took shape in the imagery of material abundance and consumerist bliss. Between 1955 and 1965, visionaries like Walt Disney developed the potent entertainment platform of the theme park to create a plausible model of what an ideal consumer society might look like and how much "fun" it could be. Disney's development of his theme parks took place alongside of the international popularity of world expos and fairs where nations put their industrial and technological accomplishments on displays that were reminiscent of the London Exhibition of 1851. To celebrate its rise to a level of unprecedented prosperity, the United States, with the help of Walt Disney, put on the grandest of world's fairs in New York in 1964. Here the United States made its most persuasive and enticing argument yet on the virtues of liberal values and the superiority of the American framework of world order.

In addition to legitimizing American power, the three episodes discussed in this chapter also represented new developments and innovations in the new type of empire that was unlike anything that came before it and would be the hallmark of American power in the future. Rather than rely chiefly on military forces, the United States conceded some decision-making responsibilities through key international institutions that formed a prominent part of world politics after the war. Rather than force open markets at the point of a rifle in order to allow trade to flow freely from imperial center to periphery, the United States used its international media and broadcasting capabilities to showcase the benefits and comforts of the manufactured products of the late industrial age to trigger demand in the periphery that would conveniently be satiated by the arrival of American goods and capital. Even the McCarthy escapades demonstrated that when the United States slipped into a xenophobic morass, the power of television ensured the proceedings were more entertaining than infuriating.

Not everyone, however, was sufficiently entertained. By 1965, the beginnings of some powerful forces of resistance to American power appeared. African-Americans, women, and students were among a large assortment of social groups inside American society who were unhappy with the spectacle of life in the imperial metropolis. Meanwhile, in those territories where American power and Soviet power clashed, nationalist groups who saw in the spread of liberal dominance the same colonial forces in new superpower guises gathered to resist the expansion of American influence. These sources of resistance waged their struggle both in material terms against the coercive power of the state as well as on the informational plane through the same media that the United States had so effectively utilized during its rise to power. The coming years were poised to be a tumultuous era of crisis for the American Empire. In the face of this, would the United States abandon its arsenal of entertainment for a more traditional deployment of coercive force, or would it continue to rely heavily on imagery, spectacle, and entertainment to pacify any explosions of dissent.

4

The Postindustrial Renewal: Guerillas, Partisans, and the Triumph of the American Empire (1965–1989)

Introduction

Radio, television, and theme park–style spectacle were instrumental components in legitimizing a tripartite domestic configuration of rule that integrated state institutions, labor, and private industry as well as an international economic order based on the principles of free trade and finance. By 1965, however, tensions embedded in these configurations of power became apparent as increased outbursts of activism among African-Americans, students, and women took shape at home while struggles against American deployments of military force erupted overseas. Though not fully apparent at the time, these disruptions were harbingers of a dramatic change to global order. Newer and more potent socioeconomic forces were arriving on the scene that would soon trigger a collapse of the postwar consensus and threaten the viability of the American Empire.

These changes in socioeconomic and political relations were made possible in part by the momentous advancements in information technologies and organization. The rise of computing technology and the internationalization of communications created a more decentralized and networked environment that increasingly mediated the way individual human beings interacted with each other. For the United States, this meant a slow but profound transformation from an industrial nation of manufacture into a postindustrial nation of information where the machines of the factory floor yielded to the computers of the suburban office park. As explained by David Harvey, the shift to an economy of information networks and post-Fordist production spawned new social groups that shook-up the compromises of post–World War II society and sparked new configurations of power at both the domestic and international level that included "forms of state sovereignty, divisions of labor, social relations, welfare provisions, technological mixes, ways of life and thought, reproductive activities, and attachments to the land and habits of the heart."[1]

The emerging information society featured an advanced industrialism based on what Daniel Bell labeled the "knowledge industry" of abstract theoretical analysis and information production, including such disciplines as research, marketing, communications—and most important for this analysis—entertainment.[2] The social and economic transformations experienced by the United States during this period bore certain similarities to those witnessed by Great Britain beginning in 1815. At the beginning of the nineteenth century, a nascent class of bourgeoisie and industrial laborers used the new technologies of the early Industrial Revolution to reconstruct a domestic political order in Great Britain that served as the foundation of the British Empire. These changes helped make Great Britain the leading nation of the world and provided the launching pad for a century of imperial expansion. Beginning in the 1960s, new groups of professionals, administrators, technocrats, and performers rose to prominence in the United States and tapped into the transformative nature of a budding information revolution to reconfigure new and more contingent coalitions of rule.

The consequences for putting the world on the path to a knowledge economy were profound. The first of these had to do with the expansion of global communications networks that compressed time and space and brought the sights and sounds of distant information or events onto the radios, television, and increasingly, computer terminals of the local home or office. In terms of material production, this meant the first steps in the globalization of industry where manufacturing operations concentrated in one country were fragmented into separated parts and scattered around the world to take advantage of lower labor costs or looser regulations available overseas. The addition of substantial amounts of research investment, advanced computing technology, and global coordination meant, "Product output is diversified, scales are reduced, and production becomes more flexible."[3] In the realm of finance, the changes were even more significant. Money was becoming far easier to move from point to point around the world and investors could seek greater returns for their investments overseas—often by financing the reconstruction of industrial assets outside more developed zones. Here again, the application of computer technologies and research capabilities played a key role, as bankers created ever-more complicated financial instruments built to hedge against the inherent risk of overseas investment in the developing world.[4]

The transformation in the assemblage of economic forces coincided with the rearrangement of social- and political-class tension and the need to forge new governing coalitions among them. Whereas the traditional form of class antagonism observable during the previous century and a half took on a bifurcated shape with an industrial bourgeoisie defending its privileged position in society from a numerically superior working class, the newer antagonisms of the late industrial era saw these tensions obscured behind social and cultural conflicts that shook up the traditional lines of class solidarity and identity. Blue-collar workers, for example, found themselves allied with captains of industry in their opposition to government programs designed by state technocrats to ease the plight of the poor and minorities. Meanwhile, affluent cultural elites in centers of East Coast privilege held fundraisers or ran guns for radical groups like the Black Panthers.[5]

All of these developments posed a mortal danger to the American apparatus of entertainment and its ability to prosecute the continued struggle for world domination with the Soviet Union.[6] The international radio broadcasts of the Voice of America (VOA), the television broadcasting networks, and the destination theme parks were all built on the industrial model of the postwar era. Heavily centralized monopolistic organizations (both in the public and the private sphere) governed by authoritarian bureaucrats or boards of directors controlled the content, scheduling, and operations of the world's major media outlets. Interaction with the public was shallow and limited while the flow of communications was almost always unidirectional in a top-down format. Audiences, while certainly enjoying the programming they were experiencing, were nevertheless unable to express any feedback or render any criticisms of the information and entertainment printed on the pages of their magazines and books or broadcasted from their radios and television sets. Unfortunately for the United States, the period between 1965 and 1980 saw a plethora of social and political groups (some marginalized, some not so much) that wished to interact with their media and shape the creation of its content.

Thus, this chapter explores how the birth of a knowledge-based postindustrial society threatened to undermine the soft power capabilities of the American Empire and forced the United States to increase its reliance on coercive force. In the crucial years between 1965 and 1973, an array of media guerillas rejected the managed liberal model of the postwar era and sought dramatic reforms to American society by waging an insurgency against the arsenal of entertainment. The first of these were the student activists, racial liberation groups, and feminists that comprised the American counterculture. At the core of their movement was the understanding that media institutions and advanced communications were a central pillar of the smothering status quo, and any successful campaign of change required the disruption, co-optation, or destruction of this media apparatus. Overseas, other movements—quite by accident—also managed to create their own counterspectacles to American power that shattered the scripted narrative of the status quo. The most momentous of these was the Tet Offensive—a surprise attack by the Viet Cong defeated by the American military, but thanks to its depiction in the media, caused proportionally more damage to the United States.

Having been outflanked by college students and peasant guerillas, the United States soon faced more powerful political agents that entered the scene between 1973 and 1980 to wage their own form of media resistance. Buoyed by the vulnerabilities in the facade of American power revealed during the Vietnam War, many of the world's underdeveloped nations attempted to create a New World Information and Communications Order (NWICO) at United Nations Economic, Social and Cultural Organization (UNESCO) during the 1970s. If successful, the NWICO would give greater autonomy to local governments to control what kind of content crossed their borders and allow developing nations a tool to resist the homogenizing entertainment output of American content producers. Back in the United States, fears that the counterculture had infiltrated the American media establishment and brought down the presidency of Richard Nixon spawned one of the most important media campaigns of the era—the development of a neoconservative entertainment capability that attracted millions of individuals alienated by the social changes wrought by the new postindustrial society and used propaganda and spectacle to turn them into a potent force in American politics.

As the neoconservatives waged their media insurrection, many of its veterans went to work for the campaign of Ronald Reagan. The victory of Reagan in 1980 signaled the end of the crisis years for American power as the new weapons and capabilities of the arsenal of entertainment were brought to bear. Reagan and the neoconservatives embraced a rebooting of the free economic principles that dated back from the heady early days of the Industrial Revolution that sought an absence of any substantial government regulation, which permitted the free flow of goods, services, and capital around the world. Dubbed "neoliberalism," one of its main effects in the realm of communications advances was the triggering of an extended period of global media consolidation with ownership of the vast arrays of communications platforms falling into the hands of fewer and fewer corporations.[7] New research and development in broadcasting technologies yielded satellite and cable television broadcasting while more widely available investment funds made possible the creation of enormously expensive (but potentially very lucrative) summer blockbuster film. With Reagan intent on bringing the Soviet Union to its knees, these new and improved media weapons played a decisive role in ending the Cold War and bringing about the final triumph of the American Empire when the Berlin Wall fell in 1989.

Insurgencies of Image: Counterculture and Guerilla Spectacle (1965–1973)

If powerful states could deploy an arsenal of entertainment as part of a larger apparatus of command, it was equally possible these weapons could fall into the "wrong" hands and be used against their masters. While the United States had confronted rival states who possessed powerful media capabilities during the world wars and in its continuing struggle with the Soviet Union, the power brokers of the American Empire did not fully recognize the idea that activist movements and political dissidents at the lowest levels of society could also create captivating spectacle to challenge the status quo. During the tumultuous years between 1965 and 1973, however, all this changed as several different dissident groups, alienated by the arrangements of global power in the mid-twentieth century, captured the attention of the world and put the ability of the United States to dominate the West through less coercive means in jeopardy.

The first of these groups were the disaffected student protestors who rebelled against the stifling conformity of postwar American society and sought to open up spaces for individual creative expression (including alternative forms of lifestyle incongruent with the nuclear family paradigm). The second group was African-American activists like Martin Luther King Jr. and Malcolm X who protested the fact that the postwar managed liberal order consigned individuals of African dissent to poverty, despair, and political repression. The third faction of the larger counterculture consisted of the women's movement, which argued that their ability to fully realize their individual potentialities were constrained by the paternalist bent of society in the mid-twentieth-century America. One of the novelties of the counterculture in pursuing their political goals in comparison with previous protest movements was their being media savvy in turning the power of the establishment media on its head. Rather than go through the very narrow and constrained media channels available in a monopolistic communications infrastructure, the counterculture movement sought to win hearts and imaginations through the creation of sensationalist spectacle and absurdist theater, and thereby capture the "hypnotic effect" of television cameras. In so doing, the counterculture struck some of the first blows against the old conventions of American power, and though it sounds counterintuitive, the raucous and iconoclastic revelers of Woodstock vilified by present-day conservatives actually broke down the first walls of the old liberal order that allowed the predecessors of today's Tea Party to take hold of a leading position in the political culture of the United States.

A second variation of this phenomenon of bottom-up spectacle took place in one of the bloodiest conflict zones of the Cold War. Motivated by a radical idea of self-determination that sought to develop a nation free from outside influence (in theory if not in practice), the Viet Cong had waged a stubborn insurgency against the American military and its indigenous allies in South Vietnam. Though materially inferior to the Americans, the Viet Cong nevertheless benefited from the increasing power of broadcast media and the decentralization of the control of media content. In launching their Tet Offensive, they contradicted the narrative disseminated into the public sphere by the American military and the dominant media outlets that the war was progressing to a rapid conclusion. With the advent of more instantaneous communications abilities, the emerging drama of insurgent guerillas attacking ostensibly secure American installations broke through the din of variety shows, situation comedies, and athletic events that were standard fare on American television. With the outbreak of the

Tet Offensive, millions of Americans who were only marginally aware of the American presence in Southeast Asia suddenly discovered that not only was the United States fighting a war in Vietnam, but also that it was quite possibly about to lose it.

Indeed, opposition to the American intervention in Vietnam was one of the animating principles of the counterculture movement. In challenging policies like the Vietnam War, leaders of the counterculture like Jerry Rubin—founder of the Youth International Party, or Yippies—understood that mass media and broadcast communications were transforming society, and in so doing, creating opportunities to challenge American power. Rubin's comprehension of the ability of mass media to rearrange ideas and perceptions of reality came about as a boy listening to his radio. Upon hearing an Elvis Presley song playing on his stereo, Rubin recognized the old conservative playlists of mainstream radio were forever changed as a flood of rock-n-roll music entered the scene of American popular culture. For listeners like the young Rubin, the effect was almost reptilian and illuminated the frustrations and limitations of the mid-twentieth-century industrial society: "The New Left sprang…from Elvis' gyrating hips…Elvis Presley ripped off Ike Eisenhower by turning our uptight young awakening bodies around. Hard animal rock energy beat surged hot through us, the driving rhythm arousing repressed passions."[8]

Contributing to the effect of Elvis's gyrating hips were other innovations that made rock music more pervasive and accessible. The placement of radios in cars, according to Rubin, had the unintended effect of arousing the repressed passions of American youth. "Affluent culture, by producing a car and car radio for every middle-class home, gave Elvis a base for recruiting." With car keys in hand and Elvis on the radio, young men and women could finally succumb to the repressed passions of industrial society: "The back seat [of the car] produced the sexual revolution, and the car radio was the medium of subversion."[9] They also provided a crude form of networked communications, with each individual car radio representing a singular node of information that individualized the listening experience.

Rubin's insights into the transformative power of media were not confined to radio—he, like Joseph McCarthy (ironically enough), also recognized the awesome power of the "hypnotic effect" of television: "Have you ever seen a boring demonstration on TV? Just being on TV makes it exciting. Even picket lines look breathtaking. Television creates myths bigger than reality."[10] Indeed, despite the boon television was for McCarthy, Rubin insisted television was a force of subversion:

> The media does not *report* "news," it creates it. An event happens when it goes on TV and becomes myth. The media is not "neutral." The presence of a camera transforms a demonstration, turning us into heroes. We take more chances when the press is there because we know whatever happens will be known to the entire world within hours [emphasis original].[11]

Rubin went further still, suggesting the hypnotic effect of television was derived not from the content of the message but from the image it presented. The actual words that went along with the televised image were of lesser importance or totally inconsequential. "The *words*," according to Rubin, "may be radical, but television is a non-verbal instrument! The way to understand TV is to shut off the sound. No one remembers any words they hear; the mind is a Technicolor movie of images, not words."[12]

As the 1968 presidential election approached, the challenge for activists was to create spectacle and commotion in sufficient tantalizing quantities that the assembled reporters and correspondents would have no choice but to point their cameras and microphones in the direction of the protestors. The intent of these high jinks was not so much to hijack the entire media apparatus toward the activities of the protestors, but to provide gaudy countertexture to the standardized pabulum of the "legitimate" media. The great master of orchestrating spontaneous spectacle was Abbie Hoffman, a man described as "a revolutionary clown, advertiser and public relations expert," who later assisted Rubin in the founding of the Youth International Party.[13] Hoffman recognized one of the key inventions of industrial age propaganda, the commercial, was the archetypal conduit of persuasion as media began to saturate society. "The commercial is information. The program is rhetoric. The commercial is the figure. The program is the ground," Hoffman insisted, going on to explain, "We [the protestors] are living TV ads, movies...There is no program. Program would make our movement sterile."[14]

Hoffman put these ideas to work in several stunts that garnered him much media attention and established himself as one of the counterculture's leading figures. In August 1967, Hoffman successfully disrupted trading on the floor of the New York Stock Exchange by dumping dollar bills from the observation gallery. The event enjoyed wide coverage on the evening news and got substantial mention in the large-circulation New York newspapers, and much to Hoffman's delight, "every news report differed."[15] Hoffman was keen to see this diversity in the portrayal of the event since it only reiterated his insistence that "reality was made up and that news was a fiction."[16] Later that year, Hoffman and his cohorts attempted to outdo themselves by launching a mass protest against the Pentagon. In the press conference to announce the event, Hoffman insisted the action was "an exorcism to cast out the evil spirits" through chants, incantations, and other symbolic actions that would cause the massive building to "rise in the air."[17] The event was significant not only for the audacity of its absurdity, but also because this absurdity had a very real effect in gathering publicity for the counterculture movement and bringing them together to form a united political front. The protest at the Pentagon marked the occasion that brought together the vanguard of the disparate dissident groups of the 1960s, including Hoffman's guerilla theater troupers, Rubin's free speech advocates, Tom Hayden's anti-Vietnam war protestors, and Bobby Seale's Black Panthers.

After the actions at the Pentagon, the stage was set for what would be the Chicago apotheosis of the counterculture's effort at facilitating revolt. Hoffman eagerly looked forward to conjuring up an endless parade of spectacles, including "rock n' roll, guerilla theater, violent confrontations, and...bloodshed in the streets."[18] Such actions would guarantee television coverage and have the effect of arousing "the masses of young people who were alienated from their parents and teachers and from American society as a whole."[19] Hoffman hoped to get a permit to put on a five-day "Festival of Life" that would serve as a sort of counterconvention to the one being held by the Democratic Party, but the city refused to issue the permit, meaning any mass gathering of protestors would be subject to police action. Though indications were that Hoffman was disappointed about not receiving the permit, as it placed his plans of using famous musicians to raise the profile of the protests in jeopardy, the denial nevertheless assured that violent confrontation between Chicago's then notoriously abusive police force and provocative protestors would create the best spectacle possible.[20] In the seven days that marked the convention week between August 23 and August 30, 1968, significant violence between police and dissidents took place on five of them, including the "police riot" on August 28 when television cameras outside the convention hall captured the aggressive "clearing of the streets" by the Chicago police through tear gas, clubbings, and beatings.

Indeed, the late summer events in Chicago represented the recognition by members of the established industrial elite and their political surrogates that their positions of authority were vulnerable—less from the radicalism of the members of the counterculture and more by the dwindling power of their vocations in a budding postindustrial society. Richard J. Daley, the notorious mayor of Chicago in 1968 who had turned the city into his own personal fiefdom in his rise to power by aligning himself with institutions of the old order (labor unions, state bureaucracies, and captains of industry) declared earlier that week that "the television industry is part of the violence [of the protests] and is creating it all over the country."[21] It was of little surprise, therefore, that when Daley ordered the police to use violence in their confrontations with the protestors, journalists also became targets of beatings along with the rabble-rousers. During an early protest on Sunday night of convention week, law enforcement agencies went after members of the media in a manner that made it "clear that police were looking for reporters, that they were the prime target."[22] On the Wednesday night of the convention when the police unleashed their full fury, 20 reporters required hospital treatment and those who escaped personal harm often saw their cameras smashed, film seized, or otherwise verbally and physically intimidated. Perhaps even more frustrating was the fact that the reports they wrote of their observations and experiences of the evening were heavily edited by their newsroom superiors in what appeared to be blatant attempt by newspaper editors loyal to the mayor to obscure the truth of the events.[23] These attempts at censorship, however, were in vain as the compelling content of the broadcast mediums of radio and television once again demonstrated their society-changing influence by "showing pictures of rioting police, [prompting] the American public...to realize something bizarre was going on in Mayor Daley's city."[24]

In the end, however, coercion still showed itself to be superior in affecting immediate political outcomes and the police activity on the streets of Chicago indicated that the information society was still in its fledgling stage. Indeed, the rapid collapse of the counterculture after 1968 demonstrated that the networked society had not yet burrowed that deeply into the foundations of the postwar assemblage of power. While the rhetoric and values of the New Left of the 1960s may have invoked Marxist ideas and symbols in their pursuit of social change, the basic industrial bourgeois values of Western society never faced an existential threat as many of the more grounded New Left intellectuals of the day pointed out on more than one occasion.[25] Moreover, most Americans did not agree with much of the political agenda being advocated by the various components of the counterculture movement. On a number of key points, public opinion was still very much behind the forces of the status quo. On the hot topic of Vietnam, for example, popular support for the intervention by the American military remained solid for much of the 1960s. While the call to end the American presence in Southeast Asia was a key demand of the counterculture and inspired some of their more outlandish actions, it was broadcast imagery coming from another group of resistors that had the effect of impacting this support far more than any attempts to "levitate" the Pentagon.

The Tet Offensive began in the predawn hours of January 31, 1968, a day that corresponded roughly with the Vietnamese New Year's holiday of Tet. Tens of thousands of North Vietnamese soldiers launched a multitude of attacks against American and South Vietnamese military installations, diplomatic buildings, and urban centers. Though the planners and participants of these attacks were likely oblivious to any abstract theory of media and society, their actions as captured by Western cameras succeeded in bringing into sharp relief the new ability of the electronic media to illuminate the contradictions of projecting power overseas in the middle of the twentieth century. In this way, the Tet Offensive taught a valuable lesson to future American leaders about how to legitimize intrusive foreign actions and further the process of radically reconfiguring the notion of empire.

One of the inescapable facts of the Tet Offensive was that in military terms, the operation was a total and complete failure. The action was intended to present the North Vietnamese military, which up to this point had been reliant on guerilla-style hit-and-run battle tactics, as a formally organized fighting force that could engage the American military in open combat. Upon seeing this show of strength, the Vietnamese population in South Vietnam would abandon their acceptance of the American military occupation and join their northern comrades in the drive to rid the land of its foreign presence.[26] But within days of the first attacks, the American and South Vietnamese forces emerged victorious in most battles, and in no place where North Vietnamese forces engaged American military units could the communists claim victory.[27] One of the few places where a prolonged struggle occurred was in the city of Hue near the border between the two Vietnams. This battle lasted 25 days, and saw the North Vietnamese take control of the city for a brief period of time before South Vietnamese and American forces retook the city in bloody urban combat.[28] A general uprising among the South Vietnamese population never occurred and it would be five more years before the American military permanently left the region.

Despite these victories, however, the Tet Offensive became a symbol of the futility of the American effort to destroy communist movements in Southeast Asia and create a stable government that was loyal to and supportive of American power in the region. Common explanations for this phenomenon point toward biased or sensationalist reporters compromised by liberal ideology epitomized by Spiro T. Agnew's famous label of journalists as "nattering nabobs of negativism."[29] Yet what many mistook for political bias was in fact a single example of the new reality of war in a world where visceral images, however momentary, fragmented, or detached from the physical reality they may be, possessed as much power to control the outcome of a conflict as the military means of destruction.

Two images from the Tet Offensive exemplify how spectacular images in broadcast media gained such a powerful influence over popular thinking about the American presence in Vietnam. The first was the commando-like raids of specialized North Vietnamese soldiers against the American embassy compound in Saigon that gave the impression that communist soldiers had taken control of the United States' primary civilian installation in the country. The second (and more iconic) image was the summary execution of a suspected Viet Cong solider by Colonel Nguyen Ngoc Loan, head of the South Vietnamese Police. In a still photo printed in American newspapers and in video footage shown on evening news broadcasts, Colonel Loan is shown raising a pistol to the temple of the unnamed man dressed in civilian clothes before casually pulling the trigger. With these sights streaming onto the television screens across the United States, the entire narrative of the war thus far was brought into question. The footage of a pitched battle taking place between communist soldiers and American troops in and around the US embassy betrayed the continual refrain from leading American politicians and military leaders of "sound evidence of progress in Vietnam" and that because of this progress, "we [the US military] are on our way out."[30] The gory spectacle of a suspected enemy solider being shot in the head with no consideration of judicial process suggested that both sides in the conflict were guilty of war crimes and the Vietnamese allied with the United States could not claim any moral high ground vis-à-vis their communist adversaries.

Despite the claims of media bias in the wake of the Tet Offensive, media coverage of the war featured mostly cooperation between military and media personnel. Addressing the media strategy of the military, James Willbanks observed that "Army and Marine press officers had reported every in-country operation, regardless of outcome, as a major step forward."[31] In looking at the media's reaction to these pronouncements, David Culbert suggested, "American television news coverage of the Vietnam War for the most part offered little of visual significance, and more often followed or reinforced elite opinion than attacked the status quo."[32] However, the sights and sounds of battles taking place in previously peaceful South Vietnamese cities and on the grounds of American diplomatic installations flew in the face of everything journalists had been told up to that point. A serious "credibility gap" appeared that made military spokespersons look like liars and journalists look like fools. Adding to these negative impressions was the fact that the Tet Offensive took place on the heels of a publicity tour by President Johnson with the unfortunate title of "The Success Campaign." Designed to shore up domestic support for the American presence in Vietnam, the campaign managed to buoy public backing for the war, only to see these spikes in support collapse when the images of Tet began their rounds on broadcast television.[33]

Faced with a profound contradiction between the statements of endless success by the political and military establishment and the compelling images of ostensible North Vietnamese strength, American reporters and journal-ists naturally reassessed the information they were reporting. Newsmen that had been content passing along the information given to them by military press personnel found themselves needing to offer editorial comments that were critical of the American effort in Vietnam in order to reclaim a sem-blance of professionalism. Mike Wallace of Columbia Broadcasting System (CBS) stated in a report that the offensive had "demolished the myth" that had been constructed over the previous years of American military strength and steady progress.[34] In a comment that later became one of the signature statements of the entire war, Walter Cronkite summed up a special CBS report on the events of the Tet Offensive by stating, "To say that we are closer to victory today is to believe, in the face of the evidence, the optimists who have been wrong in the past. To suggest we are on the edge of defeat is to yield to unreasonable pessimism. To say we are mired in stalemate seems the only realistic, yet unsatisfactory conclusion."[35]

The Tet Offensive was neither the first nor the worst setback in the his-tory of the American military. The onslaught of communist expansion after World War II provided numerous opportunities for the American public to sour on its many overseas commitments and damage the credibility of American political leaders. Indeed, at the low point of the Korean conflict, American military forces were backed up against the city of Pusan on the southern coast of Korea by invading North Korean forces before McArthur's amphibious landing at Inchon relieved the pressure. Despite this crisis, American support for the war in Korea, though often fluctuating, remained more or less steadfast, and at no point was Dwight Eisenhower's presi-dency in any serious jeopardy. With the Tet Offensive, however, powerful images and compelling storylines of a widespread insurgency throughout a supposedly secure South Vietnam proved to be the beginning of the end of extensive popular support for an American military presence in Southeast Asia, and resulted in what one commentator called the "political assassination" of President Lyndon Johnson.[36]

Whether taking form in the American counterculture or in the insurgencies of Vietnam, the beginnings of a postindustrial society built on the power of rapid communication and broadcast imagery triggered a struggle to resist and change the assemblage of American power. The social groups and political factions that fully comprehended the power of media were in an in an ideal position to help mold the future of global politics. However, the events of 1968 demonstrated that few people fully comprehended the power of captivating media images as entertaining programming in a globalizing networked structure. Only few prescient individuals like Abbie Hoffman were exceptions and helped give a marginal counterculture movement a larger and more visceral presence on the American social landscape. In Vietnam, North Vietnamese insurgents succeeded in making a failed attempt at starting a wider insurgency into a key turning point in the American presence in Vietnam and in the larger history of American foreign policy. In the wake of these events, however, the secrets of this mysterious power of media weapons were further unlocked by other segments of postindustrial society both within and outside of the United States. As the Watergate scandal broke in American newspapers, these new actors took center stage.

Neoconservative Challenges: The Rise of Partisan Entertainment (1973–1980)

The revolts of 1968, both at home and abroad, badly eroded the stability and legitimacy of the postwar international assemblage of authority as well as the American military power assigned to protect it. In both the streets of Chicago and the rain forested trails of Southeast Asia, the ideas of individual and self-determination obliterated the centralized foundations of American world order. In order to reestablish its dominant position in the face of the lingering threat of the Soviet Union, a new package of ideas that accounted for the basic changes taking place in the socioeconomic foundations of American society along with a beefing up of the American means of material power was badly needed. However, the continuing nuclear stalemate and the crisis of confidence in the American military in the aftermath of Vietnam limited the options available for launching a comeback. As the counterculture faded into obscurity and American soldiers came home from Vietnam in 1972, newer actors both at home and abroad entered the scene to lay siege to the status quo and make a bid to change the world order.

While individuals like Abbie Hoffman and Jerry Rubin were important early pioneers in exposing the contradiction between the old industrial assemblage of power and the nascent postindustrial society, this section argues that many of their ideological foes were waiting in the wings to reassert or challenge American power. The most important of these was an emerging community of political activists that took some of the radical elements of the counterculture's individualism and fused them with traditional ideas of Christian morality and the moral benefit of projecting American military power overseas. Precise labels are not easy to find, but the term "neoconservatism" best approximates the unique features of this new right-leaning movement that brought together elite intellectuals, economic libertarians, and Christian evangelists that rose to prominence amid the Watergate dirges of the 1970s.[37] The power of this new movement came in large part from its recognition of the importance of information and control of media resources in the brave new world of postindustrial society. Led by influential captains of industry like Joseph Coors, intellectuals like Paul Weyrich, and media showmen like Roger Ailes, the neoconservatives poured substantial amounts of money into the creation of a partisan entertainment capability that brought together disparate social groups into large politically active audiences.[38] Through this mass support, neoconservatives made a successful bid to take control of the governing institutions of the United States.

At the heart of the neoconservative movement was a shift in the class and social groups that formed the ruling coalitions of party politics. In the past, industrialization spawned a primary social antagonism between wealthy industrialist and bankers versus factory workers and rural peasants. The neoconservatives of the postindustrial age emphasized new antagonisms away from class and more toward ideology, culture, and identity. In its preference to see the United States rely more heavily on military force in confronting the Soviet Union, neoconservatism also shared much in common with the mature phase of British imperial policy, which sought to deal with the resistances to its expansion through colonial wars and interventions. Yet, the world of the later twentieth century was a far different place with oil-producing nations flouting the power of the United States by artificially raising the price of oil in 1973. Indeed, the Tet Offensive experience had demonstrated to many leaders in the developing world of the power of media in their struggles to remain independent and nonaligned. Together, they attempted to consolidate this resistance at the United Nations through the program known as the NWICO.

The best way to understand the new ideas of postindustrial neoconservatives comes from a comparison to their industrial forbearers. Whereas the old-guard conservatives (to take three sample issues) were tolerant of unions and political consensus building, backed segregation, and embraced isolationism in foreign policy, neoconservatives were hostile to unions and political compromise, believed in ideological purity over racial purity, and advocated a strong interventionist foreign policy overseas. Another way to track these changes is to look at the party realignments that began to take place in the 1960s that wreaked havoc on presidential electioneering for a decade. In 1964, George Wallace, a candidate that supported segregation and criticized the Vietnam policy, ran for the presidential nomination of the Democratic Party. Yet four years later, he was compelled to leave the party and run for the president at the head of a newly formed (and highly contingent) American Independence Party. In 1960, when an accommodating Richard Nixon who schmoozed with Nikita Khrushchev at the "Kitchen Debate" fell to John F. Kennedy, the Republican Party tried again four years later with the Arizonan Barry Goldwater, a man who could barely contain his contempt for welfare programs and foreign policies that coddled the Soviet Union.[39]

The ugly truth in all this was that the counterculture and neoconservatives "were reverse sides of the same political and cultural evolutionary coin."[40] Whereas members of the counterculture sought to smash a society conforming to a bland consumerism, neoconservatives were equally interested in smashing a society conforming to a rigid centralized bureaucracy. Whereas Vietnam was problematic for the likes of Jerry Rubin and Abbie Hoffman as an act of American imperialism, Vietnam was equally problematic for the likes of Paul Weyrich and Joseph Coors as an act of American impotence in the face of a grave communist threat. The principles and policies of both sides could not have been further apart ideologically, but they did share a commonality in that they were packages of ideas that were outside of the normal political assumptions of late industrial American society in 1960. As Weyrich put it in 1981,

> We want to change the existing power structure. We are not conservatives in the sense that conservative means accepting the status quo. Today isn't the same as the 1950s, when conservatives were trying to protect what was, constitutionally, economically and morally, in the control of more or less conservative people.[41]

If counterculture radicals were drawn primarily from the ranks of middle-class youth, disenfranchised African-Americans, and disgruntled women, the neoconservatives forged an uneasy alliance between established intellectuals and pious working-class masses. The brains of the movement consisted of "quite a few...New Yorkers, most of them certified members of the Eastern intelligentsia...enjoy(ing) access to the opinion-molding community from the *Wall Street Journal* to the *Washington Post*."[42] From inside the beltway at the Heritage Foundation or a short cab ride away from Wall Street at the Manhattan Institute, neoconservative ideas made their way to the suburbs and small towns of the United States through small-business associations that were drawn to an agenda of low taxes and less centralized regulation and through churches and religious organizations that agreed with the condemnations of liberalism's immorality and pandering to godless communism. Yet, the key to making this diffusion from elite centers of power to the streets of "middle" America was the development of an autonomous communications capacity built in a way so as to be completely detached from the established media apparatus of the United States.

This intense desire for independence in both medium and message stems from the Watergate scandal. In 1971, the *New York Times* began publishing a series of leaked Pentagon documents that revealed the American presence in Vietnam was the result of a deliberate effort to expand American power in Southeast Asia and not a stopgap effort against communist aggression as had long been argued. The publication of these "Pentagon Papers" soon led to disclosures about the illegal activities of Richard Nixon and several members of his administration in the pages of the *Washington Post* that eventually forced the once popular president to resign in 1974. The boisterous presence of the counterculture on the streets of the United States may have ended, but the investigations by Woodward and Bernstein showed to many conservatives that some of their authority-challenging principles penetrated key social institutions. The prospect of the *Washington Post*, one of the nation's most influential newspapers, directly attacking the sitting president during a time of domestic and international crisis bordered on treasonous. Unfortunately, it was one thing to let the police or military bludgeon the disheveled punks of the counterculture out of existence, but quite another to unleash the coercive apparatus of the state on journalists working for an ostensibly respectable media institution like the *Washington Post*. In a knowledge-based economy, struggles for power were won not with coercive force but with information, entertainment, and spectacle, and those who sought to defend America's most precious values and institutions from subversion had to learn to use these media weapons.

Fortunately for conservatives, not all the innovators of the postindustrial media and intellectual landscape were leading members of the counterculture. While the counterculture had Abbie Hoffman and Jerry Rubin, conservatives had (and continue to have) Roger Ailes. The impact Ailes had on the neoconservative is almost incalculable—whereas George Creel weaponized information for the United States in a manner that helped it win World War I, Ailes weaponized information for neoconservatives in a manner that allowed them to win the White House and other governing institutions of American power. Spending his early years learning the trade of television broadcasting in Ohio during the 1960s, Ailes appreciated the ability of televised images to manipulate the viewer. Ailes's loyalty to the "small-town values" instilled into him growing up in rural Ohio made him contemptuous of the counterculture movement, but this ideological baggage did not prevent him from recognizing and admiring the power of media images in similar way as Abbie Hoffman. In a handbook on media relations written for general consumption in the 1980s titled *You Are the Message*, Ailes said, "Everything you do in relation to other people causes them to make judgments about what you stand for and what your message is. *You Are the Message* comes down to the fact that unless you identify yourself as a walking, talking message, you miss the critical point."[43]

One of Ailes's early coups came as a media consultant for the Nixon campaign in 1968. By coaching Nixon on the fine art of public speaking and scripting his statements to the press, Ailes successfully transformed a cantankerous and jowly Richard Nixon who had famously "lost" the nation's first televised presidential debate to the telegenic John F. Kennedy in 1960 into a poised and savvy political communicator that helped him win the presidency. After this success, he began his own media consulting company that "worked for Republican political candidates, provided communications counseling to corporations, and was also involved in a number of entertainment pursuits involving records, stage productions, and television production."[44] However, manipulating the image one presented to the camera and becoming a more competent political performer was only the beginning. Because Watergate demonstrated that the American media establishment had been hopelessly compromised by the radical values of the 1960s, an entirely new media infrastructure that could churn out untainted messages and images became a necessity.

While most of the American public remained captivated by the continuing details of the Watergate scandal, conservatives quietly began to build this alternative partisan communications apparatus. As Kerwin Swint observed,

> The 70s and 80s were a watershed time for conservative movement in the mass media—new conservative publications were founded, right-wing think tanks and foundations provided research and funding, the strong conservative presence among the talking heads of TV news programs began, and most importantly, conservative talk radio emerged as a major force in American media and politics.[45]

Ailes played a key role in the construction of this force. Backed by the finding of wealthy financier Robert Pauley and industrial brewmaster Joseph Coors, Ailes was hired to consult with the staff of a start-up news network titled Television News (TVN) that would provide preedited broadcast news stories to local television stations that they would run on their airwaves as part of their news shows—a sort of "visual wire service." Several months after the operation began, Ailes was hired to be its news director. TVN was the first attempt at creating a news source that was independent of the big three networks and their loathsome liberal bias. As one senior staffer at TVN put it, "I hate Dan Rather. I hate all those network people. They're destroying the country. We have to unify the country. TVN is the moral cement."[46] The hope was that TVN would eventually become a "fourth network," but by the end of the summer of 1974, the organization ceased operations as its donors directed their funding elsewhere. This failure did not end the dream of creating an "unbiased" news service. In the succeeding years, other conservative activists made another failed attempt at a news outlet called National Empowerment Television in 1993. Five years later, however, success was finally attained with the start of Fox News Channel. It should come as no surprise that one of the founders and current president of Fox News is none other than Roger Ailes.[47]

The pioneers of conservative broadcasting also poured a great deal of their substantial funds into another outlet that proved to become an important font of partisan entertainment in the postindustrial age—the think tank. In this part of the endeavor, Joseph Coors was the key innovator. Coors "created, or helped to fund, dozens of the best known conservative political organizations in America, including the Christian Broadcasting Network, the Heritage Foundation, the Hoover Institution, the Manhattan Institute, the Ethics and Public Policy Center, and the Free Congress Foundation."[48] Though not all conservative think tanks had identical goals or founding principles, all of them spent a great deal of time and money on publicity for their ideas and policy recommendations. The typical Right-leaning think tank started in the 1970s "specializ[ed] in producing conservative books, monographs, newsletters, policy papers, and reviews on domestic and foreign issues."[49] Unlike the weighty studies of the academia, think tank publications, aside from making conclusions that fit with the agenda of the organization, were produced in a way that made them easily digestible for the busy and easily distracted casual partisan: "Most of the publications are designed to meet the 'briefcase test'—succinct enough to be read in the time it takes for an official to be driven from Washington's National Airport to a congressional committee hearing on Capitol Hill (about twenty minutes)."[50] Skillfully written executive summaries and talking points read by a sympathetic decision maker could easily slip into the text of a prepared speech or press conference, thus ensuring the idea or argument would make it into television news coverage of political events.

A crucial component, however, was missing in this emerging media machine—emotion, passion, or other forms of sentimentality to make it engaging and entertaining to the masses. Cable television and televangelism solved this problem. At about the same time all eyes were focused on the Watergate scandal, the fledgling technology of cable television slowly became commercially viable, and "Christian conservatives were among the first to exploit…new technological innovations that provided an alternative to dependence on the three major television networks at the time."[51] With much of the nation's population taken aback by the brazenness of counterculture spectacle they had seen on the traditional networks for the past few years, there was a strong demand for not only more "wholesome" programming but also criticisms and condemnations of the radicalism such groups advocated.

Indeed, if Jerry Rubin's great insight that just being on TV makes things exciting was true, then television would be a huge boon to the dull sermonizing of much religious communication or be a powerful enhancement to the lively revivalism of many American churches. Preachers like Billy Graham were pioneers at carving out spaces on traditional broadcasting networks on which to spread the word of the gospel and making the necessary connections from liturgy to policy. In the 1970s, however, as the neoconservatives arrived on the scene, the leading innovator was Pat Robertson. His Christian Broadcasting Network saw its programs syndicated on local television stations as early as 1961 before establishing a cable channel of his very own in 1977. Aside from constructing a substantial broadcasting infrastructure, Roberston's innovations also included "the use of religion in a political news talk-show format—based on the news and current-affairs style created by the CBS program *60 Minutes*."[52] Robertson also founded his own university, unimaginatively titled CBN University when it was founded in 1977, before changing it to a more dignified moniker of Regent University a few years later. In founding this university, however, Robertson was actually behind the trend, as televangelist Oral Roberts had founded his university of the same name in 1963 and Jerry Falwell had founded Lynchburg Baptist College (later Liberty University) in 1971.[53] In a matter of years, the sum total of these programs, networks, think tanks, and universities created an alternative electronic universe ideologically sealed from outside influence and poised to capture the spirits of millions of people.

Neoconservatism, with its emphasis on traditional individual morality and military strength overseas, went a long way to reconfigure the disparate social forces of American society into a semicoherent consensus after the social upheavals of 1968. Overseas, however, leaders of the developing world were also using the collapsing of the post–World War II assemblage of power to assert their own autonomy from external superpower pressures. The television drama of the Tet Offensive demonstrated that the power of the United States could be challenged and states eager to assert their own autonomy began to take steps in this direction. The first sign of this trend occurred during the oil crisis of 1973 when members of the Organization of Petroleum Exporting Countries (OPEC) artificially raised the price of oil against the wishes of the United States. By cutting production of oil and artificially spiking the price, Arab nations affected American foreign policy in a way that no group of subaltern nations could in the past. Needless to say for neoconservatives, this expression of developing world power was unnerving.

Even more unnerving, however, was the prospect that the developing world was also discovering the power of media and global communications and taking steps to destroy the American advantage at manipulating these capabilities. Through UNESCO, leading politicians of key developing nations attempted to ensure the international architecture of global communications remains free from imperial control. Their efforts began the deliberations of the NWICO. The NWICO was part of a larger effort of the New International Economic Order (NIEO). The NIEO featured an agenda that sought to reduce or eliminate the widening gaps in wealth and power between the developed world and the former colonial world that continued to struggle with poverty, underdevelopment, and repeated violations of sovereignty by superpowers. Thus, the NWICO was an inherent recognition by many nations that the decentralized nature of emerging global communication networks provided an opportunity to remain free of superpower alignments and opened space to express genuine self-determination.

Indeed, for many peripheral nations, broadcast media images and information were essential to any program attempting to alleviate economic malaise and asserting political prerogative on the global stage. The problem, as UNESCO director-general Amadou-Mahtar M'Bow stated in 1981, was that many developing countries felt "that particular items of news relating to the developing countries originating in the north do not always faithfully reflect the true state of affairs and that, at times, news is even distorted or manipulated in such a way as to give a false picture of the developing countries."[54] Even more revealing were the findings of the MacBride Commission, which concluded a study in 1980 that international information flows had been predominantly one-directional from the affluent world to the underdeveloped world and this disparity in information flows had "undesirable consequences" for these struggling states.[55] Phillip Muscat from Malta went still further, claiming, "In certain instances the international press is used as a destabilizing factor against the governments whose only crime is generally that of standing up for their rights, their sovereignty and independence."[56] Such a statement was profound in that it was among the first to see the main manifestations of the American Empire in the form of media capabilities and not military power.

News and objective information was only part of the story. The vast majority of entertainment and cultural programming on the radio and television airwaves of many developing world nations was almost exclusively American. UNESCO figures indicated that "Guatemala imported 84 percent of its television programming, Malaysia 71 percent, Zambia 64 percent, Nigeria 63 percent, the Dominican Republic [and] 50 percent."[57] Even developed nations like Canada saw 46 percent of their programming originating in the United States.[58] Within this context, indigenous language and culture were at risk of eradication not through the mass killing and repressive rule of local colonial administrations, but through the internalization and adaptation of foreign behaviors, languages, values, and ways of being learned through constant exposure to foreign media programs.

To combat this, M'Bow advocated that UNESCO adopt a resolution that would outline a basic framework of rules that could govern international information flows. The heart of this resolution, M'Bow argued, should be the principle that in order to allow peripheral nations to control the information circulating around their territory, broadcasting outlets must be under the control of the state. For M'Bow, the question centered on the principal of national sovereignty—if nations have the right to control the flow of people and goods that enter their state, should not the nations of the world also have the right and ability to control what kinds of information are disseminated within their borders? To the advocates of the NWICO, the answer was an obvious yes, and they hoped that such a position would be readily supported by the United States. Surely, the nation that promoted sovereign rights in the wake of World War I and famously refused to condone the seizure of the Suez Canal in 1956 by France and Great Britain on the grounds that it reeked of old-style European imperialism in Africa would support such an effort by postcolonial nations to control their own media environment.

The nature of empire, however, had changed, and more and more the United States was getting a better sense of this transition. The ability to shape and shift the behaviors and desires of the world's population was now done through indirect forms of command—international institutions, relations of trade, and perhaps most importantly, information and entertainment. To establish a norm in international relations that gave states the right to regulate what kinds of information entered and exited the country put this means of administration at risk. Many neoconservatives believed that behind the NIEO and NWICO were surrogates of the Soviet Union attempting to replicate the totalitarian practices of communism within their own nations. It did not help that the aforementioned resolution supported by M'Bow bore a strong resemblance to a document introduced by the Soviet Union in 1971 with the cumbersome title of "Fundamental Principles Governing the Use of the Mass Media in Strengthening Peace and International Understanding and in Combating War, Propaganda, Racialism, and Apartheid."[59] Given this history, now was not the time for the United States to cede countermeasures to its most powerful weapons to developing nations. Indeed, so real was the fear that proposed socialist reforms in Chile under the leadership of President Salvador Allende led to an American-sponsored coup in that country in 1973.[60] Interventions like this, however, were not the preferred route to maintaining control. Like the preference for indirect action in the early Victorian era, the United States favored the use of less precise but more palatable indirect tools of rule than the coercive instruments that yielded more immediate results but increased resentment and legitimacy.

Moreover, the rhetoric of a free press provided the perfect moral cover for the exercise of media hegemony in the developing world. Indeed, as partisan rancor over who was ultimately responsible for the events of Watergate continued unabated back in the United States, almost everyone across the political spectrum agreed upon the importance of keeping the media free and unencumbered of government authority or regulation. As Thomas L. McPhail observed,

> Like nothing else might have, the Watergate scandal reinvigorated a latent distrust of governmental regulations and demonstrated to the people of the United States and other core nations the need for a press free of government control. Even the mere suggestion of increased government control of the media was anathema to the U.S. public and Western journalists.[61]

Thus, the NIEO and the NWICO order met a similar fate as the counterculture of American society when it met the full political and economic weight of the United States and its control of international institutions. Using its hegemonic position in the United Nations, the United States went about alienating leaders that advocated for the NWICO by threatening to cut off direct foreign aid, or, in cases where the United Nations itself proved insufficiently malleable, withheld its payment of dues and other financial assistance.[62] Arguing that press freedom was a human right also neutralized developing world claims that communications regulations were gross violations of global media companies' right to operate free of government interference. In making this argument, the United States, as well as many of its Western allies, were clearly elevating press freedom over the rights of states to determine what images and messages passed to the consciousness of its own people.[63] Such a stance contradicted previous advocacy of the importance of the sovereign principle, but given the fears about declining American power amid insurgent blocs of developing world nations, the last thing American leaders were interested in was relinquishing their best tool of propagating American ideals and values to populations outside of its borders.

For all the economic difficulties that took place during the 1970s, the United States successfully moved toward a reconsolidation of its global power under the leadership of the neoconservatives. With the election of Ronald Reagan in the 1980s, this project accelerated as the narrative of "neoliberalism" enhanced the power of finance and used the mechanisms of debt and leverage to reconsolidate global media outlets into multinational entities that had the ability to bind the perceptions and imaginations of the world's people closer together. As the next section shows, the new global media capability combined with the charisma of a former movie star as president of the United States took the worldview of the neoconservatives and made it palatable for millions of people across the globe. The renewal of the American Empire was underway and it would soon reach unprecedented heights.

Empire Resurgent: Reagan's Election and Blockbuster Entertainment (1980–1989)

Slowly but surely, the transformation of the American economy into a decentralized network of information and imagery production was changing the prevailing arrangement of social forces, material power, and ruling institutions that constituted the American Empire. These changes ended the postwar consensus of power sharing between heavily bureaucratized government agencies, centralized corporate behemoths, and hierarchically run labor unions and replaced them with something new. What this new assemblage of power looked like was difficult to pin down at the time, but after sufficient study, the term "neoliberalism" became one of the best ways of describing the phenomenon. David Harvey defines neoliberalism as the belief "that human well-being can best be advanced by liberating individual entrepreneurial freedoms and skills within an institutional framework characterized by strong private property rights, free markets, and free trade."[64] Neoliberalism represented a vast expansion of wealth generation as new techniques and organizational models created new efficiencies in the production of goods and services. Labor was "deunionized" and forced to become more flexible (jobs became more of a "part-time" nature), corporate entities began to sell-off much of their productive capacities in favor of financial activities, and government agencies were ostracized to sidelines.[65] However, neoliberalism also represented shifts in wealth distribution and the reworking of social life that produced substantial deleterious effects. The core values of the late twentieth-century neoliberal capitalism tended to benefit the wealthy and well-to-do and left the material condition of the masses in a stagnated state.[66]

Though these kinds of disparities often produce social tensions, the 1980s instead was a period of relative stability in American society that served as a foundation for greater expansion overseas. This section examines how the media capabilities of the time and their ability to stir the populist sentiments of the American masses relaunched the American Empire and brought about its ultimate triumph. The pieces of this success, as explored in the previous section, were largely in place by the time the presidential contest of 1980 began. Advocates of free market economics, national values based on evangelical Christianity, and American expansionism had in their own ways sought to seize the reins of power away from the lingering elites of the previous industrial era. This section builds on that discussion and argues that through the appealing celebrity of Reagan these groups brought their respective constituencies together to form a populist foundation for domestic power. The deregulation at the heart of neoliberalism also allowed media companies to reconstitute themselves as global communications entities that could transmit messages to a worldwide population. Though Reagan was rarely reluctant to use military power, the enormous image-generating capacity of global media firms epitomized by the consolidated Hollywood film studio system turned the small peripheral clashes of the late Cold War into epic struggles of good versus evil.

Yet these various groups that formed the popular foundation of Reagan supporters were not natural allies. The values of avarice and hypercompetition endemic to neoliberal capitalism were at odds with Christianity's focus on compassion, charity, and universal love. Moreover, the insistence on using strong military power (or at least the appearance of such power) to batter dissenting nations and peoples into submission undermined the image of the United States as a benevolent superpower that was the world's last, best hope for freedom. Fortunately for the United States, the image of Ronald Reagan and his message of populist empowerment was sufficient rhetorical glue to keep the socioeconomic structure of neoliberalism adhered together and help bring about the collapse of the Soviet Union. Amid the backdrop of the end of communism—broadcast live around the world with the fall of the Berlin Wall in 1989—it seemed the end of history had truly arrived.

Such epic events, however, were far from the minds of anyone in 1980 when Reagan assumed the presidency. Reagan's rise to popularity began in

1976 when a small group of neoconservative intellectuals and politicians revived a mid-twentieth-century think tank known as the Committee on the Present Danger (CPD). The aim of this small group was to critically evaluate the official intelligence estimates of the threat posed by the Soviet Union and, where necessary, provide alternative assessments. More often than not, the conclusions of the CPD were far more menacing and dire than those of the Central Intelligence Agency (CIA) or other formal intelligence agencies. In 1979, the former governor of California and then presidential candidate Ronald Reagan assumed a position on the executive board of the CPD, thanks in no small part to his firm advocacy of direct and aggressive confrontation of communism and the Soviet Union.[67] However, Reagan, as the world was soon to discover, was no ordinary right of center politician. Yes, he had shown his disdain for the counterculture in 1969 by ordering police and National Guard troops to occupy the city of Berkeley amid large student demonstrations against the Vietnam War. He had also shown his neoconservative bona fides in his policies of tax cutting and regulation overturning while governor of California and his advocacy of these same policies as a presidential candidate. Yet, what made Reagan the quintessential postindustrial presidential suitor was his career as a film actor and television spokesperson throughout his professional career. As new media capabilities and platforms, such as cable television and live satellite broadcasting came online, Reagan helped consolidate the various fragments of the neoconservative ruling coalition into a successful presidential bid and a renewed effort to make the United States the world's most dominant state.[68]

With his background in acting and public relations, Reagan had already shown an innate ability to connect with a mass audience through broadcasting conduits. Yet, even the man who would soon be known as the "Great Communicator" needed occasional advice and coaching from the behind-the-scenes masters of the broadcasting medium. Though not formally part of his campaign, Roger Ailes nevertheless served as an important image consultant during Reagan's runs for president, being especially instrumental in helping Reagan recover from a poor performance in a debate with Walter Mondale in 1984.[69] Ailes helped Reagan understand that his ability to connect with large groups of people centered on his knack for showing warmth, compassion, and humor in his speeches and making millions of listeners feel like he was talking solely to them.[70] In an age when live television began to come into its own, Reagan could present a pleasing facade to a series of new policy proposals that began the controversial process of dismantling and defunding many governmental programs, reducing taxes on the wealthy, and rebuilding the military foundations of a new American imperial framework.[71]

The actual construction of this new framework, however, needed more than the smiles and wit of a telegenic politician. Aiding in Reagan's effort to consolidate power at home and overseas was a communications apparatus going through its first significant update and reorganization since the end of World War II. New technologies that where in the planning stages or in limited release for several years were finally being brought online and enjoying mass distribution. Cable television was perhaps the biggest change taking place by the time of Reagan's first presidential victory. Whereas previous television broadcasting had been controlled by a few large conglomerates who distributed their signals through the air via antennae, cable television sent its signal through a terrestrial cord that had the ability to carry several signals simultaneously. Though viewers would have to pay a fee to have the cable installed in their home and for the programming it conveyed, the happy result was a spike in the number of potential channels available and thus the opportunity to break the programming oligopoly of the major networks. Both activists on the Right and the Left saw this as a positive development as both regarded the major broadcasters as hopelessly beholden to the status quo (whether this status quo was industrial advertisers or liberal elites). More choice and more spaces for expression could only be a positive step forward. Indeed, many individuals of the time seemed to feel this way, since "by the mid-1980s, nearly half of American homes had cable television."[72]

Also of great importance, especially in the coverage of news, was the development of mobile live television feeds that permitted news outlets to cover distant events in real time without the need for recording or editing. Live television programming had already existed for several years, but these transmissions were usually restricted to scripted television shows or variety programs contained in a highly controlled sound studio. The ability to record live events "in the field" regardless of location represented a dramatic step forward in communications capability. Again, for critics who believed the elite-controlled media revealed their biases in how they edited or framed a particular piece of recorded news footage, live broadcasts provided an opportunity to deliver raw and unedited words and images to the viewing audience.[73] For a politician gifted in mass communication like Ronald Reagan, live television was a powerful tool of conveying important messages and impressions directly to constituents with minimal filters.

These advances in communications, however, were expensive. The amount of capital necessary to purchase cable and satellite capacities challenged the budgetary prowess of traditional media outlets. In this way, they resembled the problem faced by operators of print media in the middle part of the nineteenth century in Europe. During that era, the increasing costs of upgrading existing print technology, including the cost of steam presses, access to railways, and specialized staff members like professional journalists and illustrators, proved to be prohibitive for many small publishing operations, especially those who had small or niche readerships. The result was a substantive change in the style and content of newspapers and journals as they sought mass circulations of their journals in order to maximize revenue and pay for technological upgrades and professional staffs. Now, in the 1980s, a similar phenomenon was taking place, with media companies needing to find new ways of generating revenue to justify substantial investment to pay for upgrades. Some newer outlets, like the cable news channel Cable News Network (CNN), had the financial support of entrepreneurial multimillionaires (in this case Ted Turner) on which to fall back.[74] However, for other more traditional media outlets, the vast sums of money required to operate a late twentieth-century news operation required high finance and corporate consolidation. As seen with the changes in print media in the nineteenth century, the need to raise money and increase revenues meant the content of broadcast outlets changed in order to garner the largest mass audiences—even if this meant looking beyond the borders of the United States to find these audiences.

As a result, a noticeable trend in the concentration of cable television began in 1984 and continued steadily in subsequent decades.[75] Cable channels that began as independent entities or part of a small package of channels started by media companies were sold and repackaged to other companies, many of which were not even media outlets, in the hopes they might be cash cows for the larger corporate organization that often had a substantial debt burden. Music Television (MTV), in many ways the quintessential 1980s cable television station promoting celebrity and popular culture, provided a stark example. MTV began life in 1981 as a venture by Warner Communications, a large media company, and American Express, the iconic credit card brand. In 1984, the company merged several other cable channels it had started or acquired, including VH-1 and Nickelodeon, into a single entity called MTV Networks.[76] In 1985, MTV Networks, producing a reliable profit for the first time since its inception, was purchased by the media giant Viacom in the hope that its profitability would ease Viacom's debt burden. Two years later, however, Viacom was bought by Sumner Redstone's National Amusements for the hefty price of $3.2 billion, two-thirds of which was financed through bank loans. Such an enormous debt burden meant that MTV and its sister channels had to produce massive amounts of revenue quickly in order to justify the enormous amount of debt utilized to acquire it.[77]

A similar process took place with other television broadcasting outlets, including the rise of Rupert Murdoch's News Corp. Coming to life as a small company managing a package of Australian newspapers, News Corp purchased the movie studio 20th Century Fox in 1981. Leveraging its ownership of the famous movie studio, News Corp then started its own broadcast television network in the United States to rival the big three traditional broadcasters (CBS, National Broadcasting Corporation [NBC], and American Broadcasting Company [ABC]) in 1986.[78] Murdoch and News Corps, however, were merely part of a larger trend of consolidations and mergers. The 1980s also saw General Electric buy NBC in the same year as Fox Broadcasting took to the airwaves while ABC merged with Capital Cities, a conglomerate of several local television stations, before eventually being bought by the Walt Disney Company.[79]

The concentration of media ownership, however, is only part of the story. With a handful of individuals and companies loaded down with debt pulling the strings of most of the world's communications, the need to maximize ratings in an effort to generate the most lucrative of profits became a categorical imperative for all media outlets. Thus, the content, like that of the cheap newspapers in the mid-nineteenth century, focused increasingly on entertainment and amusement. Sports, in the form of Entertainment and Sports Programming Network (ESPN) made its presence on the television landscape during the 1980s), law and order (epitomized by the long running NBC drama of the same name), and news programming that prioritized human interest stories over beat reporting became the focus of new cable channels and broadcast programming.[80] As the sales and mergers of media outlets progressed, television networks were but one asset in an armada of movie studios, book publishing houses, newspapers and magazine printers, radio stations, video game developers, and almost any other type of mass market media product in existence at the time. As these various platforms came together, the term "media convergence," or "the integration of text, numbers, images and sound in the media which have largely been considered separately," becomes an increasingly important concept.[81] With media convergence, a brand or theme introduced in one medium is cross promoted in another, often creating a great deal of homogeneity, standardization, and imitation regardless of the uniqueness of the local culture.[82]

The highly concentrated (in terms of ownership) and widely distributed (in terms of global coverage) media apparatus that took shape in the 1980s provided an important opportunity to introduce new political ideas and cultural signifiers into the American psyche. With the election of a popular and charismatic political figure like Reagan who was comfortable in front of the camera, an ideal spokesperson for the package of values centered on the ideology of neoliberalism, preservation of traditional cultural institutions, and the assertion of American military power had been found. All that was left was to distill these ideas into entertaining and captivating themes on the television sets, films, and print media of the United States and to watch them diffuse throughout the world.

For chief executive officers and Wall Street bankers, the cult of personality surrounding Reagan was less relevant than the fiscal and tax policies that left their bellies and their bank accounts full. The Joint Economic Committee, a research arm for the US House and Senate on economic issues, revealed that "America's top 420,000 households alone accounted for 26.9 percent of US family net worth—in essence, 26.9 percent of the nation's wealth. The top 10 percent of households, meanwhile, controlled approximately 68 percent. Accumulation and concentration of wealth would be simultaneous hallmarks of the 1980s."[83] These beneficiaries had no difficulty at expressing populist patriotism and no doubt swooned at some of Reagan's rhetorical flourishes about it being "morning in America," but this did not prevent them from making decisions that damaged the lives of the American working classes in order to create short-term profitability or to sell-off large swathes of prime American real estate to foreign buyers.

Among the working classes, especially those who lived in rural areas, celebrations of American power had a far greater impact. With the majority of soldiers and sailors coming from working-class families, Reagan's use of symbols of American strength and invincibility in his rhetoric played especially well, and reoriented "this group's identity from being workers to patriots."[84] It also allowed Regan to engage much of the Southern region of the United States, which had long been a stronghold of the Democratic Party. As certain social programs implemented by Democratic politicians aimed at eliminating economic and political disparities in the urban core of cities alienated white voters, Reagan used his antigovernment, pro-military message to bring a large portion of these Southern voters over to his side without having to directly confront the lingering racial tensions. The fact that the American South had a plethora of military bases that were the foundation of many local economies only made the message that much more appealing.[85]

However, what clinched the South for Regan was its place as the home of American evangelical Christianity. Reagan's largest block of support came from evangelical Christians who had formed a potent political bloc in the 1970s thanks in large part to the large communications infrastructure they controlled. From their daily television shows syndicated on network television to 24-hour televangelism on their own cable channels, the Christian broadcasting apparatus provided an endless loop of support and endorsement of Reagan's presidency and his policies. Consequently, Reagan was often eager to show his gratitude to this bloc of voters even if he himself did not share their religious fervor.[86] Indeed, one of Reagan's most famous speeches, where he articulated the reasons why he believed the Soviet Union posed such a grave threat to the United States, was delivered before a Christian evangelical group. In that speech Reagan insisted, "And while they [secularists] proclaim that they're freeing us from superstitions of the past, they've taken upon themselves the job of superintending us by government rule and regulation. Sometimes their voices are louder than ours, but they are not yet a majority."[87] In making this statement, Reagan was neatly linking some of the prime elements of the neoconservatives—oppressive government constraint and regulation—with the core values of faith and its importance in American culture. Reagan went on to use these values to morally justify the buildup of American military might against the existential threat of communism. In the same "evil empire" speech, Reagan quoted part of a conversation he had with a voter who said to him, "I would rather see my little girls die now, still believing in God, than have them grow up under communism and one day die no longer believing in God."[88]

Reagan's rhetoric, while galvanizing the heartland of America, did not go down easily overseas. Given the fatigue many developing nations demonstrated with Cold War politics expressed in the various initiatives of the NIEO, the United States needed to use its global media capability to make the aggressive confrontation of the Soviet Union an enticing and captivating event. Interestingly enough, the opportunity to engage the world with a high-octane American spectacle coincided with a series of small military conflicts with peripheral nations like Grenada and Libya. An example of traditional imperial military intervention that might have triggered massive international revolt in the past became instead an opportunity to use these conflicts as global entertainment. The transformation of imperial police actions into blockbuster movie plots that drew large international audiences at theaters around the world was one of the more ingenious turns in the development of the American Empire. It not only revealed a key technique of winning hearts and minds, but also negated some of the more abrasive rhetoric of the Reagan presidency overseas.

As a presidential candidate, Reagan was sympathetic to the foreign policy concerns expressed by many neoconservatives that a viable international order required a strong American military. Upon his election, Reagan put these ideas into action by initiating an enormous program of military expansion, centering on the development of advanced weapons systems that negated the vast numerical advantage the Soviet military enjoyed over the United States. New models of warships were quickly designed and put into production while older vessels, some dating back to World War II, were brought out of mothball and integrated into the active fleet. Billions of dollars were poured into the development of new fighting vehicles like the M-1 tank and the Bradley fighting vehicle or into new aircraft like the B-2 stealth bomber.[89] The biggest project of them all was the Strategic Defense Initiative (SDI), in which billions of dollars were invested into a space-based ballistic missile interception system designed to shoot down the nuclear missiles of the Soviet Union during a potential attack. Indeed, so much money saw its way into these programs that criticisms of the program's cost and effectiveness sprang up both at home and abroad among allied nations.[90] In addition to these specific issues, the overall national debt of the United States skyrocketed as the accumulated total of all these new systems vastly outpaced the tax receipts of the nation. Yet, these problems seemed to be of little consequence during the Reagan presidency as the new and powerful military was not only a source of pride to fuel domestic patriotism, but also a means to reassert dominance around the world. Reagan, it seemed, was going back to the old way of imperial control through coercive force.[91]

Yet for all the firepower and muscle constructed by Reagan's measures to beef up the military, the actual actions of the United States during this period resembled a power that saw spectacle and posturing as a more effective way to achieve its ends rather than actual overseas violence. Some cases, of course, clearly featured more traditional material efforts to impose conformity on subordinate nations in a manner resembling the imperial model of the nineteenth or earlier twentieth century such as the funding of the anticommunist insurgents in Nicaragua or the mujahedeen fighters of Afghanistan. However, in many other cases the approach resembled the empire of entertainment that had been taking shape since the mock battles of Smith and Blackton during the Spanish-American War. Small-scale military actions where American military might was used to discipline a weak nation were sensationalized in the media to give the impression of an invincible juggernaut of freedom.

One of the earliest examples of this came in 1981 when two American warplanes shot down two Libyan warplanes over the Gulf of Sidra. The encounter resulted after several days of standoffs between the Libyan government claiming the entirety of the Gulf of Sidra as its territorial waters and the American Navy intentionally entering the gulf in the name of navigational freedom. Libyan fighter jets routinely flew directly at American ships only to turn off after being intercepted by American fighters, but in the middle of August in 1981, one of the Libyan fighters fired a missile at a pair of American jets. The missile missed its target, and the technologically superior American planes quickly shot down their attackers. The incident was of little consequence, as the standoff in the gulf continued off and on for several years, but a dramatized version of the event served as the climax of one of the most iconic movies of the Reagan era: *Top Gun*. Douglas Kellner described this film a "Reaganite wet dream" and as the embodiment of "the Reagan/Yuppie values of winning at all costs, of putting competition at the center of life, and going all out to win in every domain of social existence, from dating to sports to career."[92] The film earned $350 million globally, boosted recruitment into every branch of the military, and became an international cultural reference point that still has resonance today.[93]

In another example, American soldiers and marines invaded the tiny Caribbean nation of Grenada in 1983 after a coup d'état brought an authoritarian government to power. While the coup served a pretext for the action, Grenada drew much ire from the Reagan administration due to its alignment with Cuba and its decision to build a large runway that could ostensibly accommodate large Soviet aircraft. Thus, when members of the military deposed the socialist government, the ensuing instability and potential for a more thorough takeover by Cuban (or Soviet) actors prompted Reagan's hand. On October 25, 1983, American forces invaded, and after a few brief skirmishes from a tiny Grenadan military force that by one account was "poorly organized," the island was more or less conquered in 48 hours.[94]

Popular reaction to the invasion was generally supportive, but the event received an ornate remodeling in 1986 when Clint Eastwood made the film *Heartbreak Ridge*, where the invasion served as the background for the transformation of a handful of young slackers into patriotic warriors. The film was a success with audiences, earning $70 million at home as well as an additional $70 million overseas, suggesting the film's patriotic themes and military bravado had an impact on foreign audiences.[95] Though critical reaction to the film was mixed, especially given the splash the more critical war film *Platoon* made that same year at the Academy Awards, *Heartbreak Ridge* had the last laugh as it depicted the first significant military action by the United States since the end of the Vietnam War. The success of the invasion and the film together hinted at the new type of interventions that blended real world military actions with mass entertainment. Films like *Top Gun* and *Heartbreak Ridge* showed how global audiences who were ostensibly going out for an evening's entertainment were in reality plugging into a world where the values of neoconservatism were popularized and normalized and testified to the benefits of the transnational imperial apparatus that was constructed around these values.

Finally, there is the aforementioned example of the SDI. In its early stages, the program received the informal moniker of "Star Wars," in reference to the universally recognized space epic released in 1977. Richard Perle, one of Reagan's assistants at the Pentagon, recognized the positive imagery such an association gave to the controversial program: "It's a good movie. Besides, the good guys won."[96] However, the technology of firing lasers from high in the atmosphere of the planet resembled the actions of the evil galactic empire in the actual Star Wars film, prompting intense opposition from Left-leaning critics in the United States and antinuclear activists in the Europe.[97] Furthermore, it became apparent to many close to the project that the technology to make it work was not feasible, and that the project itself was more of an elaborate hoax than a viable defense program.[98]

However, at the Reykjavik Summit in 1986, Soviet Premier Mikhail Gorbachev was only willing to enter into a mutual disarmament pact with the United States on the condition that Reagan limit the funding and research into SDI. Gorbachev's demand suggested the images of the potency of the new weapon systems and their potential for rendering the United States invincible to nuclear attack were significant enough that they became the lynchpin on an agreement that would essentially end the nuclear stalemate of the Cold War. Reagan too, despite the skepticism in the United States over whether SDI was plausible, believed the imagery and spectacle surrounding the program and was therefore not prepared to sacrifice it in exchange for the end of 40 years of superpower tension.[99] One can see in this exasperating situation one of the crowning achievements of the American Empire of entertainment imagery—appearances and demonstrations of titanic technological strength beamed through broadcast mediums around the world and infused with rich pop-culture allusions served as key bargaining chips in superpower negotiations rather than actual physical weapons.

Reagan was harshly criticized for not being prepared to trade his SDI program for total nuclear disarmament, but in a world where images were increasingly becoming more important than physical reality, his decision was nothing short of shrewd. Indeed, five years later, the Soviet Union collapsed as its economy no longer had the ability to provide for the basic necessities of its society *and* engage in an arms race with the United States that would soon be armed with space-based weapons similar to the kind seen in the movie *Star Wars*. Had Gorbachev known the truth, perhaps he would have chosen a different bargaining strategy and saved his country, but in the end, the Soviet Union fell and the renewed American Empire used the lessons it had learned to make a bid for its right to rule by entertaining the whole world.

The trend of "militainment" was part of a larger process of the globalization of a popular culture rooted in the United States with American cultural signifiers but starting to evolve into a distinct standard of international taste. Other organs of cultural production, such as popular music channels like MTV, fast food cuisine like McDonalds's restaurants, and news brands like CNN and British Broadcasting Corporation (BBC) were becoming the frontline warriors of disseminating a package of values that explicitly or implicitly endorsed the political and economic priorities of neoliberalism.[100] Though occasionally iconoclastic (often times as a result of a preplanned marketing strategy), organizations such as these nevertheless were agents of an American-sponsored world order and in many ways made the values of neoliberalism stronger as they began to leap into areas of the world no longer dominated by a Soviet sponsor.

Conclusion

What began in the 1960s as a radical outburst of iconoclasm and a rejection of postwar American values eventually became an aggressive blend of capitalism and traditionalism that not only reorganized and resuscitated American power but also reshaped fundamental aspects of American society. In making these changes, the American Empire maintained its global dominance rooted in the control of international institutions but added new mechanisms of command and influence including a potent mass entertainment and cultural production apparatus that increased its hold on the imaginations of large populations around the world. Though the transition from the liberal postwar socioeconomic order to networked neoliberalism was tumultuous in its early stages, the narrative of neoliberalism ensured that American power remained paramount even if this power was now commanded by newer assemblage of social forces both within the United States as well as outside of it.

This process began with the counterculture movement of the late 1960s undermining the monopoly of centralized media companies through guerilla propaganda and absurdist fanfare while overseas the Tet Offensive showed how even poor insurgent peasants could turn the arsenal of entertainment against itself. Ironically, these breaches opened up by radical activists on the Left were most fully exploited by the forces of neoconservatism, which took advantage of these gaps by starting up their own news and information organizations and legitimized and normalized their interpretations of neoliberalism in the 1970s. By 1980, neoconservatives had constructed a populist base around the celebrity power of Ronald Reagan and took control of the apparatus of the state. Both the material power of the United States along with the discursive power of consolidating global media companies allowed the United States to romanticize its projections of power around the world and help strike the final blow to the Soviet Union as it was collapsing into oblivion. In 1989, with the fall of the Berlin Wall this process was complete.

So dramatic was the final fall of communism that the neoconservative political philosopher Francis Fukuyama declared that the world had reached the "end of history."[101] Embedded within this idea was the belief that American power was the guardian of a neoliberal world order that would absorb the final hinterlands of the old Soviet Empire and marked the beginning of an era of ceaseless peace and prosperity. Indeed, the idea of an "end of history" implied the American Empire was fully renewed and would not face any of the challenges and contradictions that contributed to the decline and fall of the great empires of the past. Thus far, however, this era of peace and prosperity has not materialized—indeed an era of uncertainty and upheaval quite unlike anything experienced in the past 60 years has taken shape since the fall of the Berlin Wall. Terrorist attacks in 2001 and the worst global economic crisis since the Great Depression have ushered in an era of uncertainty and dread among most of the world's population. Given the precarious nature of the global environment in the early twenty-first century, new expressions of dissent and rebellion are very likely to rise and challenge the American-sponsored prevailing assemblage of global power.

When these uprisings do occur, how will the United States react? Will it rely on its arsenal of entertainment to keep the masses content and passive? Will it take advantage of new communications technologies, especially the much ballyhooed smart phone technologies and the social media platforms they create? If so, then a pattern this book has explored will likely continue, and the new technologies of the digital age will, much like the tabloid presses and the broadcasting outlets of radio and television (perhaps after a brief period of contestation) solidify and more deeply entrench the present global ruling apparatus protected by American power. However, this book has thus far also discussed certain moments where new communications technologies radically transformed society, introduced exciting new ideas into the world, and overturned governing institutions once thought unchangeable. Are the scattered upheavals of the twenty-first century and the way people are communicating to each other within them a harbinger of a monumental shift in the direction of history? The pages that follow in the conclusion will discuss some of these intriguing questions.

Conclusion

America Overexposed? Globalization, Digital Communications, and the Fate of the American Empire (1989–Present)

By the end of the twentieth century, the arsenal of entertainment revealed itself to be the culmination of an almost two-centuries-long process. The initial stages of this development began in the heady days of the Industrial Revolution when Great Britain (and later the United States) supplemented traditional deployments of military capability with the instruments of soft power. In the succeeding years, however, information and entertainment became a means of power projection in their own right, integrating themselves into a larger assemblage of global command and authority. Today, this vast and omnipotent apparatus of spectacle assumes much of the responsibility to enforce daily imperial discipline and is poised to preserve an era of planetary stability managed under American auspices. Colonial armies, smothering bureaucracies, or any of the other previous trademarks of a stifling imperial structure are absent in a world where many of the trivial desires and discontents of subject people can be satiated or neutralized. This new global capability, made possible by the advancement of mass communication technologies, makes the American Empire unique among its imperial predecessors and gives it the ability to weather the storms of economic downturn, popular dissent, and social unrest into the foreseeable future.

This vast media apparatus, however, was but one form of soft power available to the United States as the twentieth century drew to a close. The fall of the Berlin Wall in 1989 and the collapse of the Soviet Union in 1991 opened up an opportunity for a dramatic reorganization of the global structures of power through a process known as globalization. At the heart of globalization were several phenomena.[1] The first was the expansion of neoliberal principles that grew out of the ideological hegemony of a rising financial elite and their populist base in the United States during the 1980s. The demise of the Soviet Union meant that there was no obstacle to the wide proliferation of these ideas to every nook and cranny of the world.

The second was the transfer of power away from states and toward transnational forms of global governance and social control including intergovernmental organizations, multinational corporations, nongovernmental organizations, and cadres of elite decision-making bodies (such as the G-8 or the Bilderburg Group). Some have suggested this actually indicates that the twenty-first-century world order is becoming an empire detached from the rule of a single state, but events like the American invasion of Iraq in 2003 show that American power is still preponderant, even if state sovereignty in general shows signs of waning or changing.[2] The third and perhaps most important aspect of globalization was the digitization of the global communications infrastructure that incorporated the creation of the World Wide Web, satellite communications platforms, and social media networks navigated with smart phones and digital cameras. With this network in place, there were no barriers to prevent the American arsenal of entertainment from continuing its bombardment of the imaginations of the world's populations.

Thus, one can see why there is little plausible or effective global resistance to the American Empire. No economic ideologies enjoy the same widespread elite support as neoliberalism, no global unions or social movements speak for the collective struggles of the world's underclasses, and no state with superpower status in terms of military capacity has the ability to stand up to the awesome might of the capabilities of the United States. As these pages have shown, one can now add the capabilities of communications media to the conventional understandings of the structure of American power. With their ability to disseminate compelling packages of information, dramatic spectacle, and engaging entertainment, the ability for individual subjects to critically evaluate their surroundings and organize action to change these surroundings has been all but eliminated. Even in the face of the surging influence of states like China, India, and Brazil, the flavor of globalization remains primarily American and ensures that American preferences and tastes persist even if the American command of the economic or political sphere wanes. American Empire, in some variation, is here to stay.

Or is it? This book has also recognized that there were moments in the development of this awesome global communications infrastructure when reformers, resistors, or outliers created or captured certain media capabilities and deployed against the forces of the status quo. Antislavery advocates and parliamentary reformers challenging the status quo in early nineteenth-century Great Britain were trailblazers in using print media platforms to make fundamental changes to the structure of national politics and break the British aristocracy's monopoly of power. Pioneers in the development of film and radio technologies like John Grierson and John Reith hoped their efforts led to a stronger nation or a more erudite citizen. Activists like Jerry Rubin and Abbie Hoffman discovered how the spectacular nature of television could be used against the established power structure while insurgents in Vietnam showed how compelling imagery could neutralize the military prowess of a superpower. Globalization has now brought to the world a new generation of digital media platforms with technical powers that far exceed the communications capabilities of just a few years ago. In concluding the study, this book will now inquire if the new digital platforms are indeed the tools through which the United States will solidify its global dominance or whether digital media can expose and exploit cracks in the facade of American power.

Two recent events have placed the possibility of an extended era of American administered peace and prosperity into jeopardy—the terrorist attacks of September 11, 2001, and the explosion of global protest movements that followed the financial crisis of 2008. These events were extraordinary in the disruption they caused. The attacks of September 11 and the subsequent war on terror saw a dramatic expansion of American power into the Middle East and Central Asia at the cost of tens of thousands killed, many of whom were civilians caught in the struggles between a lethal superpower army and the ruthless insurgents of Iraq and Afghanistan. The financial crisis of 2008 caused enormous suffering for people around the world as millions in the United States lost their homes and jobs, countries ran up gargantuan amounts of debt, and countless numbers of individuals in the developing world who had escaped poverty found themselves slipping back into a state of depravation. Most recently, the revolts associated with the Arab Spring have toppled three dictatorships in Northern Africa, created two sustained civil conflicts in Syria and Bahrain, and left an entire region of the globe in a state of flux.

However, these events were also extraordinary in their ability to pierce the veneer of pleasure and amusement that has become the hallmark of American soft power. For the first time since the 1960s, the United States lost the ability to either control the narrative of its power or have the controversy associated with the exercise of this power rendered innocuous through amusement and distraction. The reason for this has to do with the decentralized nature of digital media technologies. Whereas the older technologies of print, motion picture, radio, and television relied mostly on hierarchically organized structures to produce content and unidirectional platforms for dissemination, the new technologies of digital media created organic social networks where users produce their own content and disseminate them through the network via the interaction hardware (personal computers, smart phones, digital cameras) of the network.[3]

Within the more open environments of globalization, social networks can organize and concentrate a substantial amount of power at almost any point on the planet. The gravity of these networks often pale in comparison with those of states, transnational corporations, and major international institutions, however, they still can deliver substantial influence that impacts the larger actors of international politics. This helps to explain the persistence of a group like Al Qaeda, which is less a formal terrorist organization like Hezbollah or the Irish Republican Army, and more a network of scattered extremist nodal points that tap into a common Islamist ideology in pursuit of specific political objectives.[4] American military power has destroyed several nodal points in the network, including the largest symbolic node of Osama bin Laden at his hiding place in Pakistan in 2011. However, destruction of nodes does not mean the destruction of the network, which can expand into new areas as it is being destroyed elsewhere.

As one should expect from a state that relies heavily on the power of media for stabilizing world order, the United States has not been oblivious to the changes wrought by digital communications. Many of the more calculating members of the American foreign policy establishment over the past decade understood well that destroying enemy networks meant exploiting the American advantage in communications capability in order to penetrate and capture the cognitive tissue of populations sympathetic to terrorist appeals and extremist ideology. In the immediate aftermath of the September 11 attacks, the Bush administration allocated approximately $10 billion on what diplomats like to call "public diplomacy," or government expenditures designed specifically to bypass any local governmental intermediaries and speak directly "to the people" of a specific nation.[5]

This effort began with the hiring of advertising guru Charlotte Beers by the State Department as assistant secretary of public diplomacy and the contracting of the public relations firm The Rendon Group within a month of September 11 attacks.[6] As arguably the most capable advertising sage of the last two decades, Beers was charged with the responsibility of increasing the sympathy among overseas audiences for the United States and its interests and to counter the Al Qaeda "lie machine" that could occasionally gain airtime on independent Arab language satellite television networks like Al Jazeera.[7] Colin Powell justified Beers's hiring by saying,

> I wanted one of the world's greatest advertising experts, because what are we doing? We're selling. We're selling a product. That product we are selling is democracy. It's the free enterprise system, the American value system. It's a product very much in demand. It's a product that is very much needed.[8]

Charlotte Beers's strong bona fides among diplomats at the State Department was matched by the reputation and experience of John Rendon—a master image conjurer for the Pentagon. Rendon's specialty is "perception management," which includes "exploiting the technology of American campaigns— focus groups, voter databases, rapid-response teams" in an effort to shape and mold media representations of events.[9] When Marines entered Kuwait City in 1990 to the cheers of hundreds of individuals waving American flags, it was Rendon's agency that made sure those flags were distributed in time for the Marines' arrival.[10] As Beers and Rendon concocted their strategy to "rebrand" America's image abroad, the Pentagon also created the

Office of Strategic Influence (OSI). Rather than fabricate positive images of American values in the world's media, the OSI discredited individuals and institutions that might be overtly critical of American policy by planting news stories or opinion pieces in foreign media outlets—with no promise that such stories would be completely truthful.[11]

Yet, many of these efforts were met with lukewarm results, if not outright failures. Beers's signature campaign to repair the American brand in the Arab world, dubbed "Shared Values," fell flat on its face. Public opinion polling throughout the Middle East in 2003 revealed that most of the inhabitants of the Arab world retained a negative view of the United States, and while many of them enjoyed the entertainment products of the West, this did not translate into support of US foreign policy or acquiescence in the face of American interventions in the Middle East.[12] Indeed, after Beers quietly left her post at the State Department, two other publicity gurus— former State Department spokesperson Margaret Tutwiler and former communications director for the Bush administration Karen Hughes—each tried their own hand at boosting the brand of the United States around the world and each also had inauspicious results.[13] Meanwhile, the Pentagon had to scrap its OSI when the plans to plant false stories in newspapers evoked widespread criticism around the world as well as within the United States.[14] The world's most adept practitioner of soft power was losing the battle for hearts, minds, and imaginations of a significant portion of the world's people and few seemed to know why.

The problem for the United States was its apparent abandonment of the thing that had brought it so much success in exercising global authority with only modest resistance for the past 60 years. For all the attention paid toward the "battle for hearts and minds" after September 11 attacks, it was the military power of the United States that played the leading role in responding to the attacks. First, with its invasion of Afghanistan, then with the much more controversial intervention in Iraq, the United States showed a preference for traditional coercive force over the promise of information and image. When platforms of information were used, they more often than not supplemented the deployment of violence and brute force by conveying the images of strength and power associated with the American military apparatus. Indeed, while public diplomacy spending rose to $10 billion after September 11 attacks, spending on military power reached $782 billion by 2010—an all-time high.[15] With such a backdrop, it is easy to see why the efforts of someone like Charlotte Beers failed since media campaigns designed to arouse sentimentality and stir emotions about common values cannot hope to compete with the sights of falling bombs, rolling tanks, and the bloody carnage of civilian casualties—the latter of which was often transmitted through foreign-based Internet websites since such images rarely found their way onto traditional Western media.[16]

These developments echo the famous line by Marshal McLuhan in his famous tome *Understanding Media*: "The medium is the message."[17] The decentralized network structures brought about by digital media platforms recorded and transmitted the dubious activities being committed by the United States in the pursuit of the imperial discipline it feared it had lost in the aftermath of September 11 attacks. It was not that the United States had never committed such unsavory acts in the past—making the world safe for democracy during the world wars and containing the spread of communism during the Cold War required actions that contradicted the humanitarianism of the American rhetoric.[18] Yet, the interventions and dubious actions of previous ages rarely made it onto the unidirectional radios, movie screens, or television sets of American consumers. By contrast, the multidirectional and interactive platforms of smart phones and digital cameras linked together via the Internet could make even the smallest human rights abuse committed by the agents of American power become "must see TV." Thus, when the world discovered the images of prisoner abuse at the hands of American soldiers in the now infamous Iraqi prison of Abu Ghraib, the power of the United States to realize its objectives in Iraq suffered. The United States had justified its invasion of Iraq through appeals to humanitarian principles, but pictures of prisoner abuse committed by American soldiers belied the image of the United States as a universal force for good. Moreover, applications of excessive military force in civilian contexts allowed Islamist groups intent on implementing repressive theocratic regimes the means to portray themselves as heroes resisting an imperial aggressor. The instantaneous nature of global communications capabilities only heightened this problem since the ability to contextualize or neutralize negative images became far more difficult when such images could be disseminated around the world in a matter of seconds.[19]

In 2008, with the election of President Obama, the United States switched tactics. This switch coincided with two important developments—the turmoil unleashed by the financial crash (an event that discredited among many communities around the world the neoliberal approach to economics and the shortcomings of globalization) and the mass adoption of perhaps the most significant change of the digital media revolution—social media. Networks like Facebook and Twitter along with crowd-sourced sites like Wikipedia were potentially the ultimate quantum leap forward in soft power that could solve the marketing failures of the recent past. Users of social networking sites could create their own content through their ability to share information and images and in the process entertain and amuse themselves and each other. Intense market research into what kinds of content people around the world wanted would no longer be necessary because sites like Facebook or YouTube made the thoughts, ideas, and preferences of their users available to anyone who followed the blog posts, self-made videos, and "likes" of users.[20]

From the perspective of the United States, not only could social media platforms amuse millions of individuals seeking to promote themselves, but also empower groups in authoritarian countries or marginalized by extremist terror to flout the restrictive tendencies of governments in places like China and the Middle East and further expand the zone of freedom around the world. The opening up of these nations to free expression would be a boon not only to the expansion of globalization, but also in the interests of the United States. As Hillary Clinton said in a speech in 2010,

> The internet is a network that magnifies the power and potential of all others. And that's why we believe it's critical that its users are assured certain basic freedoms. Freedom of expression is first among them. This freedom is no longer defined solely by whether citizens can go into the town square and criticize their government without fear of retribution. Blogs, emails, social networks, and text messages have opened up new forums for exchanging ideas, and created new targets for censorship.[21]

In other words, the spaces opened up by social networks would support the power of the United States (since the United States ostensibly supports freedom of expression) and undermine the power of rival governments and enemy combatant groups (that oppose such freedoms of expression).

However, Clinton and other public boosters of open information and interaction through social networking failed to anticipate how the media tools that could help bring down authoritarian governments could also direct the attention of vast global audiences toward acts of authoritarianism and imperial rule committed by the United States. In the last four years, the world has seen several examples of this, but none has been as damaging as the saga of Wikileaks. Established by the controversial advocate of free information Julian Assange, Wikileaks was a site where anonymous sources of sensitive information could upload their content for public release. In 2010, a disgruntled army private names Bradley Manning (now Chelsea Manning) turned over troves of secret government documents to Wikileaks, which then passed them on to several international newspapers including the *New York Times* and London's *Guardian*. The leaks, which included the video of an American attack helicopter obliterating a small group of innocent men standing around on an Iraqi street corner, exposed the violence and brutality of wars in Iraq and Afghanistan and contradicted the narrative that American power overseas was bringing about a freer and more civilized world.[22] Moreover, the reaction of the United States to these leaks (as well as more recent revelations by National Security Agency [NSA] contractor Edward Snowden) has been similar to the one seen in the aftermath of the terrorist attacks on September 11—all hard power and very little soft power.[23] Julian Assange has been the subject of an intense investigation by the Department of Justice in the hopes of indicting him and prosecuting him for espionage while the original source of the leaked content, Private Chelsea Manning, was held before her trial in solitary confinement in a US military prison in conditions so harsh that the United Nations issued a formal protest.[24]

There are also movements afoot within the United States' communications regulatory apparatus to constrain the freedom of the Internet and allow corporations and other organizations to pay for privileged exposure in search engines and other Internet access points at the expense of individuals using cyberspace for noncommercial or nongovernmental use.[25] There is even talk of giving the president of the United States access to a "kill switch" that would instantaneously cut off access to the Internet for millions of users.[26] Even if drastic measures like these represent extreme and unlikely cases of authoritarian intrusion into cyberspace, reporters like Evgeny Morozov have pointed out how governments and corporations use information and data about individuals freely available on personal websites and social networking sites to engage, track, and constrain the activities of individuals these organizations deem a threat to their interests (and the revelations of Edward Snowden suggest these practices are not confined to authoritarian regimes).[27] While platforms like Facebook and Twitter began as tools of entertainment and amusement, in their ability to cultivate interactions among members of social groups, it is entirely possible that these communications capabilities will become notorious for making possible the massive gathering of information by the American government on individuals and communities around the world. Such developments would signal a loss of faith in entertainment as an effective means of soft power and a possible return to traditional methods of imperial discipline. The recent revelations by Edward Snowden suggest as much.[28]

If this is true, then perhaps an opportunity has been found to pick up the abandoned tools of the arsenal of entertainment and use information and spectacle to confront, critique, and challenge the American Empire. After most societies around the world become more knowledge oriented, the ability to control images and information and organize assemblages of power around these images is increasingly the standard by which influence is measured. Because recent innovations in communications technology can manipulate images and information like never before, it is here that many groups rising in resistance to American power and neoliberal globalization attain part of their transformative potential. Paul Mason gives an elegant summary of the division of labor among the various information platforms of the twenty-first century and the impact they can have:

> If you look at the full suite of information tools that were employed to spread the revolutions of 2009–11, it goes like this: Facebook is used to form groups, covert and overt—in order to establish those strong and flexible connections. Twitter is used for real-time organization and news dissemination, bypassing the cumbersome "newsgathering" operations of the mainstream media. YouTube and the Twitter-linked photographic sites—Yfrog, Flickr and Twitpic—are used to provide instant evidence of the claims being made. Link-shorteners like bit.ly are used to disseminate key articles via Twitter.[29]

In essence, there is not a word of text or pixel of imagery that cannot be gathered, compressed, processed, and disseminated to a global audience. These capabilities may not have the traditional advantages of physical power with its ability to take and hold territory, but they do have the ability to capture the imaginations and stir the emotions of millions of people when images "go viral." As dictators like Hosni Mubarak found out during the Egyptian revolution, one cannot kill or destroy this swarm of data without killing the host body politic.

One can see how this structure facilitates mutual support among different networks around the world with the events of the Arab Spring. In the aftermath of the death of Mohammed Bouazizi—the young Tunisian man who sparked the Arab Spring when he set himself on fire in protest against the authoritarian government, protests and acts of rebellion in Tunisia spawned shadow protests in other parts of the world as members of different social networks in different countries with a connection back to Tunisia organized simultaneous demonstrations. Thus, while youths in Tunis were fighting riot police, flash mobs and demonstrations were taking place in Berlin and London. When Tunisian president Ben Ali and Egyptian president Hosni Mubarak shut down the Internet in their respective nations, revolutionaries in both countries passed along tweets, photos, and blog posts to friends around the world to be redisseminated where online access was not blocked.[30] Similar mobilizations and networking also allowed for global "anticapitalist" protests of October 15, 2011, to take place with little or no centralized planning or coordination.[31] Indeed, an event that takes place in one part of the world will quickly filter to the rest via real-time tweets and Flickr and Yfrog photos (or now, Instagram and Vine clips). It is the ability to disseminate stirring images around the world instantaneously that has proven to be particularly effective in creating something akin to serial drama among millions and stirring the action of global resistance networks.

The development of mobile communication devices featuring photographic and video recording functions as well as video sharing sites like Vine has also enhanced the ability for passive spectating to give way to active political organizing, publicizing, and action. Having the ability to log onto the Internet or access social networks on the go allows for an organizational flexibility and opens up spaces for creative movement that frustrate attempts to repress or disburse public gatherings. Combined with the photographic and video capability on most devices, smart phones and video sharing platforms also provide an opportunity to document the movement's actions and record state actions that contribute to the media narrative that today's counterhegemonic forces attempt to purvey. Indeed, few things arouse more populist anger and illuminate the contradictions of government action than compelling images of state violence (where law enforcement agencies use paramilitary tactics to enforce misdemeanors and petty offenses while appearing to do nothing against those who exacerbate the misery of the age). Conversely, nothing arouses the brutality of the state more than having its corrupt lawlessness broadcasted to the world. Egyptian activist Khaled Said was beaten to death in 2011 by Egyptian police in retaliation for posting videos of government and law enforcement corruption on YouTube.[32]

Indeed, the power to use mobile device technologies allows for what Stephen Mann has dubbed "sousveillance," or "watchful vigilance from underneath."[33] Many activists like Julian Assange can be seen as master practitioners of sousveillance. Whistle-blowing websites like Wikileaks, with its emphasis on publicizing secret or sensitive information about powerful institutions and individuals from anonymous members of the general population, also captures the spirit of sousveillance as an effective tactic of a present-day counterhegemonic bloc. However, it is through the power of mobile communications devices that the potential of sousveillance is best understood. One of the more compelling examples of this took place during the protests amid the G20 summit in the spring of 2009. During a day of particularly intense scuffling between protestors and police, a local newspaper seller named Ian Tomlinson died after an encounter with riot police. Initial reports suggested he had died of a coincidental heart attack, but the revelation of footage from a tourist's cell phone camera of Tomlinson being violently struck from behind by a police officer resulting in him hitting his head on the ground opened up an investigation on the possibility that Tomlinson's death was not due to natural causes.[34]

The revelations of such videos can have a devastating effect in not only gaining the attention of the masses but also initiating procedures to have those in positions of power held accountable through existing institutions (such as what happened with the London police officer who struck Ian Tomlinson) or, perhaps more profoundly, undermine the popular legitimacy of the institution or individual involved. Indeed, once politically charged content makes it onto a video sharing site like YouTube or Instagram, there is generally no controlling the impact such images might have. This perhaps explains why the United States government has treated Chelsea Manning, the leaker of the helicopter gunship video, so harshly.[35] The video she released among the trove of other government documents did significant damage to the reputation of the United States. It also explains why someone like Edward Snowden is so keen to avoid being arrested by American law enforcement that he has sought refuge in Vladimir Putin's Russia.[36]

Suffice to say, not all deployments of mobile device technology are constructive in their challenges of the economic and political conditions of the times. The use of Blackberry Messenger during the London Riots to notify individuals of looting opportunities at stores that had their display windows broken or to avoid areas where police had concentrated serves as an example.[37] Nevertheless, this usage does demonstrate the power of instantaneous communication (even if the objectives of the users of this technology are morally dubious) and highlights how those who inhabit the lower rungs of the social and economic hierarchy often are more skilled and competent users of the technology than bureaucratic and political elites are.

Among the most recent communications innovations that have boosted the effectiveness of "sousveillance" has been live streaming technology. In the past, the ability to broadcast live images was the exclusive privilege of large corporate media operations that could afford the expensive equipment needed to capture and disseminate images of events in real time as they happened. In recent years, however, the equipment that allows for instantaneous and mobile broadcasting of images through digital cameras and smart phones has become much smaller and much more affordable. Increasingly, coy and clever protestors have deployed these broadcasting assets to give global audiences on the Internet the ability to watch actions and events live, raw, and uncut. Indeed, certain users of this technology have become unofficial "reporters" for various social movements. In New York, live streamers like Tim Pool have not only established a name for themselves with their own unique social networking sites that broadcast live images, but also serve as broadcasters for several mainstream media outlets, including Al Jazeera.[38]

Live stream represents a volatile new step in media power in that it makes the "hypnotic effect" of television available to all. Moving imagery and sound can be controlled by individual agents who no longer have to compete for camera time controlled by mainstream broadcasters that comprise part of the status quo. Combined with the other tools of the twenty-first century media age, the social movements of today are truly masters of their own media form. The stirring images of revolutionaries storming a government building or overzealous police brutalizing passive protestors has the effect of making the movements another form of mass entertainment that attract the eyes of millions. However, the power of media, as seen throughout this study, is extremely volatile and could, as seen with the example of the McCarthy Hearings, inflict more damage than entertainment. To take one example, Livestreamers at Occupy Wall Street found themselves filming a group of protestors letting the air out of the tires of a police vehicle. When they realized they were being filmed, the protestors demanded they not be filmed, and in one case, a livestreamer was physically assaulted.[39] The footage of this interaction was highly compelling, but it certainly does ingratiate the cause of those fighting for economic justice to neutral viewers.

This last example provides a much larger lesson for those who wish to use media as a weapon and build their own arsenal of entertainment. Like the implements of physical force, the media weapons of soft power are not inherently "good" or "bad," but are tools that can be applied to a host of objectives. The prevailing trends revealed in this book indicate the media technologies of the past two centuries have been developed and wielded by the interests and the institutions of the prevailing structures of global power to preserve their position of privilege and dominance and neutralize expressions of dissent.

In the nineteenth and early twentieth centuries, Great Britain discovered that platforms like international exhibitions, tabloid newspapers, music hall performances, motion pictures, and radio could arouse the emotions or stir the imaginations of the domestic citizenry (less so subjected peoples in the colonies) and serve as a plausible alterative to coercive force or stifling administration to meet the challenges of dissent. However, Britain learned these lessons slowly while many challengers of British power found that compelling words and images conveyed through these same technologies could also arouse sympathy for their resistance. By the time Britain had built a communications network that could penetrate deep enough into the collective consciousness of all the peoples of its empire, world war and racist colonial legacies ensured the empire's demise. The British experience, however, laid the foundation for new political agents to use new forms of media technology and spectacle to build new forms of empire.

Indeed, even before the end of World War II, the United States was already innovating new communications technologies and experimenting with novel forms of mass entertainment. During the Spanish-American War, audiences in major American cities first experienced the thrill of going to movies and seeing motion pictures projected onto a vertical surface. While the content of these early motion pictures tended to be pedestrian, the medium quickly evolved into a means of neutralizing the isolationist status quo of the American population and drumming up mass support for the deployment of American military force abroad. This newly discovered power increased in the years leading up to the outbreak of World War I with the blooming of a film production industry and then harnessed by the government in the form of the Committee on Public Information whose director, George Creel, conceptualized media platforms as weapons of war as important as rifles or artillery. Yet, questions remained about the true potency of information and entertainment as well as the best ways to manage and deploy it. The new and popular technologies of radio and sound cinema made substantial contributions to the Allied war effort, but debates over whether such platforms should be controlled by the state or left in the hands of the private sector prevented them from being used as effectively as they could. The debate was a tacit admission that while a consensus existed that the state had a right to use violent force when it deemed necessary, the soft power represented by mass media was too powerful to have a similar exclusive state prerogative. Soft power was becoming the new hard power.

Such debate subsided a bit in the aftermath of World War II, as an American state increasingly paranoid about the potential for communist expansion unleashed an avalanche of international radio programming against the Soviet Union and its allies in Europe. A similar effort took place domestically, with the new technology of television playing an integral part of the rise and fall of Joseph McCarthy and his anticommunist purges—an episode that demonstrated once again how the power of new media technologies was still poorly understood by those who sought to harness them. Yet, with nuclear weapons making open wars between the superpowers too risky, mass entertainment and spectacle served as an effective substitute for engaging the Soviet Union and showcasing the consumerist lifestyle. Few individuals of the time had a better grasp of the enormous potential of entertainment media than Walt Disney, whose input into the design and execution of the 1964 New York World's Fair showed how theme park–style amusement was an important part of the growth arsenal of entertainment.

As the various appendages of American power reached into more and more regions of the world, it became inevitable that the secret weapon of the rising American Empire would not only be discovered, but also deployed by those resisting American command. Within the United States, key members of the revolts of the 1960s, including Jerry Rubin and Abbie Hoffman, discovered ways of taking a media apparatus that was still heavily centralized and unidirectional and turning it against itself. Meanwhile, in Vietnam, North Vietnamese soldiers—quite by accident—showed how a few potent and well-timed images could change a military defeat into a symbolic victory. Perhaps no one suffered worse from a poor media image than Richard Nixon, whose resignation from office aroused the hatred and anger of many neoconservative politicians who blamed the demise of their president on a liberal-controlled media apparatus. Determined to take control of the battlefield of ideas, neoconservative politicians established an array of media platforms that sought to capture public opinion through content that was partisan, opinionated, and perhaps most importantly, entertaining. Their efforts contributed to the rise of Ronald Reagan, the neoliberal ideology, and an economic climate where vast sums of capital concentrated into a handful of banks and corporations. One consequence of this was media consolidation—the buying out and merging of global media companies into a few powerful entertainment behemoths that made engaging media content for a truly global audience. By the end of the Cold War, there were few communities on earth that could hide from the entertainment products of the American Empire and its surrogates.

Paradoxically, the moment when digital media is making the American Empire's soft power poised to seep into the last nooks and crannies of the global population is also the moment when the American Empire's grasp on this power appears to be at its most tenuous. The historical trends explored in this book suggest that the United States, the dominant corporate and financial institutions it protects, and the social classes that benefit from their operations, will likely muddle through the confusion and misunderstanding of digital media. Before long, dominance and command will return as those with the most to lose with the collapse of American power discover the best means to integrate and attach the platforms of digital media to the larger structure of political, economic, and cognitive power. Meanwhile, those who briefly felt the freedom of creative space and empowered to transform their surroundings through the capabilities of digital media devices and social networking platforms will slip back into a comfortable servitude and quiet despair associated with having thousands of Facebook "friends" but no meaningful interpersonal interaction.

However, this future is not certain. Contemporary developments like the Arab Spring and *indignado* movement in Europe suggest this integration will be problematic. With economic disparity and social unrest triggering a crisis of legitimacy among the fundamental assumptions of representative democracy and consumer capitalism throughout the world, the ability of entertainment to keep the masses pacified and content becomes increasingly difficult. Digital media, while certainly having the ability to perpetuate the soft power of the American Empire, can nevertheless go beyond mere entertainment and perhaps reorganize social relations. The ease with which digital media platforms and social networking capabilities can facilitate real world action means that communities will not be content with simply waiting for their media devices to amuse them and will instead use their hardware and software to bring about genuine change. Already, the world has witnessed how teams of engaged individuals can take down the websites of the powerful, organize occupations of public spaces, and expose the ugly side of contemporary imperial rule. By themselves, these events may seem inconsequential, but together they may be the first sprouts of a viable challenge to the American Empire that will set one of the tones of global politics for the rest of the twenty-first century.

Notes

Introduction   The American Empire and the Weaponization of Entertainment

1. The term "Facebook Revolution" can refer to any of the revolts that took place in the Middle East or Central Asia beginning with the Iranian uprisings of 2009, but Egypt tends to be the event most closely associated with the term. See Wael Ghonim, *Revolution 2.0: The Power of the People Is Greater than the People in Power* (New York: Houghton Mifflin Harcourt, 2012).
2. See Rahaf Harfoush, *Yes We Did: An Inside Look at How Social Media Built the Obama Brand* (Berkeley, CA: New Riders, 2009).
3. For more on these specific examples, see Paul Mason, *Why It's Kicking Off Everywhere: The New Global Revolutions* (New York: Verso, 2012).
4. While the idea of an American Empire has long been present in the critical literature of American foreign policy, it started to receive a positive analysis from more mainstream scholars at about the time of the invasion of Iraq. The most widely circulated of these newer works include Max Boot, "The Case for American Empire," *The Weekly Standard*, October 15, 2001; Niall Ferguson, *Colossus: The Price of America's Empire* (New York: Penguin Press, 2004); and Michael Ignatieff, *Empire Lite: Nation Building on Bosnia, Kosovo and Afghanistan* (New York: Random House, 2010). For a more rigorous academic treatment of the question, see Daniel H. Nexon and Thomas Wright, "What's at Stake in the American Empire Debate," *The American Political Science Review* 101, no. 2 (May 2007): 253–271.
5. Thucydides, *History of the Peloponnesian War*, Rex Warner, trans. (London: Penguin, 1972), 400–408.
6. For examples of states where governments have been toppled through some sort of American action, see Stephen Kinzer, *Overthrow: America's Century of Regime Change from Hawaii to Iraq* (New York: Times Books, 2006).
7. This theme is explored more deeply in John Mueller and Mark G. Stewart, *Terror Security and Money: Balancing the Risks, Benefits and Costs of Homeland Security* (New York: Oxford University Press, 2011); and Steven Pinker, *The Better Angels of Our Nature: Why Violence Has Declined* (New York: Penguin, 2011).
8. See Task Force on Inequality and American Democracy, *American Democracy in an Age of Rising Inequality* (American Political Science Association, 2004). http://www.apsanet.org/imgtest/taskforcereport.pdf.
9. According to Cox, clear understandings of the structures of power at the global level cannot be reduced to single variable like material capability, states and institutions, or the conviction of ideas. Rather, all three of these aspects of power mutually constitute an assemblage of command and authority that represents a harmony of social, political, and economic interests that come to define a particular era of

history or "historic bloc." These historic blocs, however, are constantly in a state of flux, as different formations of power representing the different sets of values and interests of different social groups and alliances of states struggle with each other for dominance until one emerges as triumphant. The measure of this victory is made by the ability of the prevailing interest group to control not only the political apparatus of the nation, but also the cultural, moral, and persuasive instruments of the nation as well. Victory at the international level emerges when this assemblage of power becomes internalized in the minds and imaginations of diverse subject communities in the form of a shared understanding of "common sense" or "conventional wisdom," even when this conventional wisdom in not in the interest of the specific communities. Once the conventional wisdom is established, recourse to coercive discipline is less frequent. See Antonio Gramsci, *Selections from the Prison Notebooks*, Quintin Hoare and Geoffrey Nowell Smith, eds. and trans. (New York: International Publishers, 1999), 258–276; and Robert Cox, "Gramsci, hegemony, and international relations: an essay in method," in Stephen Gill, ed., *Gramsci, Historical Materialism and International Relations* (Cambridge, UK: Cambridge University Press, 1993), 137–139.

10. This book does not attempt to explain why entertainment has the psychological effects that it does on the mind and the collective consciousness of an audience. The argument here focuses on the political consequences for these psychological effects. For more on the psychology of entertainment, see Dolf Zillmann and Peter Vorderer, eds. *Media Entertainment: The Psychology of Its Appeal* (Mahwah, NJ: Lawrence Erlbaum, 2000).

11. The theoretical assumptions being expressed here follow a substantial body of work by critical theorists who have been interested in the relationship between media and structures of power. These include Bertolt Brecht, *Brecht on Theater* (New York: Hill and Wang, 1964); Max Horkheimer and Theodor Adorno, *Dialectic of Enlightenment* (New York: Continuum, 2002); Paul A. Baran and Paul M. Sweezy, "The Quality of Monopoly Capitalist Society: Culture and Communications," *Monthly Review* 65, no. 3 (July–August 2013): 43–64; C. Wright Mills, "The Cultural Apparatus," in *The Politics of Truth* (New York: Oxford University Press, 2008), 203–212; and Robert W. McChesney, *The Political Economy of Media: Enduring Issues, Emerging Dilemmas* (New York: Monthly Review Press, 2008).

12. Herbert Marcuse called this inability to conceptualize better alternatives to the prevailing arrangement of power "one-dimensionality." Much of his analysis focused on the triumph of technical and instrumental rationality, though parts of his analysis incorporated discussions of media and communications. One aspect of the argument this book makes is to give entertainment media a larger role in bringing about this one-dimensionality. See Herbert Marcuse, *One-Dimensional Man* (Boston: Beacon Press, 1964).

13. In this interpretation, media triggers frenetic activity on the part of the audience, but only to emulate the images of lifestyle and celebrity. This usually entails a rush to purchase the various consumer goods associated with the desired lifestyle on display. See Guy Debord, *Society of the Spectacle*, Donald Nicholason-Smith, trans. (New York: Zone Books, 1999); and Benjamin Barber, *Consumed: How Markets Corrupt Children, Infantilize Adults, and Swallow Citizens Whole* (New York: W. W. Norton, 2007).

14. Joseph S. Nye, *Soft Power: The Means to Success in World Politics* (New York: Public Affairs, 2004).

15. Ibid., x.

16. Ibid., 6.

17. Ibid., 23–72.

18. Ibid., 31.
19. Ibid., 123–125.
20. Ibid., 137. For an analytically richer variation of this argument, see Jack Donnelly, "Sovereign Inequalities and Hierarchy in Anarchy: American Power and International Society," *European Journal of International Relations* 12, no. 2 (June 2006): 139–170.
21. George Creel, *How We Advertised America* (New York: Harper Brothers, 1920), 5.
22. The idea of *detournément* is first theorized in Debord, *Society of the Spectacle*, 129–148.

1   Legitimacy through Popular Entertainment: Bringing the British Empire to Life (1815–1945)

1. Myriad histories of the social and economic history of Europe exist, but this study builds its analysis from the three pivotal books written by Eric Hobsbawm: *The Age of Revolution: 1789–1848* (New York: Mentor, 1962); *The Age of Capital: 1848–1875* (New York: Vintage, 1976); and *The Age of Empire: 1875–1914* (New York: Pantheon, 1987).
2. This question was most famously posed by Elie Halévy, who used it as the basis for a six-volume study of English history. See Elie Halévy, *A History of the English People in the Nineteenth Century*, 6 vols. (London: E. Benn, 1952).
3. This was Halévy's thesis, expressed in volume one of *A History of the English People in the Nineteenth Century*, 514.
4. Emma Griffin, *Liberty's Dawn: A People's History of the Industrial Revolution* (New Haven, CT: Yale University Press, 2013).
5. Eric Hopkins, *Industrialization and Society: A Social History, 1830–1951* (New York: Routledge, 2000), 1–126.
6. See J. Crick and A. Walsham, eds., *The Uses of Script and Print. 1300–1700* (Cambridge, UK: Cambridge University Press, 2003); D. McKitterck, *Print, Manuscript, and the Search for Order, 1450–1830* (Cambridge, UK: Cambridge University Press, 2003); and Clementine Oliver, *Parliament and Political Pamphleteering in Fourteenth Century England* (Woodbridge, UK: Boydell and Brewer: 2010).
7. Adam Hochschild, *Bury the Chains: Prophets and Rebels in the Fight to Free an Empire's Slaves* (Boston: Houghton Mifflin, 2005), 3.
8. For a complete story on the public campaign to abolish the slave trade before 1807, see Hochschild, *Bury the Chains*.
9. William Wilberforce, speech before Parliament quoted in Stephen Tomkins, *William Wilberforce: A Biography* (Grand Rapids, MI: Wm. B. Eerdmans Publishing Company, 2007), 95.
10. James Walvin, "The Propaganda of Anti-Slavery," in James Walvin, ed., *Slavery and British Society, 1776–1846* (Baton Rouge: Louisiana State University Press, 1982), 60.
11. David Turley, *The Culture of English Antislavery 1780–1860* (London: Routledge, 1991), 48–49.
12. Alan Richard, "Slavery and Romantic Writing," in Duncan Wu, ed., *A Companion to Romanticism* (Oxford, UK: Blackwell, 1998), 463. Other noteworthy works included former slave Olaudah Equiano's autobiography *The Interesting Narrative of the Life of Olaudah Equiano, or Gustavus Vassa, the African*, Robert Southey's *Poems Concerning the Slave Trade*, Samuel Coleridge's poem *The Rime of the Ancient Marinere*, and James Montgomery's epic *The West Indies*.

13. Hochshild, *Bury the Chains*, 128–129.

14. Turley, *Culture of English Antislavery*, 48.

15. Marcus Wood, *Blind Memory: Visual Representations of Slavery in England and America 1780–1865* (New York: Routledge, 2000), 59–60.

16. Ibid., 48.

17. Anti-Slavery Society Minute Book quoted in Turley, *Culture of English Antislavery*, 48.

18. Turley, *Culture of English Antislavery*, 49.

19. Seymour Drescher, *Capitalism and Antislavery: British Mobilization in Comparative Perspective* (Oxford, UK: Oxford University Press, 1987), 156.

20. A few examples include Henry Vincent, William Lovett, John Collins, and Bronterre O'Brien. See Betty Fladeland, "Our Cause being One and the Same: Abolitionists and Chartism," in Walvin, *Slavery and British Society*, 92.

21. Thomas Buxton Howell, *The Slave Trade in Africa* (London: John Murray, 1839), 281–282.

22. Italics in the original. Ibid., 282.

23. Christopher Lloyd, *The Navy and the Slave Trade: The Suppression of the African Slave Trade in the Nineteenth Century* (London: Longmans, Green and Co., 1949), 12–23.

24. Ibid., 89–90.

25. In the case of Cuba, the number of slaves transported dropped from 40,000 in 1835 to 3,150. In the case of Brazil, the numbers dropped from 65,000 in 1836 to 14,200. These numbers represent only those individuals who survived transport and does not account for the countless thousands who were thrown overboard en route due to disease, dissent, or for insurance reasons. See Lloyd, *Navy and the Slave Trade*, 90.

26. Catherine Hall, *Civilizing Subjects: Metropole and Colony in the English Imagination 1830–1867* (Chicago: University of Chicago Press, 2002), 299.

27. *Missionary Herald*, October 1840, quoted in Hall, *Civilizing Subjects*, 332–333.

28. See, for example, Société française pour l'abolition d'esclavage, *No. 16. Banquet offert à la deputation de la Société central britannique pour l'abolition universelle d'esclavage, 10 fervier, 1840* (Paris: Hingray, 1840), 2–13.

29. Reverend Edward Bickersteth, "Memoirs from the Rev. Edward Bickersteth," *Edinburgh Christian Magazine* 3 (April 1851–March 1852): 306.

30. A small group of so-called anticoercionists, centered around radical abolitionists Josiah Sturge and William Hutt, advocated economic development in Africa as the antidote to the slave trade rather than deployments of military force. See Lloyd, *Navy and the Slave Trade*, 105–108.

31. Ronald Robinson, John Gallagher, and Alice Denny, *Africa and the Victorians: The Climax of Imperialism in the Dark Continent* (New York: St. Martin's Press, 1961), 29.

32. Chartism was a movement among the British working classes for the expansion of the right to vote and other basic political rights not extended to those who did not own property or could demonstrate substantial wealth or financial means. See Max Beer, *A History of British Socialism* (Manchester, NH: Ayer, 1979).

33. The Corn Laws were tariffs Great Britain placed on the importation of foodstuffs from Europe that kept the price of food artificially high. Amid the poverty and depravation of the 1830s and 1840s, many advocates of free trade (as well as some working-class Chartists) insisted that these social problems could be solved with the repeal of these laws. See Justin McCarthy, *The Epoch of Reform: 1830–1850* (London: Longmans, Green, and Co., 1882).

34. Jeffrey A. Auerbach, *The Great Exhibition of 1851: A Nation on Display* (New Haven, CT: Yale University Press, 1999), 10–14.

35. Yvonne Ffrench, *The Great Exhibition: 1851* (London: Harvill Press, 1950), 9–12.

36. Prince Albert quoted in Ffrench, *Great Exhibition*, 22.

37. The term "Crystal Palace" was originally a term of subtle mockery used in an article about the Great Exhibition in *Punch*. See Marion Harry Spielman, *The History of "Punch"* (London: Cassell, 1895), 84.

38. Thomas Richards, *The Commodity Culture of Victorian England: Advertising and Spectacle, 1851–1914* (Stanford, CA: Stanford University Press, 1990), 22.

39. Patrick Howarth, *The Year Is 1851* (London: Collins, 1951), 220.

40. Richards, *Commodity Culture of Victorian England*, 23.

41. The sheer volume of material on display was astounding. For a complete list of everything exhibited, see *Great Exhibition of the Works of Industry of All Nations: Official and Illustrated Catalogue* (London: Spicer Brothers, 1851).

42. Richards, *Commodity Culture of Victorian England*, 25.

43. Auerbach, *Great Exhibition of 1851*, 165.

44. "The Exhibition—The Crystal Palace," *The Economist*, May 10, 1851. See also Richards, *Commodity Culture of Victorian England*, 29.

45. "The Opening of the Great Exhibition," *The Times*, May 2, 1851; and Auerbach, *Great Exhibition of 1851*, 1.

46. This view reflected the foreign policy of Lord Palmerston, who was prime minister at the time of the Great Exhibition. See Martin Kingsley, *The Triumph of Lord Palmerston: A Study of Public Opinion in England before the Crimean War* (London: G. Allen and Unwin Ltd., 1924).

47. Auerbach, *Great Exhibition of 1851*, 112–113.

48. Richards, *Commodity Culture of Victorian England*, 33.

49. Auerbach, *Great Exhibition of 1851*, 167.

50. *The Times*, commenting on the variety of social and political perspectives represented at the exhibition suggested the event was planned with "perfect impartiality," and that "every shade of political opinion in the country, and every great interest in the State," was represented and that "Protectionism, the Peerage, the commonality, science, art, (and) the East India Company" all had their voices heard. See Auerbach, *Great Exhibition of 1851*, 29.

51. Auerbach, *Great Exhibition of 1851*, 165.

52. This point is discussed more fully in Robinson, Gallagher, and Denny, *Africa and the Victorians*.

53. Hannah Arendt referred to this group as "the mob," and she interpreted it as an important point in the eventual development of totalitarianism in Europe. See Hannah Arendt, *The Origins of Totalitarianism* (Orlando, FL: Harcourt, 1976), 123–304.

54. For more on the Indian Revolt and its effect on British society, see Christopher Herbert, *War of No Pity: The Indian Mutiny and Victorian Trauma* (Princeton, NJ: Princeton University Press, 2008).

55. Peter Harrington, "Images and Perceptions: Visualizing the Sudan Campaign," in Edward M. Spiers, ed. *Sudan: The Reconquest Reappraised* (London: Frank Cass, 1998), 83.

56. Kevin Williams, *Get Me a Murder a Day!: A History of Mass Communication in Britain* (London: Arnold, 1998), 49–50.

57. Jane Chapman, *Comparative Media History: An Introduction 1789 to the Present* (Malden, MA: Polity, 2005), 39.

58. Raymond L. Schults, *Crusader in Babylon: W.T. Stead and the* Pall Mall Gazette (Lincoln: University of Nebraska Press, 1972), 60.
59. W. T. Stead, "Government by Journalism," *Contemporary Review* 49 (January/June 1886): 653.
60. Ibid.
61. Ezekiel 33:3–4 quoted in Stead, "Government by Journalism," 667–668.
62. Stead, "Government by Journalism," 671.
63. Williams, *Get Me a Murder a Day!*, 49–50.
64. On Stead's affinity for interviews, see Schults, *Crusader in Babylon*, 83–87.
65. See *History of* The Times, 23–24.
66. Schults, *Crusader in Babylon*, 70.
67. Ibid.
68. "The Catastrophe in the Soudan" *Pall Mall Gazette*, November 22, 1883. Also see Schults, *Crusader in Babylon*, 69.
69. Schults, *Crusader in Babylon*, 71.
70. "Chinese Gordon for the Congo," *Pall Mall Gazette*, January 5, 1884. See also Schults, *Crusader in Babylon*, 71.
71. "Chinese Gordon on the Soudan," *Pall Mall Gazette*, January 9, 1884. See also Schults, *Crusader in Babylon*, 72.
72. Schults, *Crusader in Babylon*, 74–75.
73. Ibid., 76.
74. "General Gordon's Mission to the Soudan," *Pall Mall Gazette*, January 19, 1884. See also Schults, *Crusader in Babylon*, 76.
75. Chapman, *Comparative Media History*, 77–78.
76. See Sigmund Freud, "Civilization and Its Discontents," in Peter Gay ed., *The Freud Reader* (New York: W. W. Norton, 1995), 751–753; and Hans Morgenthau, *Politics among Nations* (New York: Knopf, 1954), 93–101.
77. J. A. Hobson, *The Psychology of Jingoism* (London: Grant Richards, 1901), 9.
78. J. A. Hobson, *Imperialism: A Study* (Ann Arbor: University of Michigan Press, 1965), 215.
79. Ibid., 48.
80. F. Verschoyle, *Cecil Rhodes: His Political Life and Speeches: 1881–1900* (London: Chapman and Hall, 1900), 7.
81. Johannes Stephanus Marais, *The Fall of Kruger's Republic* (Oxford, UK: Clarendon Press, 1961), 318.
82. Penny Summerfield, "Patriotism and Empire: Music Hall Entertainment 1870–1914," in John MacKenzie, ed., *Imperialism and Popular Culture* (Manchester, UK: University of Manchester Press, 1986), 22.
83. John MacKenzie, *Propaganda and Imperialism:The Manipulation of British Public Opinion, 1880–1960* (Manchester, UK: University of Manchester Press, 1984), 40.
84. Hobson, *Psychology of Jingoism*, 4.
85. Ibid., 3.
86. Steve Attridge, *Nationalism, Imperialism, and Identity in Late-Victorian Culture: Civil and Military Worlds* (Basingstoke, UK: Palgrave, 2003), 23.
87. Ibid., 23.
88. Ibid., 27.
89. Donal Lowry, ed., *The South African War Reappraised* (Manchester, UK: University of Manchester Press, 2000), 1.
90. Letter from Milner to Schreiner, December 8, 1898. See also Denis Judd and Keith Surridge, *The Boer War* (London: John Murrary, 2002), 44.
91. George Sturt, *The Journals of George Sturt, 1890–1927* (Cambridge, UK: Cambridge University Press, 1967), 302.

92. Quoted in Paul Ward, *Red Flag and Union Jack: Englishness, Patriotism, and the British Left 1881–1924* (Woodbridge, Sufflolk, UK: Boydell Press, 1998), 59.

93. Leslie Stephen, *Selected Letters of Leslie Stephen: Volume I, 1864–1882* (Columbus: University of Ohio Press, 1996), 509.

94. Paula M. Krebs, *Gender, Race, and the Writing of Empire: Public Discourse and the Boer War* (Cambridge, UK: Cambridge University Press), 14.

95. William E. Carson, *Northcliffe: Britain's Man of Power* (New York: Dodge Publishing, 1918), 154.

96. Jacqueline Beaumont, "The British Press during the South African War," in Mark Connelly and David Welch, eds., *War and Media: Reportage and Propaganda, 1900–2003* (London: I. B. Tauris, 2005), 11.

97. See Antonio Gramsci, *Selections from the Prison Notebooks*, Quintin Hoare and Geoffrey Nowell Smith, eds. and trans. (New York: International Publishers, 1999), 277–318; and Robert Cox, *Production, Power and World Order: Social Forces in the Making of History* (New York: Columbia University Press, 1987), 211–273.

98. Paul Kennedy, *The Rise and Fall of the Great Powers: Economic Change and Military Conflict from 1500 to 2000* (New York: Vintage, 1987), 198–202.

99. Andrew S. Thompson, *Imperial Britain: The Empire in British Politics, c. 1880–1932* (Harlow, UK: Longman, 2000), 158.

100. Philip M. Taylor, *British Propaganda in the 20th Century: Selling Democracy* (Edinburgh, UK: Edinburgh University Press, 1999), 38.

101. Ibid.

102. Upton Sinclair quoted in Taylor, *British Propaganda in the 20th Century*, 44.

103. Taylor, *British Propaganda in the 20th Century*, 43–46.

104. Ibid.

105. Ibid.

106. R. W. Setson-Watson quoted in A. J. May, *The Passing of the Habsburg Monarchy 1914–18*, 2 vols. (Philadelphia: University of Pennsylvania Press, 1966), vol. 2, 605.

107. Taylor, *British Propaganda in the 20th Century*, 56–57.

108. Ibid., 58.

109. For this and other examples of Irish counterpropaganda, see Ben Novick, *Conceiving Revolution: Irish Nationalist Propaganda during the First World War* (Portland, OR: Four Courts Press, 2001), 72–102.

110. Ibid.

111. Ibid., 210.

112. Thomas Fleming, *The Illusion of Victory: America in World War I* (New York: Basic Books, 2003), 63.

113. In the case of Australia and New Zealand, see Eric Montgomery Andrews, *The ANZAC Illusion: Anglo-Australian Relations during World War I* (Cambridge, UK: Cambridge University Press, 1993), 126.

114. Jacquie L'Etang, *Public Relations in Britain: A History of Professional Practice in the Twentieth Century* (New York: Routledge, 2004), 32.

115. Mariel Grant, *Propaganda and the Role of the State in Inter-war Britain* (Oxford, UK: Clarendon Press, 1994), 18. The rise of public relations is discussed more deeply in the next chapter.

116. Ibid., 17.

117. Grierson quoted in Grant, *Propaganda and the Role of the State*, 17.

118. L'Etang, *Public Relations in Britain*, 33.

119. Ibid.

120. Anandi Ramamurthy, *Imperial Persuaders: Images of Africa and Asia in British Advertising* (Manchester, UK: Manchester University Press, 2003), 133–134.

121. Ibid.

122. Grant, *Propaganda and the Role of the State*, 18.
123. John MacKenzie, ed., *Imperialism and Popular Culture* (Manchester, UK: University of Manchester Press, 1986), 209.
124. Ibid.
125. Ibid., 218.
126. Eric Louw, *The Media and Political Process* (Los Angeles: Sage, 2010), 122.
127. Ibid.
128. Ibid.
129. Taylor, *British Propaganda in the Twentieth Century*, 76–78.
130. Winston Churchill, "Civilization: An Address to the University of Bristol, July 2, 1938," in Winston Churchill and Randolph Churchill, *Blood, Sweat and Tears* (Camden, NJ: Haddon Craftsmen, 1941), 46.
131. Lord Windelsham, *Broadcasting in a Free Society* (London: Blackwell, 1980).
132. Regarding the potential for the popularization of radio, Reith said, "To have exploited so great a scientific invention for the purpose and pursuit of entertainment alone would have been a prostitution of its powers and an insult to the character and intelligence of the people." See John Reith, quoted in Windelsham, *Broadcasting in a Free Society*, 17.
133. John Reith quoted in Williams, *Get Me a Murder a Day!*, 94.
134. Williams, *Get Me a Murder a Day!*, 94–95.
135. John MacKenzie, "In Touch with the Infinite: The BBC and the Empire," in *Imperialism and Popular Culture*, 186.
136. Ibid., 167–168 and 180.
137. Ibid., 175.
138. Taylor, *British Propaganda in the 20th Century*, 98–99.
139. Nicholas John Cull, *Selling the War: The British Propaganda Campaign against American "Neutrality" in World War II* (New York: Oxford, 1995), 136–137.
140. Burton Paulu, *British Broadcasting* (Minneapolis, MN: Jones Press, 1956), 392.
141. M. A. Doherty, *Nazi Wireless Propaganda: Lord Haw-Haw and British Public Opinion in the Second World War* (Edinburgh, UK: Edinburgh University Press, 2000), 101–102.
142. See Cull, *Selling the War*, 136.
143. For further elaborations on the nature of "black propaganda," see Garth S. Jowett and Vitoria O'Donnell, *Propaganda and Persuasion*, 3rd ed. (Thousand Oaks, CA: Sage, 1999).
144. Eric Barnouw, *Media Lost and Found* (New York: Fordham University Press, 2001), 109.
145. Taylor, *British Propaganda in the Twentieth Century*, 129.
146. Ibid., 131.
147. Ibid., 132–133.
148. Cull, *Selling the War*, 136.
149. Dwight Eisenhower quoted in Frederick Taylor, "Breaking the German Will to Resist: Allied Efforts to End the Second World War in Europe by Non-Military Means, 1944–45," *The Historical Journal of Film, Radio and Television* 18, no. 1 (1998): 5.

2 Overcoming Isolationism: Film, Radio, and the Rise of the American Empire (1898–1945)

1. Frederick Taylor, "Breaking the German Will to Resist: Allied Efforts to End the Second World War in Europe by Non-Military Means, 1944–45," *The Historical Journal of Film, Radio and Television* 18, no. 1 (1998): 5.

2. Both Fiske and Strong were social Darwinists who argued the United States must survive by expanding. See John Fiske, *American Political Ideas Viewed from the Standpoint of Universal History* (New York: Harper and Brothers, 1885), 101–152; and Josiah Strong, *Our Country: Its Possible Future and Its Present Crisis* (New York: Baker and Taylor, 1891), 208–227. Burgess gave a primarily racial defense of American imperialism by arguing Anglo-Saxons had a "superior national character," which made them best suited for political rule. See John W. Burgess, *Political Science and Comparative Constitutional Law* (Boston: Ginn and Company, 1890–1891), I, 30–39. Alfred T. Mahan gave the most practical expression of a vision of American empire in his book *The Influence of Sea Power upon History* wherein he argued that the prosperity and wealth of all the great civilizations in human history required great navies of global reach to protect the nation's interests. See *The Influence of Sea Power upon History, 1660–1783* (Boston: Little, Brown and Company 1890), 35–90.

3. Ray Phillips, *Edison's Kinetoscope and Its Films: A History to 1896* (Westport, CT: Greenwood Press, 1997).

4. Douglas Gomery, *Shared Pleasures: A History of Movie Presentation in the United States* (Madison: University of Wisconsin Press, 1992), 13–17.

5. David W. Griffith, "Motion Pictures as a Means of Foreign Advertising," *Compressed Air* 24, no. 9 (1919): 9331.

6. Gerald Linderman, *The Mirror of War: American Society and the Spanish-American War* (Ann Arbor: University of Michigan Press, 1974), 1–8.

7. Walter LaFeber, *The New Empire: An Interpretation of American Expansion* (Ithaca, NY: Cornell University Press, 1963), 7–16.

8. Ibid., 36.

9. John Fiske, "Manifest Destiny," *Harper's New Monthly Magazine* LXX, 578–590. A thorough review of all major expansionist publications prior to the Spanish-American War can be found in Julius W. Pratt, *Expansionists of 1898* (Chicago: Quadrangle, 1936), 1–33.

10. Pratt, *Expansionists*, 21. All of Mahan's periodical essays appear in two volumes: *The Interests of America in Sea Power, Present and Future* (Boston: Little, Brown and Company, 1897); and *Lessons of the War with Spain, and Other Articles* (Boston: Little, Brown and Company, 1899).

11. Pratt, *Expansionists*, 279–316.

12. See Marcus M. Wilkerson, *Public Opinion and the Spanish-American War: A Study in War Propaganda* (Baton Rouge: Louisiana State University Press, 1932); and Joseph E. Wisan, *The Cuban Crisis as Reflected in the New York Press, 1895–1898* (New York: Octagon, 1965).

13. Wilkerson includes many samples of this reporting, which was often as sensationalistic as it was fabricated. James Creelman, a correspondent for the *World*, gives a rather juicy example when he writes, "The horrors of a barbarous struggle for the extermination of the native population are witnessed in all parts of the country. Blood on the roadsides, blood in the fields, blood on the doorsteps, blood, blood, blood! The old, the young, the weak, the cripple—all are butchered without mercy." See Wilkerson, *Public Opinion and the Spanish-American War*, 32.

14. Ibid., 6.

15. Pratt, *Expansionists*, 244–278.

16. Ibid., 247 and 274.

17. See Stuart Creighton Miller, *Benevolent Assimilation: The American Conquest of the Philippines, 1899–1903* (New Haven, CT: Yale University Press, 1982).

18. Stratemeyer was a big admirer of Theodore Roosevelt and his belief that "time spent in the military—ideally, during war—was perhaps the ultimate making of a man, and his love of soldiering is echoed in Stratemeyer's works." See Diedre

Johnson, *Edward Stratemeyer and the Stratemeyer Syndicate* (New York: Twayne Publishers, 1993), 68.

19. Ibid., 70–71.
20. Pat Hodgson, *The War Illustrators* (New York: Macmillan, 1977), 178–180.
21. Ibid., 28. Remington's most famous painting in this regard is titled *The Charge of the Rough Riders at San Juan Hill, 1 July 1898* and features the depiction of Theodore Roosevelt on horseback leading a band of American soldiers into battle.
22. Hodgson, *The War Illustrators*, 29 and 181–182.
23. W. K. McNeil, "We'll Make the Spanish Grunt: Popular Songs about the Sinking of the *Maine*," *Journal of Popular Culture* 2 (1968): 543.
24. For examples, see Horace S. Fiske, *The Ballad of Manila Bay and Other Verses* (Chicago: University of Chicago Press, 1900); and George Ade, *The Sultan of Sulu* (New York: R. H. Russell, 1903).
25. David Martin Reynolds, *Masters of American Sculpture: The Figurative Tradition from the American Renaissance to the Millennium* (New York: Abbeville Press, 1993), 154.
26. Charles Musser, "The American Vitagraph, 1897–1901: Survival and Success in a Competitive Industry," in John L. Fell, ed., *Film before Griffith* (Berkeley: University of California Press, 1983), 22–29.
27. Ibid., 29.
28. Raymond Fielding, *The American Newsreel 1911–1967* (Norman: University of Oklahoma Press, 1972), 2.
29. Louis Pizzitola, *Hearst over Hollywood: Power, Passion and Propaganda in the Movies* (New York: Columbia University Press: 2002), 67.
30. Fielding, *American Newsreel*, 29–30.
31. Pizzitola, *Hearst over Hollywood*, 67.
32. Regarding the role of the Rendon Group in the liberation of Kuwait, see Franklin Foer, "Flacks Americana: John Rendon's Shallow PR War on Terrorism," *The New Republic*, May 20, 2002. Regarding the orchestrated nature of the toppling of the statue of Saddam Hussein, see Peter Maass, "The Toppling," *The New Yorker*, January 10, 2011.
33. Musser, in Fell, "The American Vitagraph, 1897–1901," *Film before Griffith*, 32.
34. Library of Congress, "'Remembering the *Maine*'—The Beginnings of War," http://memory.loc.gov/ammem/sawhtml/sawsp2.html.
35. Patrick Loughney, "Movies and Entrepreneurs," in Andre Gauderault, ed., *American Cinema 1890–1909: Themes and Variations* (Piscataway, NJ: Rutgers University Press, 2009), 82.
36. Bonnie M. Miller, *From Liberation to Conquest: The Visual and Popular Cultures of the Spanish-American War of 1898* (Amherst: University of Massachusetts Press, 2011), 116.
37. Library of Congress.
38. Ibid.
39. Loughney, "Movies and Entrepreneurs," 84.
40. *New York World* quoted in Charles Musser, *The Emergence of Cinema: The American Screen up to 1907* (Berkeley: University of California Press, 1990), 241.
41. "Enthusiasm at the Theatres," *New York Tribune*, February 25, 1898.
42. Ibid.
43. Deposition of Albert E. Smith, April 9, 1900, equity no. 6990, 6991, US Circuit Court, Southern District Court of New York, Federal Archive and Record Center, Bayonne, New Jersey, 1. See also Musser in Fell, "The American Vitagraph, 1897–1901," *Film before Griffith*, 28–29.

44. Andre Gaudreault and Tom Gunning, "American Cinema Emerges," in Andre Gaudreault, ed., *American Cinema 1890–1909: Themes and Variations* (Piscataway, NJ: Rutgers University Press, 2009), 11.
45. Jacqueline Najuma Stewart, *Migrating to the Movies: Cinema and Black Urban Modernity* (Berkeley: University of California Press, 2005), 301.
46. Frank Ninkovich, *The United States and Imperialism* (Malden, MA: Blackwell, 2001), 103.
47. Mark Kurlansky, *Nonviolence: The History of a Dangerous Idea* (New York: Random House, 2009), 117.
48. Rodney Ross, "Anti-Imperialist League," in Martin J. Manning and Clarence R. Vyatt, eds., *Encyclopedia of Media and Propaganda in Wartime American*, 2 vols. (Santa Barbara, CA: ABC-CLIO, 2011), 390.
49. The story of American efforts in the Caribbean Sea after the Spanish-American War can be found in Ninkovich, *The United States and Imperialism*, 91–152.
50. A good general study of the American counterinsurgency effort in the Philippines can be found in Miller, *Benevolent Assimilation*.
51. Miller, *Benevolent Assimilation*, 196–215; and Ninkovich, *The United States and Imperialism*, 48–90.
52. See Musser, *Emergence of Cinema*, 337–370.
53. Theodore Roosevelt's thoughts on pre–World War I preparedness can be found in the compilation *For God and Take Your Own Part* (New York: George H. Doran Company, 1916). For a full overview of the preparedness movement, see John Patrick Finnegan, *Against the Specter of a Dragon: The Campaign for American Military Preparedness, 1914–1917* (Westport, CT: Greenwood Press, 1974).
54. See LaFeber, *New Empire*, 7–16.
55. Lewis Jacobs, *The Rise of American Film: A Critical History* (New York: Harcourt, Brace and Company, 1939), 85.
56. Ibid.
57. Ibid., 52–62.
58. Ibid., 55.
59. Jack C. Ellis, *A History of Film* (Englewood Cliffs, NJ: Prentice Hall, 1979), 41–44.
60. Jacobs, *Rise of American Film*, 43–46.
61. Benjamin B. Hampton, *History of the American Film Industry from Its Beginning to 1931* (New York: Dover, 1970), 85–86.
62. Ibid., 86–89.
63. Jacobs, *Rise of American Film*, 159.
64. Ibid.
65. For a complete overview of World War I films, see Gerald Herman, "The Great War Revisioned: A World War I Filmography," in Peter C. Collins and John E. O'Connor, eds., *Hollywood's World War I: Motion Picture Images* (Bowling Green, OH: Bowling Green State University Popular Press, 1997), 245–282.
66. Larry Wayne Ward, *The Motion Picture Goes to War: The U.S. Government Film Effort during World War I* (Ann Arbor, MI: UMI Research Press, 1985), 36.
67. Herman, "The Great War Revisioned," 249.
68. Douglas Gomery and Clara Pafort-Overduin, *Movie History: A Survey*, 2nd ed. (New York: Routledge, 1991), 74.
69. Ibid.
70. Emily Rosenberg, *Spreading the American Dream: American Economic and Cultural Expansion 1890–1945* (New York: Hill and Wang, 1982), 100–101.
71. *Birth of a Nation*, directed by David W. Griffith (1915; Los Angeles: Image Entertainment, 2002), DVD.

72. Jacobs, *Rise of American Film*, 174.
73. Mark Sachleben and Kevan M. Yenerall, *Seeing the Bigger Picture: Understanding Politics through Film and Television* (New York: Peter Lang, 2004), 125–126. The lines quoted in the film are, "Adventurers swarmed out of the North, as much enemies of the one race as of the other, to cozen, beguile, and use the negroes...In the villages the negroes were the office holders, men who knew none of the uses of authority, except its insolences. The policy of the congressional leaders wrought...a veritable overthrow of civilization in the South...in their determination to put the white South under the heel of the black South. The white men were roused by a mere instinct of self-preservation...until at last there had sprung into existence a great Ku Klux Klan, a veritable empire of the South, to protect the Southern country."
74. Ibid., 125.
75. Ibid.
76. Gerald Wood, "From *The Clansman* and *Birth of a Nation* to *Gone with the Wind*: The Loss of American Innocence," in Darden Asbury Pyron, ed., *Recasting: Gone with the Wind in American Culture* (Miami: University Presses of Florida, 1983) 124–125.
77. Catherine Squires, "Black Audiences, Past and Present: Commonsense Media Critics and Activists," Robin R. Means Coleman, ed., *Say It Loud!: African American Audiences, Media and Identity* (New York: Routledge, 2002), 51. Interestingly enough, reception of the film was quite positive, especially in Great Britain. See Michael Hammond, "'A Soul-Stirring Appeal to Every Briton': The Reception of *Birth of a Nation* in Britain," *Film History* 11, no. 3 (1999): 353–370.
78. George Creel, *How We Advertised America* (New York: Harper and Brothers, 1920), 5.
79. Ibid.
80. Ibid., 3.
81. Ibid., 5.
82. Ibid., 73.
83. Ibid., 17.
84. Ibid., 3; and Stephen Vaughn, *Holding Fast the Inner Lines: Democracy, Nationalism, and the Committee on Public Information* (Chapel Hill: University of North Carolina Press, 1980), 141.
85. Barbara Jones and Bill Howell, *Popular Arts and the First World War* (New York: McGraw-Hill, 1972), 7.
86. See Conclusion.
87. James R. Mock and Cedric Larson, *Words That Won the War: The Story of the Committee on Public Information 1917–1919* (New York: Russell and Russell, 1939), 77.
88. Vaughn, *Holding Fast the Inner Lines*, 200.
89. Creel, *How We Advertised America*, 146.
90. Ibid.
91. Ibid.
92. Ibid., 150.
93. Ibid., 85.
94. Ibid., 93.
95. Ibid., 94. Italics in the original.
96. Ibid., 160–165 and 223–226; and Vaughn, *Holding Fast the Inner Lines*, 201.
97. Creel, *How We Advertised America*, 281.
98. Ibid., 117.
99. Ibid., 271.

100. Ibid., 275. Italics are mine.
101. Ibid., 277.
102. See Ernest R. May, *The World War and American Isolation, 1914–1917* (Chicago: Quadrangle, 1959).
103. See Bertrand Russell, *Free Thought and Official Propaganda,* (New York: B. W. Huebsch, 1922); Harold D. Lasswell, *Propaganda Technique in World War I* (Cambridge, MA: MIT Press, 1927); and José Ortega y Gasset, *The Revolt of the Masses* (New York: Norton, 1960).
104. Mariel Grant, *Propaganda and the Role of the State in Inter-war Britain* (Oxford, UK: Clarendon Press, 1994), 16.
105. Creel wrote an extended appendix to his book that addresses these accusations. See Creel, *How We Advertised America*, 445–454.
106. Alan Axelrod, *Selling the Great War: The Making of American Propaganda* (New York: Palgrave Macmillan, 2009), 211–226.
107. Grierson quoted in Grant, *Propaganda and the Role of the State*, 17–18.
108. Stuart Ewen, *PR!: A Social History of Spin* (New York: Basic Books, 1996), 3–4.
109. Edward Bernays, *Propaganda* (Brooklyn, NY: IG Publishing, 2005), 164–165.
110. Ibid., 166.
111. Ibid.
112. See note 1.
113. Eric Hobsbawm, *The Age of Extremes: A History of the World, 1914–1991* (New York: Vintage, 1994), 87–100.
114. On John Reith's view of radio in British society, see Lord Windelsham, *Broadcasting in a Free Society* (London: Blackwell, 1980), 17.
115. Edward Berkowitz, *Mass Appeal: The Formative Age of the Movies, Radio and TV* (Cambridge, UK: Cambridge University Press: 2010), 42.
116. Ibid., 45.
117. Ibid., 43–45.
118. H. W. Heinsheimer, "Music and the American Radio," *Tempo* 3 (March 1947): 10–14.
119. Berkowitz, *Mass Appeal*, 44–56.
120. William C. Ackerman, "The Dimensions of American Radio Broadcasting," *The Public Opinion Quarterly* 9 (Spring 1945): 9.
121. Franklin Roosevelt quoted in Robert J. Brown, *Manipulating the Ether: The Power of Broadcast Radio in Thirties America* (Jefferson, NC: McFarland and Company, 1999), 9.
122. For an analysis of the effectiveness of Roosevelt's fireside chats, see Ibid., 57–74.
123. Berkowitz, *Mass Appeal*, 45.
124. This debate on the virtues of OWI was most prominently visible in the organization's leadership. Its first director, the famed poet Arthur Macleish, saw the OWI as an organ promoting not only national cohesion, but also an optimistic view of a postwar future under the tenets of the Atlantic Charter and President Franklin Roosevelt's "four freedoms" speech. MacLeish's rival at the OWI, Milton Eisenhower, however, referenced the boisterousness of Creel's CPI propaganda and insisted the OWI be little more than a neutral clearinghouse of war-related news and information. A middle ground was forged with limited success, and the agency eventually took responsibility for coordinating the messages and media put forth by mostly private producers of content. The OWI produced no original content of its own and was thus a much less potent organization then Creel's CPI. The debates surrounding the creation and authorization for the OWI can be found in Allan M. Winkler, *The Politics of Propaganda: The Office of War*

Information 1942–1945 (New Haven, CT: Yale University Press, 1978), 39–43; and Betty Houchin Winfield, FDR and the News Media (New York: Columbia University Press, 1994).

125. Many elites in the private sector were irritated that the government seemed to be taking a standoff approach to information management and demanded the government become more active in putting out nationalist propaganda. See Clayton D. Laurie, The Propaganda Warriors: America's Crusade against Nazi Germany (Lawrence: University Press of Kansas, 1996), 29.

126. Gerd Horten, Radio Goes to War: The Cultural Politics of Propaganda During World War II (Berkeley: University of California Press), 1.

127. Ibid.

128. Alexander Russo, "A Dark(ened) Figure on the Airwaves: Race, Nation, and The Green Hornet," in Michele Hilmes and Jason Loviglio, eds., Radio Reader (New York: Routledge, 2002), 257–276; and Horten, Radio Goes to War, 44–48.

129. Ibid., 63.

130. Rosenberg, Spreading the American Dream, 208.

131. Rockefeller insisted the OIAA be autonomous from the OWI. See Rosenberg, Spreading the American Dream, 209.

132. Laurie, Propaganda Warriors, 213.

133. This total was still less than the British Broadcasting Company, who was able to out-broadcast the United States and the Soviet Union combined. Rosenberg, Spreading the American Dream, 211.

134. A fuller discussion of the homogenizing trend in international cinema brought about by sound technologies can be found in Charles O'Brien, Cinema's Conversion to Sound: Technology and Film Style in France and the U.S. (Bloomington: University of Indiana Press, 2005), 17–43.

135. For a full discussion of the star power of the 1930s and 1940s, see Berkowitz, Mass Appeal, 57–75.

136. Berkowitz, Mass Appeal, 20–21.

137. Robert Fyne, The Hollywood Propaganda of Word War II (Metuchen, NJ: Scarecrow Press, 1994), 15.

138. Clayton R. Koppes and Gregory D. Black, Hollywood Goes to War: How Politics, Profits, and Propaganda Shaped World War II Movies (New York: The Free Press, 1987), 25–37.

139. Ibid., 32.

140. Lawrence H. Suid, Guts and Glory: The Making of the American Military Image in Film (Lexington: University Press of Kentucky, 2002), 634.

141. For more on the film, see Aljean Harmetz, The Making of Casablanca: Bogart, Bergman and World War II (New York: Hyperion, 2002); and Howard Kock, Casablanca: Script and Legend (New York: Overlook, 1973).

142. Charles Roetter, The Art of Psychological Warfare: 1914–1945 (New York: Stein and Day, 1974), 131.

143. Winkler, Politics of Propaganda, 80–90.

144. Ibid., 80.

145. Ibid., 115.

146. Ibid., 209–210.

3 Spreading Liberalism: Broadcasting, Consumerism, and the Maturity of the American Empire (1945–1968)

1. The conception of postwar international institutions being a component of American dominance has long been argued by historical materialist scholars of

international politics. See Robert Cox, *Production, Power, and World Order: Social Forces in the Making of History* (New York: Columbia University Press, 1987), 253–263. More recently, some more conservative scholars have offered a similar position. See Niall Ferguson, *Colossus: The Price of America's Empire* (New York: Penguin, 2004), 132–167.

2. Frederick Taylor, "Breaking the German Will to Resist: Allied Efforts to End the Second World War in Europe by Non-Military Means, 1944–45," *The Historical Journal of Film, Radio and Television* 18, no. 1 (1998): 5.

3. Cox, *Production, Power, and World Order*, 130–139.

4. Robert Dahl and Charles Lindblom, *Politics, Economy, and Welfare: Planning and Politico-Economic Systems Resolved in Basic Social Processes* (New York: Harper, 1953).

5. Cox, *Production, Power, and World Order*, 220.

6. George Kennan, "Long Telegram" quoted in Jussi Hanhimäki and Odd Arne Westad, *The Cold War: A History in Documents and Eyewitness Accounts* (Oxford, UK: Oxford University Press, 2003), 110.

7. Ibid., 111.

8. Ibid.

9. Laura A. Belmonte, *Selling the American Way: U.S. Propaganda and the Cold War* (Philadelphia: University of Pennsylvania, 2008), 16.

10. George Marshall, speech at Harvard University, June 7, 1947, quoted in Hanhimäki and Westad, *Cold War*, 121–122.

11. Belmonte, *Selling the American Way*, 29.

12. Report by the Committee on Foreign Affairs, *The United States Information Service in Europe*, 80th Congress, 2nd session, 1948, 1–23.

13. For the distinction between informational diplomacy and cultural diplomacy, see Frank Ninkovich, *The Diplomacy of Ideas: US Foreign Policy and Cultural Relations 1938–1950* (Cambridge, UK: Cambridge University Press, 1981), 113–139.

14. Ambassador Walter Smith to William Benton, February 18, 1947, *Foreign Relations of the United States, 1947*, 4:534.

15. Philip M. Taylor, *British Propaganda in the 20th Century: Selling Democracy* (Edinburgh, UK: Edinburgh University Press, 1999), 129–133.

16. David F. Krugler, *The Voice of America and the Domestic Propaganda Battles, 1945–1953* (Columbia: University of Missouri Press, 2000), 1

17. Ibid., 12.

18. Ambassador Walter Smith to William Benton, *Foreign Relations of the United States*, 533–534.

19. Belmonte, *Selling the American Way*, 23. See also "U.S. to Liven Broadcasts to Russia with Jazz Tunes and More News," *New York Times*, February 27, 1947.

20. Elena I. Bashkirova, "The Foreign Radio Audience in the USSR during the Cold War: An Internal Perspective," in A. Ross Johnson and R. Eugene Parta, eds., *Cold War Broadcasting: Impact on the Soviet Union and Eastern Europe* (Budapest: Central European University Press, 2010), 112–113.

21. Wilson P. Dizard Jr., *Inventing Public Diplomacy: The Story of the U.S. Information Agency* (Boulder, CO: Lynne Rienner, 2004), 70.

22. Bashkirova, "Foreign Radio Audience," 111.

23. Ibid., 113.

24. Ibid., 66–67.

25. Ibid., 75–80.

26. For a study of the similarities and differences of US rebuilding efforts in Germany and Japan, including cultural and educational reforms, see Masako Shibata,

Germany and Japan under the U.S. Occupation: A Comparative Analysis of the Post-War Education Reform (Lanham, MD: Lexington Book, 2005).

27. Richard T. Arndt, *The First Resort of Kings: American Cultural Diplomacy in the Twentieth Century* (Washington, DC: Potomac Books, 2005), 213–236.

28. These depictions included claims that "New England was founded on hypocrisy and sin" and that "naked Indian girls" could be seen walking around in Cheyenne, Wyoming. See Belmonte, *Selling the American Way*, 33.

29. Ibid., 34–35.

30. *Wheeling Intelligener*, "McCarthy Charges Reds Hold U. S. Jobs," February 10, 1950. See also Robert Shogan, *No Sense of Decency: The Army-McCarthy Hearings: A Demogague Falls and Television Takes Charge of American Politics* (Chicago: Ivan R. Dee, 2009), 68–69.

31. David Sarnoff quoted in Shogan, *No Sense of Decency*, 27.

32. Ellen Schrecker, *The Age of McCarthyism: A Brief History with Documents* (Boston: Bedford, 1994), 77. There was no formal government blacklist, but the names listed in the pamphlet *Red Channels* was the de facto list used by most public officials. See American Business Consultants, *Red Channels* (New York: American Business Consultants, 1950).

33. John Crosby, "The Arguments of Live TV," *New York Herald Tribune*, March 16, 1953.

34. Thomas Doherty, *Cold War, Cool Medium: Television, McCarthyism, and American Culture* (New York: Columbia University Press, 2003), 105.

35. Ibid., 106.

36. Nancy E. Bernhard, *U.S. Television News and Cold War Propaganda, 1947–1960* (Cambridge, UK: Cambridge University Press, 1999), 5, 47.

37. Doherty, *Cold War, Cool Medium*, 4.

38. For more on this debate, see Lyn Gorman and David McLean, *Media and Society in the Twentieth Century: A Historical Introduction* (Malden, MA: Blackwell, 2003), 132–134.

39. Ibid., 128–129.

40. Schrecker, *Age of McCarthyism*, 11.

41. Ibid., 9–15.

42. Shogan, *No Sense of Decency*, 67.

43. Ibid., 67–68.

44. Ibid., 60–62.

45. *Broadcasting/Telecasting*, "Crime Hearings, Commercial Shows Cancelled," February 26, 1951.

46. Doherty, *Cold War, Cool Medium*, 107–116.

47. "Lattimore Heard by Tense Crowd," *New York Times*, April 7, 1950.

48. Doherty, *Cold War, Cool Medium*, 116.

49. Ibid., 106.

50. Ibid., 120.

51. William O. Douglas, "The Black Silence of Fear," *New York Times Magazine*, January 13, 1952, 37–38.

52. Doherty, *Cold War, Cool Medium*, 128.

53. Senate Committee on Government Operations, Hearings on the State Department Information Program—Voice of America, 83rd Congress, February 16–17, 1953, 1–11.

54. Doherty, *Cold War, Cool Medium*, 128.

55. Krugler, *Voice of America*, 189

56. Ibid., 190–191.

57. Belmonte, *Selling the American Way*, 54–55.

58. Marya Mannes, "Channels: Comments on TV," *The Reporter*, March 31, 1953, 34.

59. Doherty, *Cold War, Cool Medium*, 129; and Krugler, *Voice of America*, 190–191.

60. Doherty, *Cold War, Cool Medium*, 83–90.

61. "Voice Aide Sees McCarthy Aiming at 'My Public Neck,'" *New York Times*, March 4, 1953.

62. Murrow had three on-air platforms from which to launch broadsides against McCarthy: *Edward R. Murrow with the News*, a 15-minute weekday radio show at 7:45 p.m., *See It Now* on Tuesdays at 10:30 p.m., and *Person to Person* on Fridays at 10:30 p.m. See Doherty, *Cold War, Cool Medium*, 168.

63. Joseph Wershba quoted in Doherty, *Cold War, Cool Medium*, 169.

64. Joseph McCarthy quoted in Thomas C. Reeves, *The Life and Times of Joe McCarthy* (New York: Stein and Day, 1982), 372; and Doherty, *Cold War, Cool Medium*, 170.

65. Doherty, *Cold War, Cool Medium*, 170.

66. Ibid., 173.

67. Ibid., 173–174.

68. Ibid., 174.

69. Ibid., 175.

70. Ibid., 190–196.

71. CBS actually backed out of its commitment to cover the hearings live, as it would mean preempting daytime soap operas and reimbursing advertisers who had already paid for the spots. See Doherty, *Cold War, Cool Medium*, 202.

72. Ibid., 202.

73. Joseph Welch, "The Army-McCarthy Hearings, 1954," in Robert D. Marcus and Anthony Marcus, eds., *On Trail: American History through Court Proceedings and Hearings*, vol. II (St. James, NY: Brandywine, 1998), 136–151.

74. Doherty, *Cold War, Cool Medium*, 204.

75. Paul Scott Rankie quoted in Doherty, *Cold War, Cool Medium*, 87.

76. Dizard, *Inventing Public Diplomacy*, 57.

77. Belmonte, *Selling the American Way*, 111.

78. Shawn J. Parry-Giles, *The Rhetorical Presidency, Propaganda, and the Cold War, 1945–1955*, (Westport, CT: Praeger, 2002), 120–123.

79. For the story of Mossadegah's toppling, see Stephen Kinzer, *Overthrow: America's Century of Regime Change from Hawaii to Iraq* (New York: Times Books, 2006), 111–128.

80. For the story of Arbenz's toppling, see Kinzer, *Overthrow*, 129–147.

81. For detail of the campaign, see Edward S. Herman, "Returning Guatemala to the Fold," in Gary D. Rawnsley, ed., *Cold War Propaganda in the 1950s* (New York: MacMillan, 1999).

82. Michael H. Hunt, *The World Transformed: 1945 to the Present* (New York: St. Martin's, 2004).

83. According to Robert Cox, tripartism was the distribution of social power in the mid-twentieth-century United States among the industrial elite, organized industrial trade unions, and government bureaucrats. This structure was the social manifestation of the managed liberal ideology the United States sought to promote after the war. See Cox, *Production, Power, and World Order*, 74–78.

84. See Robert E. Stripling and H. A. Smith, "Testimony of Walter E. Disney before the House Committee on Un-American Activities," in Kathy Merlock Jackson, ed., *Walt Disney: Conversations* (Jackson: University Press of Mississippi, 2006), 34–41.

85. Walt Disney quoted in "After Hours," *Harper's*, June 1948, 573.
86. William Makepeace Thackeray, *Miscellanies*, Vol. V (New York: Harper and Brothers, 1877), 556.
87. Walt Disney quoted in "A New Disneyland in Burbank!," *Burbank Daily Review*, March 27, 1952.
88. Walt Disney quoted in Michael Sorkin, "See You at Disneyland," in Michael Sorkin, ed., *Variations on a Theme Park: The New American City and the End of Public Space* (New York: Hill and Wong, 1992), 206.
89. As argued by Paul Baran and Paul Sweezy, spurring massive consumer spending became an important element in ensuring the health of the global economy since by the mid-twentieth century many large industries had consolidated into large monopolies and needed constant sales to avoid stagnation, cuts in employment, and the threat of social strife. See Paul A. Baran and Paul M. Sweezy, *Monopoly Capital: An Essay on the American Economic and Social Order* (New York: Monthly Review Press, 1966).
90. Robert H. Haddow, *Pavilions of Plenty: Exhibiting American Culture Abroad in the 1950s* (Washington, DC: Smithsonian Institution Press, 1997), 74.
91. Khrushchev's response to the displays of these technologically advanced kitchen appliances was to ask, "Don't you have a machine that puts food in mouth and pushes it down?" See, "The Two Worlds: A Day-Long Debate," *New York Times*, July 25, 1959, 3.
92. "The Two Worlds: A Day-Long Debate," 1.
93. Jack Masey and Conway Lloyd Morgan, *Cold War Confrontations: US Exhibitions and Their Role in the Cultural Cold War* (Baden: Lars Müller, 2008), 36–57.
94. Ibid., 108–151.
95. Lawrence R. Samuel, *The End of the Innocence: The 1964–1965 New York World's Fair* (Syracuse, NY: Syracuse University Press, 2007), 5–6.
96. Ibid.
97. Steven Watts, *The Magic Kingdom: Walt Disney and the American Way of Life* (Boston: Houghton Mifflin, 1997), 414.
98. Ibid.
99. Ibid.
100. Ibid., 415.
101. Ibid., 416.
102. Ibid.
103. Samuel, *End of the Innocence*, 142–143.
104. Michael Hardt and Antonio Negri, *Empire* (Cambridge, MA: Harvard University Press, 2000), 148.
105. Samuel, *End of the Innocence*, 130.
106. Watts, *Magic Kingdom*, 417.
107. Ibid., 418.
108. Samuel, *End of the Innocence*, 126–127.
109. Ibid., 185.
110. Ibid.
111. On several occasions, the visitors waiting to board busses from the limited parking facilities to the fairgrounds began small riots at the slow pace of the transportation. Police soon had to supervise these areas. See Samuel, *End of the Innocence*, 41.
112. See Timothy Leary, *Turn on, Tune in, Drop out* (Berkeley, CA: Ronin, 1965).
113. Carson's book is generally credited with jumpstarting the modern environmentalist movement. See Philip Shabecoff, *A Fierce Green Fire: The American Environmental Movement* (New York: Island Press, 2003), 99–101.

114. Samuel, *End of the Innocence*, 87.
115. Robert Rosenblum, "Remembrance of Fairs Past," in *Remembering the Future: The New York World's Fair From 1939 to 1964* (New York: Rizzoli, 1989), 18–19.
116. Samuel, *End of the Innocence*, 88.
117. Illen Sheppard, "Icons and Images: The Cultural Legacy of the Fair," in Rosenblum, *Remembering the Future*, 177.

4   The Postindustrial Renewal: Guerillas, Partisans, and the Triumph of the American Empire (1965–1989)

1. David Harvey, *A Brief History of Neoliberalism* (Oxford, UK: Oxford University Press, 2005), 3.
2. For more on the idea of knowledge-based economy and society, see Daniel Bell, *The Coming of Post-Industrial Society* (New York: Basic Books, 1973), 212–264.
3. Robert Cox, *Production, Power, and World Order: Social Forces in the Making of History* (New York: Columbia University Press, 1987), 273–308.
4. For a fuller explanation of the dynamics of the rise of American-sponsored financialization in the later twentieth century, see Giovanni Arrighi, *The Long Twentieth Century: Money, Power, and the Origins of Our Times* (London: Verso, 1994), 269–299.
5. For more on how such cultural luminaries of the 1960s like Leonard Bernstein and Jean Seberg worked for radical causes like the Black Panthers, see Amy Abugo Ongiri, *Spectacular Blackness: The Cultural Politics of the Black Power Movement and the Search for a Black Aesthetic* (Charlottesville: University of Virginia Press, 2010), 58–87.
6. As it turned out, the Soviet Union was having its own problems with its rapidly rusting industrial infrastructure and the pressure put on it by the changing postindustrial dynamics to make political and economic reforms.
7. For a full expression of the idea of neoliberalism, see Harvey, *Brief History of Neoliberalism*, 1–38.
8. Jerry Rubin, *Do It!: Scenarios of the Revolution* (New York: Simon and Schuster, 1970), 17–18.
9. Ibid., 19.
10. Ibid., 106.
11. Ibid., 107.
12. Ibid., 108.
13. Jonah Raskin, *For the Hell of It: The Life and Times of Abbie Hoffman* (Berkeley: University of California Press, 1996), 140.
14. See Abbie Hoffman, *Revolution for the Hell of It* (New York: Thunder's Mouth Press, 2005), 133 and 80.
15. Ibid., 33.
16. Raskin, *For the Hell of It*, 116.
17. Ibid., 119.
18. Hoffman likely meant the last part of his comment facetiously, but in retrospect it proved to be an apt description of what happened during the convention. See Raskin, *For the Hell of It*, 143.
19. Ibid.
20. Ibid., 145.
21. David Farber, *Chicago '68* (Chicago: University of Chicago Press, 1994), 252.
22. Mike Royko quoted in Raskin, *For the Hell of It*, 160.

23. Mark Kurlansky, *1968: The Year That Rocked the World* (New York: Ballantine, 2004), 279.
24. Royko quoted in Raskin, *For the Hell of It*, 161.
25. See *Marcuse and the Frankfurt School* [videorecording] BBC Worldwide Americas, presented by Janet Hoenig, directed by Tony Tyler, Films for the Humanities & Sciences (Princeton, NJ: Films for the Humanities & Sciences, 2003).
26. James Arnold, *Tet Offensive 1968: Turning Point in Vietnam* (London: Osprey, 1990), 13.
27. See Peter Braestrup, *Big Story* (Boulder, CO: Westview Press, 1976) for more on how images of the Tet Offensive deceived key decision makers about the status of the war.
28. James H. Willbanks, *The Tet Offensive: A Concise History* (New York: Columbia University Press, 2007), 43–55.
29. Sprio T. Agnew, "Address to the California State Convention, San Diego, California, September 11, 1970," *Congressional Record*, September 16, 1970, vol. 16, p. 32107.
30. See Willbanks, *Tet Offensive*, 111; and Daniel C. Hallin, *The "Uncensored War": The Media and Vietnam* (Oxford, UK: Oxford University Press, 1986), 159.
31. Willbanks, *Tet Offensive*, 110.
32. David Culbert, "American Television Coverage of the Vietnam War: The Loan Execution Footage, The Tet Offensive (1968) and the Contexualization of Visual Images," in Mark Connelly and David Welch, eds., *War and Media, 1900–2003* (London: I. B. Tauris, 2005), 204–205. See also Hallin, *Uncensored War*, 159–210.
33. Willbanks, *Tet Offensive*, 111.
34. William M. Hammond, *Reporting Vietnam: Media and Military at War* (Lawrence: University of Kansas Press, 1998), 111.
35. Walter Cronkite, transcript from *Who? What? When? Where? Why?: A Report from Vietnam by Walter Cronkite*, broadcast February 27, 1968, in Willbanks, *Tet Offensive*, 205–206.
36. Howard K. Smith quoted in Kevin Phillips, *Post-Conservative America: People, Politics and Ideology in a Time of Crisis* (New York: Random House, 1982), 170.
37. "Neoconservatism" lacks a widely accepted definition, but the account provided by Kevin Phillips is among the most comprehensive. See Phillips, *Post-Conservative America*.
38. Ibid., 41–47.
39. See Kevin Phillips, *The Emerging Republican Majority* (New Rochelle, NY: Arlington House, 1969). This famous book best describes the changes in party alignment due to the shifts in social and geographical demographics taking place during the 1960s.
40. Phillips, *Post-Conservative America*, 32.
41. Paul Weyrich, "Conscience of the New Right," *Conservative Digest* (July 1981): 2–8.
42. Phillips, *Post-Conservative America*, 44.
43. Roger Ailes, *You Are the Message* (New York: Doubleday, 1995), 25.
44. Kerwin Swint, *Dark Genius: The Influential Career of Legendary Political Operative and Fox News Founder Roger Ailes* (New York: Union Square, 2008), 70.
45. Ibid., 129.
46. Dan Baum, *Citizen Coors* (New York: Perennial, 2000), 113.
47. Swint, *Dark Genius*, 75.
48. Ibid., 61.

49. Jean Stefanic and Richard Delgado, *No Mercy: How Conservative Think Tanks Changed America's Social Agenda* (Philadelphia, PA: Temple University Press, 1996), 53.
50. Ibid., 53.
51. Michael Ryan and Les Switzer, *God in the Corridors of Power: Christian Conservatives, the Media, and Politics in America* (Santa Barbara, CA: Praeger, 2009), 108.
52. Ibid., 119.
53. Ibid., 47.
54. Amadou-Mahtar M'Bow, *Speech before the International Diplomatic Academy*, Paris, October 27, 1981.
55. Ulla Carlsson, *The Rise and Fall of NWICO—and Then?*, conference paper delivered at Euricom Colloquium (Venice, Italy: May 2003), 16.
56. Phillip Muscat quoted in Thomas L. McPhail, *Global Communication: Theories, Stakeholders, and Trends* (Boston: Allyn and Bacon, 2002), 186.
57. Frederick Henry Gareau, *The United Nations and Other International Institutions: A Critical Analysis* (Chicago: Burnham, 2002), 128.
58. Ibid., 128–129.
59. McPhail, *Global Communication*, 181.
60. Stephen Kinzer, *Overthrow: America's Century of Regime Change from Hawaii to Iraq* (New York: Times Books, 2006) 170–184.
61. McPhail, *Global Communication*, 66.
62. Gareau, *United Nations and Other International Institutions*, 130–137.
63. McPhail, *Global Communication*, 181.
64. Harvey, *Brief History of Neoliberalism*, 2.
65. For a fuller description of the effects of neoliberalism, see Harvey, *Brief History of Neoliberalism* and *The Condition of Postmodernity* (Malden, MA: Wiley-Blackwell, 1991).
66. See Task Force on Inequality and American Democracy, *American Democracy in an Age of Rising Inequality* (American Political Science Association, 2004). http://www.apsanet.org/imgtest/taskforcereport.pdf.
67. Sean Wilentz, *The Age of Reagan: A History 1974–2008* (New York: HarperCollins, 2008), 153.
68. Countless biographies of Ronald Reagan exist, however, the one that best sees his presidency through the lens of his experience as an actor and entertainer is Lou Cannon, *President Reagan: The Role of a Lifetime* (New York: Public Affairs, 1991).
69. Swint, *Dark Genius*, 4.
70. In this way, Reagan epitomized a key tenant of Ailes's advice on media relations, namely to "develop a curiosity about what you see in other people's faces." See Ailes, *You Are the Message*, 7.
71. For more on the cleavage between Reagan's media image and his actual governing, see John W. Sloan, *The Reagan Effect: Economics and Presidential Leadership* (Lawrence: University of Kansas Press, 1999).
72. Asa Briggs and Peter Burke, *A Social History of the Media: From Gutenberg to the Internet*, 2nd ed. (Malden, MA: Polity, 2005), 238.
73. Stephanie Marriot gives an excellent dissertation on the power and effects of live television in her book *Live Television: Time, Space and the Broadcast Event* (London: Sage, 2007).
74. Reese Schonfeld, *Me and Ted against the World: The Unauthorized Story of the Founding of CNN* (New York: HarperCollins, 2001), 12–17.
75. Eli M. Noam, *Media Ownership and Concentration in America* (Oxford, UK: Oxford University Press, 2009), 298.

76. Jack Banks, *Monopoly Television: MTV's Quest to Control the Music* (Boulder, CO: Westview Press, 1996), 31.

77. Ibid., 117–119.

78. Gary R. Edgerton, *The Columbia History of American Television* (New York: Columbia University Press, 2007), 303–304.

79. Ibid., 350.

80. For a comprehensive review of these various content changes, see Edgerton, *Columbia History of American Television*, 285–322.

81. Briggs and Burke, *Social History of the Media*, 216.

82. Todd Gitlin called this phenomenon the "recombinant style," in which past products or ideas are mixed together to create ostensibly new outputs, but are in reality mere "cultural givens reshuffled into pastiche." See Todd Gitlin, *Inside Prime Time* (New York: Pantheon, 1983), 78–79.

83. Kevin Phillips, *The Politics of Rich and Poor: Wealth and the American Electorate in the Reagan Aftermath* (New York: Random House, 1990), 11.

84. Andrew E. Busch, *Ronald Reagan and the Politics of Freedom* (Lanham, MD: Rowman and Littlefield, 2001), 231.

85. Ibid., 231–232.

86. Reagan did not identify himself as an evangelical Christian and often suffered criticisms from members of the Christian Right. See Daniel K. Williams, *God's Own Party: The Making of the Christian Right* (Oxford, UK: Oxford University Press, 2010), 187–212.

87. Ronald Reagan, "The 'Evil Empire' Speech," in J. Michael Waller, ed., *The Public Diplomacy Reader* (Washington, DC: Institute of World Politics Press, 2007), 137–143.

88. Ibid., 141.

89. For more on Reagan's defense policies, see Daniel Wirls, *Buildup: The Politics of Defense in the Reagan Era* (Ithaca, NY: Cornell University Press, 1992).

90. For samples of these criticisms, see Mira Duric, *The Strategic Defense Initiative: US Policy and the Soviet Union* (Aldershot, UK: Ashgate, 2003), 37–39.

91. A flattering study of the SDI program and its ostensible boost to the American psyche is found in Frances Fitzgerald, *Way Out There in the Blue: Reagan, Star Wars, and the Cold War* (New York: Simon and Schuster, 2000).

92. Douglas Kellner, *Media Culture: Cultural Studies, Identity and Politics between the Modern and the Post-Modern* (New York: Routledge, 1995), 53.

93. Ibid., 80.

94. *Grenada Invasion*, Special NBC News Broadcast, October 25, 1983.

95. Marc Eliot, *American Rebel: The Life of Clint Eastwood* (New York: Harmony Books, 2009), 231.

96. Richard Perle quoted in FitzGerald, *Way Out There in the Blue*, 39.

97. Duric, *Strategic Defense Initiative*, 37–39.

98. Skeptics of SDI within the government included the Congressional Office of Technological Assessment. See Alan F. Geyer, *Ideology in America: Challenges to Faith* (Louisville, KY: John Knox Press, 1997), 62.

99. Reagan's willingness to entertain the possibility of eliminating the American nuclear arsenal put him at odds with his neoconservative backers. See Jim Mann, *The Rebellion of Ronald Reagan: A History of the End of the Cold War* (New York: Viking, 2009).

100. For more on the idea that the entertainment output of American media companies now has a more internationalist orientation, see Benjamin Barber, *Jihad vs. McWorld: How Globalism and Tribalism Are Reshaping the World* (New York: Ballantine, 1996), 23–154.

101. See Francis Fukuyama, *The End of History and the Last Man* (New York: Avon, 1992).

Conclusion   America Overexposed? Globalization, Digital Communications, and the Fate of the American Empire

1. Though globalization is a "contested concept" with differing opinions of what it is and how it impacts the world, the discussion of the concept here is informed by the very good overview of the idea provided by Manfred Steger, *Globalization: A Brief Insight* (New York: Sterling, 2009).

2. This position was argued in Michael Hardt and Antonio Negri, *Empire* (Cambridge, MA: Harvard University Press, 2000).

3. For a complete analysis on the how social networks operate and the impact they can have on human relations, see Clay Shirky, *Here Comes Everybody: The Power of Organizing without Organizations* (New York: Penguin, 2008).

4. See Jason Burke, *Al Qaeda: The True Story of Radical Islam* (London: I. B. Tauris, 2003).

5. See United States Government Accountability Office, *U.S. Public Diplomacy: Key Issues for Congressional Oversight* (Washington, DC: G. A. O., 2009), 2.

6. David Boyle, "A Timely Lesson in Propaganda," *The New Statesman*, November 19, 2001.

7. Philip Van Munching, "The Devil's Adman," *Brandweek*, November 12, 2001.

8. "Selling a Nation," *Marketing Week*, November 8, 2001.

9. Franklin Foer, "Flacks Americana," *The New Republic*, May 20, 2002.

10. Sheldon Rampton and John Stauber, "How to Sell a War," *In These Times*, September 1, 2003.

11. "A Nation Challenged: Hearts and Minds; Pentagon Readies Efforts to Sway Sentiment Abroad," *The New York Times*, February 19, 2002.

12. Pew Research Center for the People and the Press, *Pew Global Attitudes Project: Views of a Changing World*, June 2003, http://people-press.org.

13. A fuller recounting and critique of the efforts to market the United States to the world after September 11, can be found in Edward Comor and Hamilton Bean, "America's 'Engagement' Delusion: Critiquing a Public Diplomacy Consensus," *International Communications Gazette* 74, no. 3 (2012): 203–220.

14. "Rumsfeld Formally Disbands Office of Strategic Infuence," *The New York Times*, February 26, 2002.

15. See *United States Department of Defense Handbook*, 2 vols. (Washington, DC: International Business Publications, 2011), vol. 1, 22.

16. Images of battle carnage and civilian casualties was but one of the differences in how the American invasions of Afghanistan and Iraq were portrayed in the Western versus non-Western media. See Anthony DiMaggio, *Mass Media, Mass Propaganda: Examining American News in the "War on Terror"* (Lanham, MD: Lexington Books, 2008).

17. Marshall McLuhan, *Understanding Media: The Extensions of Man* (Cambridge, MA: MIT Press, 1994), 7–21.

18. The most significant of these actions have been chronicled in Stephen Kinzer, *Overthrow: America's Century of Regime Change from Hawaii to Iraq* (New York: Times Books, 2006).

19. For a fuller discussion of these issues as they pertained to the American presence in Iraq, see Lila Rajiva, *The Language of Empire: Abu Ghraib and the American Media* (New York: Monthly Review Press, 2005).

20. See Shirky, *Here Comes Everybody*, 55–80 and 109–142.

21. See "Remarks on Internet Freedom," http://www.state.gov/secretary/rm/2010/01/135519.htm.

22. See David Leigh and Luke Harding, *Wikileaks: Inside Julian Assange's War on Secrecy* (Philadelphia, PA: Public Affairs, 2010).

23. The revelations of mass digital communications surveillance by the NSA came to light as this book was being finished.

24. Ewen MacAskill, "Bradley Manning Case Sparks UN Criticism of US Government," *The Guardian*, April 11, 2011.

25. Brian Stelter, "F.C.C. Faces Challenges to Net Rules," *New York Times*, December 10, 2010.

26. John Swartz, "'Kill Switch' Internet Bill Alarms Privacy Experts," *USA Today*, February 15, 2011.

27. Evgeny Morozov, *The Net Delusion: The Dark Side of Internet Freedom* (Philadelphia, PA: Public Affairs, 2011).

28. For all the newspaper stories on the topic of Edward Snowden's leaks about NSA surveillance, see "The NSA Files," http://www.theguardian.com/world/the-nsa -files.

29. See Paul Mason, *Why It's Kicking Off Everywhere: The New Global Revolutions* (New York: Verso, 2012), 75.

30. Ahmed Shihab-Eldin and Ben Connors, "The Network Revolution," *Al Jazeera*, http://www.aljazeera.com/programmes/empire/2011/02/201121614532116986 .html.

31. Adam Gabbatt, Mark Townsend, and Lisa O'Carroll, "'Occupy' Anticapitalism Protests Spread around the World," *The Guardian*, October 15, 2011. http://www .guardian.co.uk/world/2011/oct/16/occupy-protests-europe-london-assange.

32. Mason, *Why It's Kicking Off Everywhere*, 11.

33. Stephen Mann, "Sousveillance: Inverse Surveillance in Multimedia Imaging," in *Proceedings of the 12th Annual ACM Conference on Multimedia, New York, 2004*, 620–627.

34. Paul Lewis, "Video Reveals G20 Police Assault on Man Who Died," *The Guardian*, April 7, 2009. http://www.guardian.co.uk/uk/2009/apr/07/video-g20-police -assault.

35. Bradley Manning was eventually found guilty of several charges for his leaking of classified material to Wikileaks. In August of 2013, he was sentenced to 35 years in military prison. After the passing of this sentence, Manning announced his desire to live as a woman and be called by the name Chelsea Manning. See Adam Gabbatt, "'I am Chelsea Manning,' Says Jailed Soldier Formerly Known as Bradley," *The Guardian*, August 22, 2013. http://www.theguardian.com/world/2013/aug/22 /bradley-manning-woman-chelsea-gender-reassignment.

36. In a rather remarkable letter requesting Snowden's extradition, the Department of Justice went out of its way to assure the Russian government that Snowden would not be tortured while in American custody and that he would enjoy all the rights of an accused person as articulated in the US Constitution. See Adam Gabbatt, "US Will Not Seek Death Penalty for Edward Snowden, Holder Tells Russia," *The Guardian*, July 26, 2013. http://www.theguardian.com/world/2013/jul/26/us-no -death-penalty-edward-snowden-russia.

37. Josh Halliday, "London Riots: How BlackBerry Messenger Played a Key Role," *The Guardian*, August 8, 2011. http://www.theguardian.com/media/2011/aug/08 /london-riots-facebook-twitter-blackberry.

38. See "Occupy Wall Street's Live Streamer Tim Pool," *Time*, August 31, 2013. http:// www.time.com/time/video/player/0,32068,1279751069001_2099632,00.html.

39. Ryan Devereaux, "Occupy Wall Street: 'There's a Militant Animosity Bred by Direct Action,'" *The Guardian*, February 3, 2012. http://www.guardian.co.uk /world/2012/feb/03/occupy-wall-street-animosity-direct-action.

Bibliography

Abugo Ongiri, Amy. *Spectacular Blackness: The Cultural Politics of the Black Power Movement and the Search for a Black Aesthetic.* Charlottesville: University of Virginia Press, 2010.

Ade, George. *The Sultan of Sulu.* New York: R. H. Russell, 1903.

Ailes, Roger. *You Are the Message.* New York: Doubleday, 1995.

Aldrich, Robert. *Greater France: A History of French Overseas Expansion.* New York: St. Martin's, 1996.

Altick, Richard D. *Punch: The Lively Youth of a British Institution 1841–1851.* Columbus: Ohio State University Press, 1997.

American Business Consultants. *Red Channels.* New York: American Business Consultants, 1950.

Andrew, William P. *Indian Railways.* London: W. H. Allen and Co., 1884.

Andrews, Alexander. *Chapters in the History of British Journalism.* 2 vols. London: Chatto and Windus, 1887.

Andrews, Eric Montgomery. *The ANZAC Illusion: Anglo-Australian Relations during World War I.* Cambridge, UK: Cambridge University Press, 1993.

Arendt, Hannah. *The Origins of Totalitarianism.* San Diego, CA: Harcourt, 1968.

Arndt, Richard T. *The First Resort of Kings: American Cultural Diplomacy in the Twentieth Century.* Washington, DC: Potomac Books, 2005.

Arnold, James. *Tet Offensive 1968: Turning Point in Vietnam.* London: Osprey, 1990.

Arrighi, Giovanni. *The Long Twentieth Century: Money, Power, and the Origins of Our Times.* London: Verso, 1994.

Attridge, Steve. *Nationalism, Imperialism, and Identity in Late-Victorian Culture: Civil and Military Worlds.* Basingstoke, UK: Palgrave, 2003.

Auerbach, Jeffrey A. *The Great Exhibition of 1851: A Nation on Display.* New Haven, CT: Yale University Press, 1999.

Axelrod, Alan. *Selling the Great War: The Making of American Propaganda.* New York: Palgrave Macmillan, 2009.

Ayerst, David. *The Manchester Guardian: Biography of a Newspaper.* Ithaca, NY: Cornell University Press, 1971.

Bacevich, Andrew J., ed. *The Imperial Tense.* Chicago: Ivan R. Dee, 2003.

———. *American Empire: The Realities and Consequences of U.S. Diplomacy.* Cambridge, MA: Harvard University Press, 2002.

Banks, Jack. *Monopoly Television: MTV's Quest to Control the Music.* Boulder, CO: Westview Press, 1996.

Baran, Paul A., and Paul M. Sweezy. *Monopoly Capital: An Essay on the American Economic and Social Order.* New York: Monthly Review Press, 1966.

Barber, Benjamin R. *Consumed: How Markets Corrupt Children, Infantalize Adults, and Swallow Citizens Whole*. New York: W. W. Norton, 2007.

———. *Fear's Empire: War, Terrorism, and Democracy*. New York: W. W. Norton, 2003.

———. *Jihad vs. McWorld: How Globalism and Tribalism Are Reshaping the World*. New York: Ballantine, 1996.

Barclay, Oliver. *Thomas Fowell Buxton and the Liberation of the Slaves*. York, UK: William Sessions, 2001.

Barkawi, Tarak. *Globalization and War*. Lanham, MD: Rowman and Littlefield, 2006.

Barnouw, Eric. *Media Lost and Found*. New York: Fordham University Press, 2001.

Barrow, John Henry, ed. *The Mirror of Parliament: The Third Session of the Fourteenth Parliament of Great Britain and Ireland*. London: Longman et al., 1840.

Baum, Dan. *Citizen Coors*. New York: Perennial, 2000.

Bearce, George D. *British Attitudes toward India: 1784–1858*. London: Oxford University Press, 1961.

Beer, Max. *A Brief History of British Socialism*. Manchester, NH: Ayer, 1979.

Bell, Daniel. *The Coming of Post-Industrial Society*. New York: Basic Books, 1973.

Belmonte, Laura A. *Selling the American Way: U.S. Propaganda and the Cold War*. Philadelphia: University of Pennsylvania, 2008.

Bergmeier, Horst J. P., and Rainer E. Lotz. *Hitler's Airwaves: The Inside Story of Nazi Radio Broadcasting and Propaganda Swing*. New Haven, CT: Yale University Press, 1997.

Berkowitz, Edward. *Mass Appeal: The Formative Age of the Movies, Radio and TV*. Cambridge, UK: Cambridge University Press: 2010.

Bernays, Edward. *Propaganda*. Brooklyn, NY: IG Publishing, 2005.

Bernhard, Nancy E. *U.S. Television News and Cold War Propaganda, 1947–1960*. Cambridge, UK: Cambridge University Press, 1999.

Bettes, Raymond. *Tricouleur: The French Overseas Empire*. London: Gordon and Cremonesi, 1978.

Blackburn, Robin. *The Overthrow of Colonial Slavery 1776–1848*. London: Verso, 1988.

———. *The Savage Wars of Peace: Small Wars and the Rise of American Power*. New York: Basic Books, 2002.

Bourne, Henry Richard Fox. *English Newspaper: Chapters in the History of Journalism*. 2 vols. London: Spotiswoode and Co., 1887.

Braestrup, Peter. *Big Story*. Boulder, CO: Westview Press, 1976.

Brecht, Bertolt. *Brecht on Theater*. New York: Hill and Wang, 1964.

Briggs, Asa, and Peter Burke. *A Social History of the Media: From Gutenberg to the Internet*. Malden, MA: Polity, 2005.

Bright, John. *The Public Letters of John Bright*. H. J. Leech, ed. London: Sampson, Low, Marston, Searle & Rivington, 1885.

Brown, Robert J. *Manipulating the Ether: The Power of Broadcast Radio in Thirties America*. Jefferson, NC: McFarland and Company, 1999.

Bryan, William Jennings. *American Imperialism*. Chicago: Bentley and Company, 1900.

Burgess, John W. *Political Science and Comparative Constitutional Law*. Boston: Ginn and Company, 1890–1891.

Burke, Jason. *Al Qaeda: The True Story of Radical Islam*. London: I. B. Tauris, 2003.

Burnand, Francis Cowley. *Poems from Punch*. London: Harrap, 1908.

Burton, Antoinette. *After the Imperial Turn: Thinking with and through the Nation*. Durham, NC: Duke University Press, 2003.

Busch, Andrew E. *Ronald Reagan and the Politics of Freedom*. Lanham, MD: Rowman and Littlefield, 2001.

Cain, P. J., and A. G. Hopkins. *British Imperialism 1688–2000*. Harlow, UK: Pearson, 2002.

Cannadine, David. *Ornamentalism: How the British Saw Their Empire*. Oxford, UK: Oxford University Press, 2001.

Cannon, Lou. *President Reagan: The Role of a Lifetime*. New York: Public Affairs, 1991.

Carr, Edward Hallet. *The Twenty Years Crisis*. London: Macmillan, 1946.

Carson, William E. *Northcliffe: Britain's Man of Power*. New York: Dodge Publishing, 1918.

Chamberlain, M. E. *The New Imperialism*. London: Historical Association, 1970.

Chapman, Jane. *Comparative Media History: An Introduction 1789 to the Present*. Malden, MA: Polity, 2005.

Chomsky, Noam. *Hegemony or Survival: America's Quest for Global Dominance*. New York: Metropolitan Books, 2003.

Churchill, Winston, and Randolph Churchill. *Blood, Sweat and Tears*. Camden, NJ: Haddon Craftsmen, 1941.

Collin, Richard H. *Theodore Roosevelt, Culture, Diplomacy and Expansion: A New View Of American Imperialism*. Baton Rouge: Louisiana State University Press, 1985.

Collins, Peter C., and John E. O'Connor, eds. *Hollywood's World War I: Motion Picture Images*. Bowling Green, OH: Bowling Green State University Popular Press, 1997.

Connelly Mark, and Daivd Welch, eds. *War and Media: Reportage and Propaganda, 1900–2003*. London: I. B. Tauris, 2005.

Cooper, Frederick, and Anna Laura Stoler. *Tensions of Empire: Colonial Cultures in a Bourgeois World*. Berkley: University of California Press, 1997.

Cox, Robert. *Approaches to World Order*. Cambridge, UK: Cambridge University Press, 1996.

———. *Production, Power and World Order: Social Forces in the Making of History*. New York: Columbia University Press, 1987.

Creel, George. *How We Advertised America*. New York: Harper Brothers, 1920.

Crick, J., and A. Walsham, eds. *The Uses of Script and Print. 1300–1700*. Cambridge, UK: Cambridge University Press, 2003.

Cull, Nicholas John. *Selling the War: The British Propaganda Campaign against American "Neutrality" in World War II*. New York: Oxford, 1995.

Cumpston, I. M. *The Growth of the British Commonwealth 1880–1932*. New York: St. Martin's Press, 1973.

Dahl, Robert, and Charles Lindblom. *Politics, Economy, and Welfare: Planning and Politico-Economic Systems Resolved in Basic Social Processes*. New York: Harper, 1953.

Danmolé, Mashood. *The Heritage of Imperialism: A Study in Historical and Economic Analysis*. New York: Asia Publishing House, 1974.

Dawson, Graham. *Soldier Heroes: British Adventure, Empire and the Imagining of Masculinities*. New York: Routlege, 1994.

Debord, Guy. *Society of the Spectacle*. Donald Nicholason-Smith, trans. New York: Zone Books, 1999.

Deleuze, Gilles, and Felix Guttari. *A Thousand Plateaus: Capitalism and Schizophrenia*. Minneapolis: University of Minnesota Press, 1987.

DiMaggio, Anthony. *Mass Media, Mass Propaganda: Examining American News in the "War on Terror."* Lanham, MD: Lexington Books, 2008.

Dizard Jr., Wilson P. *Inventing Public Diplomacy: The Story of the U.S. Information Agency.* Boulder, CO: Lynne Rienner, 2004.

Doherty, M. A. *Nazi Wireless Propaganda: Lord Haw-Haw and British Public Opinion in the Second World War.* Edinburgh, UK: Edinburgh University Press, 2000.

Doherty, Thomas. *Cold War, Cool Medium: Television, McCarthyism, and American Culture.* New York: Columbia University Press, 2003.

Doyle, Michael. *Empires.* Ithaca, NY: Cornell University Press, 1986

Drescher, Seymour. *Capitalism and Antislavery: British Mobilization in Comparative Perspective.* Oxford, UK: Oxford University Press, 1987.

Driver, Felix, and David Gilbert, eds. *Imperial Cities.* Manchester, UK: University of Manchester Press, 1999.

Duric, Mira. *The Strategic Defense Initiative: US Policy and the Soviet Union.* Aldershot, UK: Ashgate, 2003.

Edgerton, Gary R. *The Columbia History of American Television.* New York: Columbia University Press, 2007.

Eliot, Marc. *American Rebel: The Life of Clint Eastwood.* New York: Harmony Books, 2009.

Ellis, Jack C. *A History of Film.* Englewood Cliffs, NJ: Prentice Hall, 1979.

Etherington, Norman. *Theories of Imperialism: War, Conquest, and Capital.* London: Groom Helm, 1984.

Ewen, Stuart. *PR!: A Social History of Spin.* New York: Basic Books, 1996.

Fanon, Frantz. *A Dying Colonialism.* New York: Grove Press, 1965.

———. *The Wretched of the Earth.* New York: Grove Press, 1963.

Farber, David. *Chicago '68.* Chicago: University of Chicago Press, 1994.

Fell, John F., ed. *Film before Griffith.* Berkeley: University of California Press, 1983.

Ferguson, Niall. *Colossus: The Price of America's Empire.* New York: Penguin, 2004.

———. *The Rise and Demise of the British World Order and the Lessons of Global Power.* New York, Basic Books, 2003.

Ffrench, Yvonne. *The Great Exhibition: 1851.* London: Harvill Press, 1950.

Fielding, Raymond. *The American Newsreel 1911–1967.* Norman: University of Oklahoma Press, 1972.

Finnegan, John Patrick. *Against the Specter of a Dragon: The Campaign for American Military Preparedness, 1914–1917.* Westport, CT: Greenwood Press, 1974.

Fiske, Horace S. *The Ballad of Manila Bay and Other Verses.* Chicago: University of Chicago Press, 1900.

Fiske, John. *American Political Ideas Viewed from the Standpoint of Universal History.* New York: Harper and Brothers, 1885.

Fitzgerald, Frances. *Way Out There in the Blue: Reagan, Star Wars, and the End of the Cold War.* New York: Simon and Schuster, 2000.

Fleming, Thomas. *The Illusion of Victory: America in World War I.* New York: Basic Books, 2003.

Friedman, Thomas. *The Lexus and the Olive Tree.* New York: Anchor Books, 1999.

Fukuyama, Francis. *The End of History and the Last Man.* New York: Avon, 1992.

Fullerton, Jami A., and Alice Kendrick. *Advertising's War on Terror: The Story of the US State Department's Shared Values Initiative.* Spokane, WA: Marquette Books, 2006.

Fyne, Robert. *The Hollywood Propaganda of World War II.* Metuchen, NJ: Scarecrow Press, 1994.

Gallagher, John. *The Decline, Revival and Fall of the British Empire.* Cambridge, UK: Cambridge University Press, 1982.

Gareau, Frederick Henry. *The United Nations and Other International Institutions: A Critical Analysis.* Chicago: Burnham, 2002.

Gash, Norman. *Age of Peel.* New York: St. Martin's Press, 1968.

Gaudreault, Andre, ed. *American Cinema 1890–1909: Themes and Variations.* Piscataway, NJ: Rutgers University Press, 2009.

Gay, Peter, ed. *The Freud Reader.* New York: W. W. Norton, 1995

Geyer, Alan F. *Ideology in America: Challenges to Faith.* Louisville, KY: John Knox Press, 1997.

Ghonim, Wael. *Revolution 2.0: The Power of the People Is Greater than the People in Power.* New York: Houghton Mifflin Harcourt, 2012.

Gill, Stephen, ed. *Gramsci, Historical Materialism and International Relations.* Cambridge, UK: Cambridge University Press, 1993.

Gitlin, Todd. *Inside Prime Time.* New York: Pantheon, 1983.

Goering, Joseph. *The Goebbels Diaries 1942–1943.* Louis P. Lochner, ed. and trans. Garden City, NJ: Greenwood, 1970.

Gomery, Douglas. *Shared Pleasures: A History of Movie Presentation in the United States.* Madison: University of Wisconsin Press, 1992.

Gomery, Douglas, and Clara Pafort-Overduin. *Movie History: A Survey.* 2nd ed. New York: Routledge, 1991.

Gorman Lyn, and McLean, David. *Media and Society in the Twentieth Century: A Historical Introduction.* Malden, MA: Blackwell, 2003.

Gramsci, Antonio. *Selections from the Prison Notebooks.* Quintin Hoare and Geoffrey Nowell Smith, eds. and trans. New York: International Publishers, 1971.

Grant, Mariel. *Propaganda and the Role of the State in Inter-war Britain.* Oxford, UK: Clarendon Press, 1994.

Great Exhibition of the Works of Industry of All Nations: Official and Illustrated Catalogue. London: Spicer Brothers, 1851.

Griffin, Emma. *Liberty's Dawn: A People's History of the Industrial Revolution.* New Haven, CT: Yale University Press, 2013.

Habermas, Jürgen. *The Structural Transformation of the Public Sphere: An Inquiry into a Category of Bourgeois Society.* Cambridge, MA: MIT Press, 1991.

———. *The Theory of Communicative Action.* 2 vols. Boston: Beacon, 1984.

Haddow, Robery H. *Pavilions of Plenty: Exhibiting American Culture Abroad in the 1950s.* Washington, DC: Smithsonian Institution Press, 1997.

Halévy, Elie. *A History of the English People in the Nineteenth Century.* 6 vols. London: E. Benn, 1952.

Hall, Catherine. *Civilizing Subjects: Metropole and Colony in the English Imagination 1830–1867.* Chicago: University of Chicago Press, 2002.

———, ed. *Cultures of Empire: A Reader.* New York: Routledge, 2000.

Hallin, Daniel C. *The "Uncensored War": The Media and Vietnam.* Oxford, UK: Oxford University Press, 1986.

Hammond, William M. *Reporting Vietnam: Media and Military at War.* Lawrence: University of Kansas Press, 1998.

Hampton, Benjamin B. *History of the American Film Industry from Its Beginning to 1931.* New York: Dover, 1970.

Hanes III, W. Travis, and Frank Sanello. *The Opium Wars: The Addiction of One Empire and the Corruption of Another.* Naperville, IL: Sourcebooks, 2002.

Hanhimäki, Jussi, and Odd Arne Westad. *The Cold War: A History in Documents and Eyewitness Accounts.* Oxford, UK: Oxford University Press, 2003.

Hardt, Michael, and Antonio Negri. *Empire.* Cambridge, MA: Harvard University Press, 2000.

Harfoush, Rahaf. *Yes We Did: An Inside Look at How Social Media Built the Obama Brand.* Berkeley, CA: New Riders, 2009.

Harmetz, Aljean. *The Making of* Casablanca: *Bogart, Bergman and World War II.* New York: Hyperion, 2002.

Hartley, John. *The Politics of Pictures: The Creation of the Public in an Age of Popular Media*. New York: Routledge, 1992.

Harvey, David. *A Brief History of Neoliberalism*. New York: Oxford University Press, 2005.

————. *The Condition of Postmodernity*. Cambridge, MA: Blackwell, 1990.

————. *The Enigma of Capital and the Crises of Capitalism*. New York: Oxford University Press, 2010.

————. *The New Imperialism*. New York: Oxford University Press, 2003.

Herbert, Christopher. *War of No Pity: The Indian Mutiny and Victorian Trauma*. Princeton, NJ: Princeton University Press, 2008.

Herman, Edward S., and Noam Chomsky. *Manufacturing Consent: The Political Economy of Mass Media*. New York: Pantheon, 2002.

Herzstein, Robert Edwin. *The War That Hitler Won: The Most Infamous Propaganda Campaign in History*. New York: G. P. Putnam's Sons, 1978.

Hibbert, Christopher. *The Illustrated London News' Social History of Victorian Britain*. London: Angus and Robertson, 1975.

Hichberger, Joan Winifred Martin. *Images of the Army: The Military in British Art*. Manchester, UK: University of Manchester Press, 1988.

Hilferding, Rudolf. *Finance Capital*. London: Routledge, 1981.

Hilmes, Michele, and Jason Loviglio, eds. *Radio Reader*. New York: Routledge, 2002.

Hinden, Rita. *Empire and After: A Study of British Imperial Attitudes*. London: Essential Books, 1949.

History of The Times. London: Times Publishing Limited, 1939.

Hobsbawm, Eric. *The Age of Capital: 1848–1875*. New York: Vintage, 1976

————. *The Age of Empire: 1875–1914*. New York: Pantheon, 1987.

————. *The Age of Extremes: A History of the World, 1914–1991*. New York: Vintage, 1994.

————. *The Age of Revolution: 1789–1848*. New York: Mentor, 1962.

Hobson, John. A. *Imperialism: A Study*. Ann Arbor: University of Michigan Press, 1965.

————. *The Psychology of Jingoism*. London: Grant Richards, 1901.

Hochschild, Adam. *Bury the Chains: Prophets and Rebels in the Fight to Free an Empire's Slaves*. Boston: Houghton Mifflin, 2005.

Hodgson, Pat. *The War Illustrators*. New York: Macmillan, 1977.

Hoe, Susanna, and Dereck Roebuck. *The Taking of Hong Kong: Charles and Clara Elliot in China Waters*. Hong Kong: Hong Kong University Press, 2009.

Hoffman, Abbie. *Revolution for the Hell of It*. New York: Thunder's Mouth Press, 2005.

Hopkins, Eric. *Industrialization and Society: A Social History, 1830–1951*. New York: Routledge, 2000.

Horkheimer, Max, and Theodor W. Adorno. *Critical Theory: Selected Essays*. New York: Continuum, 1999.

————. *Dialectic of Enlightenment*. New York: Continuum, 2002.

————. *The Eclipse of Reason*. New York: Continuum, 1974.

Horten, Gerd. *Radio Goes to War: The Cultural Politics of Propaganda During World War II*. Berkeley: University of California Press.

Howarth, Patrick. *The Year Is 1851*. London: Collins, 1951.

Howell, Thomas Buxton. *The Slave Trade in Africa*. London: John Murray, 1839.

Hudson, Micahel. *Super-Imperialism: The Origin and Fundamentals of US World Dominance*. London: Pluto Press, 2003.

Hunt, Michael H. *The World Transformed: 1945 to the Present*. New York: St. Martin's, 2004.

Huntington, Samuel P. *The Clash of Civilizations and the Remaking of World Order.* New York: Simon and Schuster, 1996.

Hutchins, F. G. *The Illusions of Permanence: British Imperialism in India.* Princeton, NJ: Princeton University Press, 1967.

Hyam, Ronlad. *Britain's Imperial Century, 1815–1914.* Basingstoke, UK: Palgrave, 2002.

Ignatieff, Michael. *Empire Lite: Nation Building on Bosnia, Kosovo and Afghanistan.* New York: Random House, 2010.

Ishay, Micheline. *The History of Human Rights: From Ancient Times to the Globalization Era.* Berkeley: University of California Press, 2004.

Jackson, Kathy Merlock, ed. *Walt Disney: Conversations.* Jackson: University Press of Mississippi, 2006.

Jacobs, Lewis. *The Rise of American Film: A Critical History.* New York: Harcourt, Brace and Company, 1939.

James, Laurence. *Raj: The Making and Unmaking of British India.* New York: St. Martin's, 2007.

———. *The Rise and Fall of the British Empire.* New York: St. Martin's, 1994.

Johnson, A. Ross, and R. Eugene Parta, eds. *Cold War Broadcasting: Impact on the Soviet Union and Eastern Europe.* Budapest: Central European University Press, 2010.

Johnson, Chalmers. *Blowback: The Costs and Consequences of American Empire.* New York: Henry Holt and Company, 2000.

———. *The Sorrows of Empire.* New York: Metropolitan Books, 2004.

Johnson, Diedre. *Edward Stratemeyer and the Stratemeyer Syndicate.* New York: Twayne Publishers, 1993.

Jones, Barbara, and Bill Howell. *Popular Arts and the First World War.* New York: McGraw-Hill, 1972.

Jowett, Garth S., and Vitoria O'Donnell. *Propaganda and Persuasion.* Thousand Oaks, CA: Sage, 1999.

Judd, Denis, and Keith Surridge. *The Boer War.* London: John Murrary, 2002.

———. *Empire: The British Imperial Experience from 1765 to the Present.* New York: Basic Books, 1996.

Kamen, Michael. *Visual Shock: A History of Art Controversies in American Culture.* New York: Vintage, 2006.

Kellner, Douglas. *Media Culture: Cultural Studies, Identity and Politics between the Modern and the Post-Modern.* New York: Routledge, 1995.

Kennedy, Paul. *The Rise and Fall of the Great Powers: Economic Change and Military Conflict from 1500 to 2000.* New York: Vintage, 1987.

Kiernan, Victor G. *America: The New Imperialism.* New York: Verso: 2005.

Kingsley, Martin. *The Triumph of Lord Palmerston: A Study of Public Opinion in England before the Crimean War.* London: G. Allen and Unwin Ltd., 1924.

Kinzer, Stephen. *Overthrow: America's Century of Regime Change from Hawaii to Iraq.* New York: Times Books, 2006.

Kissinger, Henry. *Does America Need a Foreign Policy?: Towards a Diplomacy for the 21st Century.* New York: Simon and Schuster, 2002.

Kock, Howard. *Casablanca: Script and Legend.* New York: Overlook, 1973.

Koppes, Clayton R., and Gregory D. Black. *Hollywood Goes to War: How Politics, Profits, and Propaganda Shaped World War II Movies.* New York: The Free Press, 1987.

Krebs, Paula M. *Gender, Race, and the Writing of Empire: Public Discourse and the Boer War.* Cambridge, UK: Cambridge University Press.

Krugler, David F. *The Voice of America and the Domestic Propaganda Battles, 1945–1953.* Columbia: University of Missouri Press, 2000.

Kurlansky, Mark. *1968: The Year That Rocked the World*. New York: Ballantine, 2004.

———. *Nonviolence: The History of a Dangerous Idea*. New York: Random House, 2009.

LaFeber, Walter. *John Quincy Adams and American Continental Empire*. Chicago: Quadrangle, 1965.

———. *The New Empire: An Interpretation of American Expansion*. Ithaca, NY: Cornell University Press, 1963.

Laffey, John. *Imperialism and Ideology*. New York: Consortium, 1999.

Lang, Sean. *Parliamentary Reform: 1785–1928*. New York: Routledge, 1999.

Lasswell, Harold D. *Propaganda Technique in World War I*. Cambridge, MA: MIT Press, 1927.

Laurie, Clayton D. *The Propaganda Warriors: America's Crusade against Nazi Germany*. Lawrence: University Press of Kansas, 1996.

Leary, Timothy. *Turn on, Tune in, Drop out*. Berkeley, CA: Ronin, 1965.

Leigh, David, and Luke Harding. *Wikileaks: Inside Julian Assange's War on Secrecy*. Philadelphia, PA: Public Affairs, 2010.

Lenin, Vladimir. *Imperialism: The Highest Stage of Capitalism*. New York: International Publishers, 1939.

L'Etang, Jacquie. *Public Relations in Britain: A History of Professional Practice in the Twentieth Century*. New York: Routledge, 2004.

Linderman, Gerald. *The Mirror of War: American Society and the Spanish-American War*. Ann Arbor: University of Michigan Press, 1974.

Lloyd, Christopher. *The Navy and the Slave Trade: The Suppression of the African Slave Trade in the Nineteenth Century*. London: Longmans, Green and Co., 1949.

Louw, Eric. *The Media and Political Process*. Los Angeles: Sage, 2010.

Lowry, Donal, ed. *The South African War Reappraised*. Manchester, UK: University of Manchester Press, 2000.

Luxemburg, Rosa. *Accumulation of Capital*. New York: Routledge, 2003.

Maass, Peter. "The Toppling," *The New Yorker*, January 10, 2011.

Maass, Peter, and Nicolai Bukharin. *Imperialism and the Accumulation of Capital*. Kenneth J. Tarbuck ed. London: Penguin, 1972.

MacKenzie, John M., ed. *Imperialism and Popular Culture*. Manchester, UK: University of Manchester Press, 1986.

———. *Propaganda and Empire: The Manipulation of British Public Opinion, 1880–1960*. Manchester, UK: Manchester University Press, 1984.

Magdoff, Henry. *Imperialism without Colonies*. New York: Monthly Review Press, 2003.

Mahan, Alfred T. *The Influence of Sea Power upon History, 1660–1783*. Boston: Little, Brown and Company, 1890.

Maier, Charles S. *Among Empires: American Ascendancy and Its Predecessors*. Cambridge, MA: Harvard University Press, 2006.

Majeed, Javed. *Ungoverned Imaginings: James Mill's the History of British India and Orientalism*. Berkeley: University of California Press, 1992.

Mangan, J. A., ed. *'Benefits Bestowed'? Education and British Imperialism*. Manchester, UK: Manchester University Press, 1988.

Mann, Jim. *The Rebellion of Ronald Reagan: A History of the End of the Cold War*. New York: Viking, 2009.

Mann, Michael. *Incoherent Empire*. New York: Verso Books, 2003.

Mannes, Marya. "Channels: Comments on TV," *The Reporter*, March 31, 1953.

Manning, Martin J., and Clarence R. Vyatt, eds. *Encyclopedia of Media and Propaganda in Wartime American*. 2 vols. Santa Barbara, CA: ABC-CLIO, 2011.

Marais, Johannes Stephanus. *The Fall of Kruger's Republic*. Oxford, UK: Clarendon Press, 1961.

Marburg, Theodore. *Expansion*. New York: Garland Publishing, 1971.

Marcus Aurelius. *Meditations*. New York: Modern Library, 2003.

Marcus, Robert D., and Anthony Marcus, eds. *On Trail: American History through Court Proceedings and Hearings*. 2 vols. St. James, NY: Brandywine, 1998.

Marcuse, Herbert. *One-Dimensional Man*. Boston: Beacon Press, 1964.

Marriot, Stephanie. *Live Television: Time, Space and the Broadcast Event*. London: Sage, 2007.

Marx, Karl, and Frederick Engels. *On Colonilaism*. New York: International Publishers, 1972.

Masey, Jack, and Conway Lloyd Morgan. *Cold War Confrontations: US Exhibitions and Their Role in the Cultural Cold War*. Baden: Lars Müller, 2008.

Mason, Paul. *Why It's Kicking Off Everywhere: The New Global Revolutions*. New York: Verso, 2012.

May, A. J. *The Passing of the Habsburg Monarchy 1914–18*. 2 vols. Philadelphia: University of Pennsylvania Press, 1966.

May, Ernest R. *The World War and American Isolation, 1914–1917*. Chicago: Quadrangle, 1959.

McCarthy, Justin. *The Epoch of Reform: 1830–1850*. London: Longmans, Green, and Co., 1882.

McChesney, Robert W. *The Political Economy of Media: Enduring Issues, Emerging Dilemmas*. New York: Monthly Review Press, 2008.

McKitterck, D. *Print, Manuscript, and the Search for Order, 1450–1830*. Cambridge, UK: Cambridge University Press, 2003.

McLuhan, Marshall. *Understanding Media: The Extensions of Man*. Cambridge, MA: MIT Press, 1994.

McPhail, Thomas L. *Global Communication: Theories, Stakeholders, and Trends*. Boston: Allyn and Bacon, 2002.

Means Coleman, Robin R., ed. *Say It Loud!: African American Audiences, Media and Identity*. New York: Routledge, 2002.

Melancon, Glenn. *Britain's China Policy and the Opium Crisis*. Burlington, VT: Ashgate, 2003.

Meszáros, István. *Socialism or Barbarism: From "American Century" to the Crossroads*. New York: Monthly Review Press, 2001.

Miles, Hugh. *Al-Jazeera: The Inside Story of the Arab News Channel That Is Challenging the West*. New York: Grove, 2005.

Miller, Bonnie M. *From Liberation to Conquest: The Visual and Popular Cultures of the Spanish-American War of 1898*. Amherst: University of Massachusetts Press, 2011.

Miller, Richard H. *American Imperialism in 1898: The Quest for National Fulfillment*. New York: Wiley, 1970.

Miller, Stuart Creighton. *Benevolent Assimilation: The American Conquest of the Philippines, 1899–1903*. New Haven, CT: Yale University Press, 1982.

Mills, C. Wright. *The Politics of Truth*. New York: Oxford University Press, 2008.

Mills, William Haslam. *The Manchester Guardian: A Century of History*. New York: Henry Holt: 1922.

Mock, James R., and Cedric Larson. *Words That Won the War: The Story of the Committee on Public Information 1917–1919*. New York: Russell and Russell, 1939.

Morgenthau, Hans J. *Politics among Nations*. New York: Knopf, 1954.

Morozov, Evgeny. *The Net Delusion: The Dark Side of Internet Freedom*. Philadelphia, PA: Public Affairs, 2011.

Mueller, John, and Mark G. Stewart. *Terror Security and Money: Balancing the Risks, Benefits and Costs of Homeland Security.* New York: Oxford University Press, 2011.

Münkler, Herfried. *Empires.* Malden, MA: Polity, 2007.

Murphy, Agnes. *The Ideology of French Imperialism: 1871–1881.* Washington, DC: Catholic University Press, 1948.

Musser, Charles. *The Emergence of Cinema: The American Screen up to 1907.* Berkeley: University of California Press, 1990.

Nabudere, D. Wadada. *Essays on the Theory and Practice of Imperialism.* London: Onyx Press, 1979.

Nakamura, Kennon H., and Matthew C. Weed. *US Public Diplomacy: Background and Current Issues.* Washington, DC: US Congressional Research Service. 2009.

Nearing, Scott. *The Tragedy of Empire.* New York: Island Press, 1945.

Negri, Antonio, and Michael Hardt. *Multitude: War and Democracy in the Age of Empire.* New York: Penguin Press, 2004.

Nesbitt, George. *Benthamite Reviewing: The First Twelve Years of* The Westminster Review. New York: Columbia University Press, 1934.

Ninkovich, Frank. *The Diplomacy of Ideas: US Foreign Policy and Cultural Relations 1938–1950.* Cambridge, UK: Cambridge University Press, 1981.

———. *The United States and Imperialism.* Malden, MA: Blackwell, 2001.

Noam, Eli M. *Media Ownership and Concentration in America.* Oxford, UK: Oxford University Press, 2009.

Novick, Ben. *Conceiving Revolution: Irish Nationalist Propaganda during the First World War.* Portland, OR: Four Courts Press, 2001.

Nye, Joseph. *The Paradox of American Power.* New York: Oxford University Press, 2002.

———. *Soft Power: The Means to Success in World Politics.* New York: Public Affairs, 2004.

O'Brien, Charles. *Cinema's Conversion to Sound: Technology and Film Style in France and the U.S.* Bloomington: University of Indiana Press, 2005.

Oliver, Clementine. *Parliament and Political Pamphleteering in Fourteenth Century England.* Woodbridge, UK: Boydell and Brewer: 2010.

Ortega y Gasset, José. *The Revolt of the Masses.* New York: Norton, 1960.

Owen, Robert, and Bob Sutcliffe, eds. *Studies in the Theory of Imperialism.* London: Longman, 1972.

Pagden, Anthony. *Lords of All the Worlds: Ideologies of Empire c. 1500- c. 1800.* New Haven, CT: Yale University Press, 1995.

Parry-Giles, Shawn J. *The Rhetorical Presidency, Propaganda, and the Cold War, 1945–1955.* Westport, CT: Praeger, 2002.

Paulu, Burton. *British Broadcasting.* Minneapolis, MN: Jones Press, 1956.

Persell, Stuart Michael. *The French Colonial Lobby: 1889–1938.* Stanford, CA: Hoover Institution Press, 1983.

Petras, James F. *Globalization Unmasked: Imperialism in the 20th Century.* New York: Zed Books, 2001.

Petras, James F., and Henry Veltmeyer. *Globalization Unmasked: Imperialism in the 21st Century.* New York: Zed Books, 2001.

Phillips, Kevin. *The Emerging Republican Majority.* New Rochelle, NY: Arlington House, 1969.

———. *The Politics of Rich and Poor: Wealth and the American Electorate in the Reagan Aftermath.* New York: Random House, 1990.

———. *Post-Conservative America: People, Politics and Ideology in a Time of Crisis.* New York: Random House, 1982.

Phillips, Ray. *Edison's Kinetoscope and Its Films: A History to 1896*. Westport, CT: Greenwood Press, 1997.

Pickering, Paul A., and Alex Tyrell. *The People's Bread: A History of the Anti-Corn Law League*. London: Leicester University Press, 2000.

Pinker, Steven. *The Better Angels of Our Nature: Why Violence Has Declined*. New York: Penguin, 2011.

Pizzitola, Louis. *Hearst over Hollywood: Power, Passion and Propaganda in the Movies*. New York: Columbia University Press: 2002.

Polychroniou, Chronis. *Marxist Perspectives on Imperialism: A Theoretical Analysis*. New York: Praeger, 1991.

Pomeranz, Kenneth, and Steven Topik. *The World That Trade Created: Society, Culture, and the World Economy, 1400 to the Present*. Armonk, NY: M. E. Sharpe, 1999.

Potter, Simon J., ed. *Newspapers and Empire in Ireland and Britain: Reporting the British Empire, 1857–1921*. Dublin, Ireland: Four Courts Press, 2004.

Pratkanis, Anthony, and Elliot Aronson. *Age of Propaganda: The Everyday Use and Abuse of Persuasion*. New York: Henry Holt, 2001.

Pratt, Julius W. *Expansionists of 1898*. Chicago: Quadrangle, 1936.

Pyron, Darden Asbury, ed. *Recasting: Gone with the Wind in American Culture*. Miami: University Presses of Florida, 1983.

Quinn, Frederick. *The French Overseas Empire*. Westport, CT: Praeger, 2000.

Rajiva, Lila. *The Language of Empire: Abu Ghraib and the American Media*. New York: Monthly Review Press, 2005.

Ramamurthy, Ananadi. *Imperial Persuaders: Images of Africa and Asia in British Advertising*. Manchester, UK: Manchester University Press, 2003.

Raskin, Jonah. *For the Hell of It: The Life and Times of Abbie Hoffman*. Berkeley: University of California Press, 1996.

Rawnsley, Gary D., ed. *Cold-War Propaganda in the 1950s*. New York: Palgrave MacMillan, 1999.

Read, Donald. *Press and People 1790–1850: Opinion in Three English Cities*. London: Edward Arnold, 1961.

Reeves, Thomas C. *The Life and Times of Joe McCarthy*. New York: Stein and Day, 1982.

Reynolds, Charles. *Modes of Imperialism*. New York: St. Martin's Press, 1981.

Reynolds, David Martin. *Masters of American Sculpture: The Figurative Tradition from the American Renaissance to the Millennium*. New York: Abbeville Press, 1993.

Richards, Thomas. *The Commodity Culture of Victorian England: Advertising and Spectacle, 1851–1914*. Stanford, CA: Stanford University Press, 1990.

Robinson, Ronald, John Gallagher, and Alice Denny. *Africa and the Victorians: The Climax of Imperialism in the Dark Continent*. New York: St. Martin's Press, 1961.

Roetter, Charles. *The Art of Psychological Warfare: 1914–1945*. New York: Stein and Day, 1974.

Roosevelt, Theodore. *For God and Take Your Own Part*. New York: George H. Doran Company, 1916.

Rosenblum, Mort. *Mission to Civilize: The French Way*. San Diego, CA: Harcourt, 1986.

Rosenblum, Robert. *Remembering the Future: The New York World's Fair from 1939 to 1964*. New York: Rizzoli, 1989.

Rosenberg, Emily. *Spreading the American Dream: American Economic and Cultural Expansion 1890–1945*. New York: Hill and Wang, 1982.

Rubin, Jerry. *Do It!: Scenarios of the Revolution*. New York: Simon and Schuster, 1970.

Ruchkoff, Douglas. *Coercion: Why We Listen to What "They" Say*. New York: Riverhead, 1999.

Ruggie, John Gerald. *Constructing the World Polity: Essays on International Institutionalization*. New York: Routledge, 1998.

Rushling, Josh. *Mission Al Jazeera: Build a Bridge, Seek the Truth, Change the World*. New York: Palgrave MacMillan, 2007.

Russell, Bertrand. *Free Thought and Official Propaganda*. New York: B. W. Huebsch, 1922.

Ryan, Michael, and Les Switzer. *God in the Corridors of Power: Christian Conservatives, the Media, and Politics in America*. Santa Barbara, CA: Praeger, 2009.

Sachleben, Mark, and Kevan M. Yenerall. *Seeing the Bigger Picture: Understanding Politics through Film and Television*. New York: Peter Lang, 2004.

Said, Edward. *Culture and Imperialism*. New York: Knopf, 1993

———. *Orientalism*. New York: Pantheon Books, 1978.

Samuel, Lawrence R. *The End of the Innocence: The 1964–1965 New York World's Fair*. Syracuse, NY: Syracuse University Press, 2007.

Sanders, M. L., and Philip M. Taylor. *British Propaganda during the First World War, 1914–18*. London: Macmillan, 1982.

Schneider, William H. *An Empire for the Masses: The French Popular Image of Africa, 1870–1900*. Westport, CT: Greenwood, 1982.

Schonfeld, Reese. *Me and Ted against the World: The Unauthorized Story of the Founding of CNN*. New York: HarperCollins, 2001.

Schrecker, Ellen. *The Age of McCarthyism: A Brief History with Documents*. Boston: Bedford, 1994.

Schults, Raymond L. *Crusader in Babylon: W.T. Stead and the* Pall Mall Gazette. Lincoln: University of Nebraska Press, 1972.

Schumpeter, Joseph A. *Imperialism and Social Classes*. New York: Augustus M. Kelly Inc., 1951.

Semmel, Bernard. *The Liberal Ideal and the Demons of Imperialism*. Baltimore, MD: Johns Hopkins University Press, 1993.

Shabecoff, Philip. *A Fierce Green Fire: The American Environmental Movement*. New York: Island Press, 2003.

Shibata, Masako. *Germany and Japan under the U.S. Occupation: A Comparative Analysis of the Post-War Education Reform*. Lanham, MD: Lexington Book, 2005.

Shirky, Clay. *Here Comes Everybody: The Power of Organizing without Organizations*. New York: Penguin, 2008.

Shogan, Robert. *No Sense of Decency: The Army-McCarthy Hearings: A Demogague Falls and Television Takes Charge of American Politics*. Chicago: Ivan R. Dee, 2009.

Sloan, John W. *The Reagan Effect: Economics and Presidential Leadership*. Lawrence: University of Kansas Press, 1999.

Slosson, Preston William. *The Decline of the Chartist Movement*. New York: Longmans, Green and Co., 1916.

Smith, Neil. *American Empire, Roosevelt's Geographer, and the Prelude to Globalization*. Berkley: University of California Press, 2003.

Snyder, Louis L., ed. *The Imperialism Reader*. New York: D. Van Nostrand, 1962.

Sorkin, Michael, ed. *Variations on a Theme Park: The New American City and the End of Public Space*. New York: Hill and Wong, 1992.

Spielmann, Marion Harry. *The History of "Punch."* London: Cassell, 1895.

Spiers, Edward M., ed. *Sudan: The Reconquest Reappraised*. London: Frank Cass, 1998.

Stefanic, Jean, and Richard Delgado. *No Mercy: How Conservative Think Tanks Changed America's Social Agenda*. Philadelphia, PA: Temple University Press, 1996.

Steger, Manfred. *Globalization: A Brief Insight*. New York: Sterling, 2009.

Stephen, Leslie. *Selected Letters of Leslie Stephen: Volume I, 1864–1882*. Columbus: University of Ohio Press, 1996.

Stewart, Jacqueline Najuma. *Migrating to the Movies: Cinema and Black Urban Modernity*. Berkeley: University of California Press, 2005.

Strong, Josiah. *Our Country: Its Possible Future and Its Present Crisis*. New York: Baker and Taylor, 1891.

Sturt, George. *The Journals of George Sturt, 1890–1927*. Cambridge, UK: Cambridge University Press, 1967.

Suid, Lawrence H. *Guts and Glory: The Making of the American Military Image in Film*. Lexington: University Press of Kentucky, 2002.

Swint, Kerwin. *Dark Genius: The Influential Career of Legendary Political Operative and Fox News Founder Roger Ailes*. New York: Union Square, 2008.

Szymanski, Albert. *The Logic of Imperialism*. New York: Praeger, 1981.

Task Force on Inequality and American Democracy. *American Democracy in an Age of Rising Inequality*. American Political Science Association, 2004. http://www.apsanet.org/imgtest/taskforcereport.pdf.

Taylor, Philip M. *British Propaganda in the 20th Century: Selling Democracy*. Edinburgh, UK: Edinburgh University Press, 1999.

———. *The Projection of Britain: British Overseas Publicity and Propaganda 1919–1939*. Cambridge, UK: Cambridge University Press, 1981.

Temperley, Howard. *White Dreams, Black Africa: The Antislavery Expedition to the River Niger 1841–1842*. New Haven, CT: Yale University Press, 1991.

Terdiman, Richard. *Making the News: Modernity and the Mass Press in Nineteenth Century France*. Amherst: University of Massachusetts Press, 1999.

Thackery, William Makepeace. *Miscellanies*. vol. V. New York: Harper and Brothers, 1877.

Thomas, Julia. *Pictorial Victorians: The Inscription of Values Word and Image*. Athens: Ohio University Press, 2004.

Thomas, Nicholas. *Colonialism's Culture*. New Haven, CT: Yale University Press, 1994.

Thompson, Andrew S. *Imperial Britain: The Empire in British Politics, c. 1880–1932*. Harlow, UK: Longman, 2000.

Thompson, J. Lee. *Politicians, the Press, and Propaganda: Lord Northcliffe, the Great War, 1914–1919*. Kent, OH: Kent State University Press, 1999.

Thornton, A. P. *Doctrines of Imperialism*. New York: John Wiley and Sons, 1965.

Thucydides. *History of the Peloponnesian War*. Rex Warner, trans. London: Penguin, 1972.

Tomkins, Stephen. *William Wilberforce: A Biography*. Grand Rapids, MI: Wm. B. Eerdmans Publishing Company, 2007.

Trevelyan, Charles Edward. *The Letters of Indophilus to* The Times. London: Longmans, Brown, Green, Longmans, and Poberts, 1858.

Tucker, Robert. *A New Isolationism: Threat or Promise?*. New York: Universe Books, 1972.

Turley, David. *The Culture of English Antislavery 1780–1860*. London: Routledge, 1991.

Vaughn, Stephen. *Holding Fast the Inner Lines: Democracy, Nationalism, and the Committee on Public Information*. Chapel Hill: University of North Carolina Press, 1980.

Verschoyle, F. *Cecil Rhodes: His Political Life and Speeches: 1881–1900*. London: Chapman and Hall, 1900.

Waller, J. Michael, ed. *The Public Diplomacy Reader*. Washington, DC: Institute of World Politics Press, 2007.

Wallerstein, Immanuel. *The Decline of American Power: The US in a Chaotic World*. New York: New Press, 2003.

Walvin, James, ed. *Slavery and British Society, 1776–1846*. Baton Rouge: Lousiana State University Press, 1982.

War-Time Speeches: A Compilation of Public Utterances in Great Britain. New York: George H. Doran Company, 1942.

Ward, Larry Wayne. *The Motion Picture Goes to War: The U.S. Government Film Effort during World War I*. Ann Arbor, MI: UMI Research Press, 1985.

Ward, Paul. *Red Flag and Union Jack: Englishness, Patriotism, and the British Left 1881–1924*. Woodbridge, Sufflolk, UK: Boydell Press, 1998.

Warren, Bill. *Imperialism: Pioneer of Capitalism*. London: Verso, 1981.

Watts, Steven. *The Magic Kingdom: Walt Disney and the American Way of Life*. Boston: Houghton Mifflin, 1997.

Wilentz, Sean. *The Age of Reagan: A History 1974–2008*. New York: HarperCollins, 2008.

Wilkerson, Marcus M. *Public Opinion and the Spanish-American War: A Study in War Propaganda*. Baton Rouge: Louisiana State University Press, 1932.

Willbanks, James H. *The Tet Offensive: A Concise History*. New York: Columbia University Press, 2007.

Williams, Daniel K. *God's Own Party: The Making of the Christian Right*. Oxford, UK: Oxford University Press, 2010.

Williams, Kevin. *Get Me a Murder a Day!: A History of Mass Communication in Britain*. London: Arnold, 1998.

Windelsham, (Lord). *Broadcasting in a Free Society*. London: Blackwell, 1980.

Winfield, Betty Houchin. *FDR and the News Media*. New York: Columbia University Press, 1994.

Winkler, Allen M. *The Politics of Propaganda: The Office of War Information 1942–1945*. New Haven, CT: Yale University Press. 1978.

Winks, Robert W. *The Age of Imperialism*. Englewood Cliffs, NJ: Prentice Hall, 1969.

Winslow, E. M. *The Pattern of Imperialism*. New York: Columbia UniversityPress, 1948.

Wirls, Daniel. *Buildup: The Politics of Defense in the Reagan Era*. Ithaca, NY: Cornell University Press, 1992.

Wisan, Joseph E. *The Cuban Crisis as Reflected in the New York Press, 1895–1898*. New York: Octagon, 1965.

Wood, Marcus. *Blind Memory: Visual Representations of Slavery in England and America 1780–1865*. New York: Routledge, 2000.

Wu, Duncan, ed. *A Companion to Romanticism*. Oxford, UK: Blackwell, 1998.

Zillmann, Dolf, and Peter Vorderer, eds. *Media Entertainment: The Psychology of Its Appeal*. Mahwah, NJ: Lawrence Erlbaum, 2000.

Index

Printed and bound in the United States of America